Study Guide Plus

for

Henslin

Essentials of Sociology
A Down-to-Earth Approach

Seventh Edition

prepared by

Lori Ann Fowler
Tarrant County College

PEARSON

Boston   New York   San Francisco
Mexico City   Montreal   Toronto   London   Madrid   Munich   Paris
Hong Kong   Singapore   Tokyo   Cape Town   Sydney

ISBN-13: 978-0-205-52472-3
ISBN-10: 0-205-52472-9

Printed in the United States of America

10 9 8 7 6 5 4 3 2 1   11 10 09 08 07

TABLE
OF
CONTENTS

Successful Study Strategies

Welcome to Sociology! You are about to embark on a fascinating journey in which you will discover all sorts of new and interesting information about yourself and the world around you. This study guide has been prepared to accompany the textbook *Essentials of Sociology: A Down To Earth Approach* by James M. Henslin. This introductory chapter describes what you will find in this study guide, explains how to use it in order to maximize your learning, and gives you some suggestions on how to approach different types of test questions. It is intended to help you learn the material and achieve academic success.

GETTING STARTED

The course syllabus that the professor hands out at the beginning of class is the place to look for information about what is important in any course. This syllabus should provide you with an outline of the topics that will be covered in the class and information on the course work expected of you as a student. For instance, it should tell you how many tests and quizzes there will be, the nature of these tests and quizzes, and when they are scheduled throughout the semester. It will also give you deadlines and due dates for written assignments and other class projects, and should include information on how the professor will calculate your final grade; you can determine which course work he or she emphasizes most by looking at how much each component in the course counts toward that final grade.

MAKING THE MOST OF COURSE MATERIALS

You will be expected to purchase the required text or texts for the course. The professor may include some recommended reading — it is up to you whether or not you read these additional texts. Increasingly, courses such as the one you are taking in sociology offer study guides like this one that accompany the text. This particular study guide includes the following for each chapter:

- a **Chapter Summary** that summarizes the main ideas found in the chapter.

- a set of **Learning Objectives** that state what you should know once you have read the textbook and learned the material. Make sure that you can meet each of the listed objectives. If you are not sure you can, reread that section.

- a **Chapter Outline** that parallels the chapter in the textbook. Review the chapter outline; if there is information in the outline that is still unfamiliar to you, go back to the textbook and reread that section. The outline can also be used to review material just before a test.

- a list of the **Key Terms** that are introduced within the chapter. Review the definition for each word and use it in a sentence. If you need help refer back to the textbook chapter.

- a list of **Key People**, sociologists whose work is discussed within the chapter. In some cases, these are early sociologists who contributed theoretical understanding and research insights to the discipline; in other cases, they are contemporary sociologists who are doing research and developing theory on the subject. Review the list and see how many names you know and whether you can identify their contribution to sociology. If you can not, go to the Index at the back of the textbook and then refer to the page listed.

- a **Self-Test** that provides you with an opportunity to see how much of the information you have retained. Each self-test includes 30 multiple choice questions, 20 true-false questions, 15 fill-in-the-blank questions, a set of 10 matching items, 5 essay questions, and 2 student projects. You will find a chapter-by-chapter **Answer Key** at the end of the study guide. This key provides answers for all of the questions in the self-test. Check your answers using the Key; if your answer is incorrect, refer to the pages in the textbook and read those again. Mark those questions that were incorrect; a few days later try them again to see if you have now learned the material. This section of the study guide will be particularly helpful to you in preparing to take tests.

SCORING HIGH MARKS ON TESTS

If you have made good use of the study guide, you should be well prepared when it comes time to take tests. Some students also find it helpful to organize study groups prior to major tests. Whether or not this is a help or a hindrance depends on your own personal study style, and the character of the group; you will need to assess both before making a decision about getting involved with such an activity. In addition, there are some specific ideas for approaching tests, including understanding the different types of tests and developing strategies for taking them.

Strategies for taking objective tests

Most of you reading this guide are quite familiar with objective tests — multiple choice, true-false, fill-in-the-blank and matching questions. In fact, these types of questions are included in the self-tests contained in this study guide for each chapter. These types of questions focus on more detailed information and on your ability to recognize the correct answer. In general, when studying for objective tests focus on details — definitions of key concepts, accomplishments of key figures, specific facts, etc. Here are some strategies that will help you do well on tests of this nature:

- **Read instructions carefully.** Many students, anxious to begin the test, do not take enough time to read the instructions carefully. Consequently they end up making mistakes when it comes to selecting and recording the correct answers.

- **Take time to read each question.** Likewise, students read questions and answers too quickly, missing important clues that would help them select the correct answer.

- **Pace yourself.** Some students may rush because they are afraid they will not have enough time to complete the exam. To avoid this problem and improve your chances of getting high marks, find out in advance how many questions will be on the test and use this information to calculate about how much time you will have for each question. During the test you can then pace yourself so that you don't run out of time and rush at the end.

- **Learn to recognize qualifiers.** In writing the test questions, the professor will use qualifying words to change the meaning of seemingly straightforward statements; *all, always, only, most, usually,* *some, sometimes, none,* and *never* are frequently used in this way. Notice that these range along a continuum from positive to negative — italicized words on each end of this continuum set up a qualification that applies 100 percent of the time, those in the middle mean that sometimes the condition exists and sometimes it doesn't. If you see an absolute qualifier and you know that condition occurs only sometimes, then you can eliminate that choice; likewise, you can rule out statements that contain variable qualifiers if you are certain that the condition occurs all of the time.

For instance, the following multiple-choice question makes use of qualifiers:

> Sanctions:
> a.   are *always* material.
> b.   can be positive or negative.
> c.   have *very little* impact on *most* people today.
> d.   All of the above.

In approaching the question, begin by asking yourself whether or not there are sanctions that are non-material. Since there are non-material sanctions — a smile, a frown, a compliment or a reprimand — then "a" is incorrect. Likewise, since sanctions do have an impact on most people, "c" is incorrect. The correct answer is "b".

- **Watch for negatives.** In addition to qualifiers, learn to notice negatives. Obvious negatives are words like *not, no,* and *never*; negatives can also be created by adding prefixes like "un-" to words like "important." If you read a question too quickly, you may overlook these negatives and end up answering incorrectly. Another common use of the negative is to ask that you identify which of the following is *not*, as is illustrated by the following question:

> All of the following are ways of neutralizing deviance, *except*:
> a.   appeal to higher loyalties.
> b.   denial of responsibility.
> c.   denial of deviant labels.
> d.   denial of injury and of a victim.

In answering this question, identify which *are* ways of neutralizing deviance, and three of these four are. The correct answer would be "c"; "denial of deviant labels" is *not* one of the ways in which people neutralize deviance.

Besides the general guidelines listed above, here are some hints about each type of question likely to be found on the typical objective test:

- **Multiple Choice questions:** Begin by reading all the answer choices and ruling out those options that you know are incorrect. You may discover that only one option is left. If more than one option remains and you have been instructed to choose only one, give some further thought to the answers. Are there any qualifiers that you need to consider? Are there grammatical clues — subject/verb agreement issues, correct fit between the stem and the answer, etc? Is there an option "all of the above" or "A and C"? It may very well be that there is more than one correct answer, but unless you have been given such an option, you need to rule out all but one.

- **True/False questions:** Remember that you have a 50/50 chance of being correct, regardless of what you choose, on this type of question. It is easier to write a true statement than a false one, and most professors want to make sure that students leave the course remembering what is true rather than being confused about what is false. You are very likely, therefore, to find more true statements than false ones. For this reason, when you really don't know the answer, it is better to choose "true" than "false." Again, pay attention to the use of qualifying words and negatives.

- **Fill-in-the-Blank questions:** Often fill-in-the-blank questions can be challenging for students. In order to prepare for fill-in-the-blank questions study key terms and key people; reading the chapters in the book more than one time will help you remember key terms and key people. When making a final decision on an answer in a fill-in-the-blank question, try each of your possible answers in the blank; choose the answer that you think makes the sentence complete and correct.

- **Matching questions:** One of the biggest problems with matching questions, especially if there is a long list to match, is becoming confused about which options you've already chosen and which you haven't. If you're recording your answers on a separate answer sheet, ask the professor if it is okay to mark on the test; if the answer is yes, get into the habit of marking which ones you've chosen as you go along. Match those that are most familiar first; by the process of elimination, you will end up with only those you don't know and you can then make the best possible guess among what is left.

Strategies for taking essay tests

Although the previous tips may help you get through the objective test, they are not suited to essay tests, which are written to maximize your recall of the material as you synthesize and summarize what you have learned. When studying for essay tests you will want to review more global information — trends, theories, and perspectives.

Just as there are strategies for managing an objective test, there are also ways of managing an essay test to maximize your results.

- Once again **read the directions carefully.** Ascertain how many essay questions you are expected to answer and whether they are drawn from separate parts of the test—for instance, the professor may want you to answer two from section A and one from section B or one each from sections A, B, and C.

- Once you have gone over the directions, **plan how you will divide the allotted time** among the questions; you want to have enough time to answer all the questions fully. Ask the professor if it makes any difference in what order you answer the questions. If it doesn't, decide for yourself the sequence in which to answer them; you may find that getting the easiest question(s) out of the way first allows you to spend more time on those that are more difficult.

- Make sure you **understand what the question is asking** you to do. Essay questions may ask you to compare (show similarities); contrast, differentiate, or distinguish (discuss differences); discuss, evaluate, or criticize (present strengths and weaknesses); demonstrate, justify, prove, show, or support (give evidence that supports an idea or statement); list, identify, enumerate, or state (list with or without a brief discussion or example). As you can see, each is asking something different, and you need to understand exactly what the professor wants you to do before you begin.

- When answering an essay question, **start with a rough outline**, jotting down ideas that you want to cover. Include both the main ideas and the supporting evidence in your quick outline. By taking a few minutes in the beginning to do this, you are assured that your information will be organized carefully and completely.

- In your response, **get right to the point**; your introduction should contain a statement of what position you will take to answer the question. The paragraphs that follow should provide supporting statements linked to theories, research and key concepts you have learned in the course of the semester.

- **Avoid using personal opinions in your essays**, unless otherwise asked to. Remember, even when asked to take a position, you should be prepared to support your position with facts, not personal opinions. Your concluding paragraph should summarize what you have stated, perhaps connecting your argument with some body of knowledge within the particular discipline.

- In general, **stay focused on the subject** and avoid using irrelevant facts simply to pad your essay. Likewise, don't try to stretch a short essay by restating the same thesis several times. The professor may conclude that you really don't have anything to say and will give you the same grade as if you had written the thesis only once in a briefer essay.

- You should also take care to **write neatly** so the professor can read what you've written. By the time you get to college, you are well aware of whether your handwriting is legible. If it is not, try printing your response. An essay that is illegible, regardless of how good the ideas and organization are, will most likely not be read or graded by the professor.

BECOMING A BETTER STUDENT

Become Familiar with Campus Resources

One key to student success is becoming more familiar with resources available on your college campus and using those resources to your advantage. Here are just a few that may be open to you:

✓ **Student services:** Many colleges have student services centers where you are likely to find counselors who provide academic, personal and career counseling, seminars and workshops on topics such as health and wellness or learning how to achieve a balanced lifestyle, and information on a wide range of issues of special concern to you.
✓ **Services for special populations:** If you are a student returning to college after many years, a student with physical or learning disabilities, a minority student, or a student from another country, there may be a center to assist you in meeting your specific academic goals.
✓ **Instructional support services:** You may also discover that your college offers instructional support services, perhaps through a learning lab or a tutoring center. These are set up to assist you in developing study, reading, and writing skills, all of which are essential if you want to succeed, not only in this sociology course, but in every course you take over your college career.

Work Out Your Own Strengths and Weaknesses

Think about your strengths and weaknesses as a student. Begin by assessing what kind of learner you are. Do you remember material best when you have heard it or when you have read it for yourself? Do you learn best when you cover all the material in one large unit or when you break the material up into smaller units? A counselor in a student services office or an on-campus learning center may be able to help you determine your personal learning style.

Besides understanding how you learn, evaluate your current study habits. Do you study better when you are alone or in a group? Do you study best when your study periods have a definite beginning and ending time and tasks are clearly outlined? Do other commitments, such as work, family, or friends, interfere with your study time? Do you find it hard to identify which information in the course is important? Do you get anxious when it comes to taking tests? Do essay tests intimidate you?

Manage Your Time Efficiently

Another important step toward college success is learning to manage your time. Beyond the time spent sleeping and eating, you have some flexibility in allocating the remaining hours. Take a few minutes and jot down what a "typical" day looks like, noting tasks that must be accomplished and the time each involves. Please note that a "typical" day will look differently for students who are working full time and going to college. Study and time management tips apply to all students, but the key for full time working students is to not take more courses in one semester than one can realistically handle. Be sure to sit down before the semester and plan your schedule, allowing yourself enough time to study and prepare for your courses.

Develop a schedule for the entire semester. Figure 1 provides an example of a weekly schedule; the days of the week are listed across the top, and the hours in the day run down the side. Activities that are done regularly, such as sleep, meals, job, classes, exercise, and volunteer commitments, are noted within the appropriate boxes. The blank boxes represent "free time." What happens during these times will change from week to week depending on what comes up. By mapping out fixed commitments at the beginning of the semester, you will be able to maximize your use of the resulting discretionary time. On weeks when you have a lot of tests or paper assignments, you may decide to forego the workout or cut back on the time you spend with your friends. By remaining flexible with your free time, you will be able to balance the competing demands on your time.

WEEKLY SCHEDULE FOR FALL SEMESTER							
	Sunday	Monday	Tuesday	Wednesday	Thursday	Friday	Saturday
7:00 am		wake up	wake up	wake up	wake up	wake up	
8:00		breakfast/ school	breakfast/ school	breakfast/ school	breakfast/ school	breakfast/ school	
9:00		class — SOC	class — BIO	class — SOC	class — BIO	class — SOC	wake up
10:00	wake up	class — ART	class — LIT	class — ART	BIO lab	class — ART	
11:00							
12:00 pm		lunch		lunch		lunch	work
1:00	volunteer	class — HIS	lunch	class — HIS	lunch — HIS	class	
2:00		work	work	work	work	work	
3:00							
4:00							
5:00	workout	workout	workout	workout	workout	workout	workout
6:00	dinner	dinner	dinner	dinner	dinner	dinner	dinner
7:00	study	study	study	study	study	party with friends	party with friends
8:00							
9:00	study break	study break	study break	study break	study break		
10:00	study	study	study	study	study		
11:00	bed	bed	bed	bed	bed		
12:00 am						bed	bed

Figure 1: AN EXAMPLE OF A TYPICAL SEMESTER SCHEDULE

ASSIGNMENT SCHEDULE – FALL SEMESTER					
	Sociology	Art	History	Biology	Literature
WK 1					
WK 2	essay on culture	charcoal project due	proposal on research topic	quiz —Ch 1-2 lab assign. 1	
WK 3				quiz — Ch 3-4	review *Pride and Prejudice*
WK 4	observation at day care center			quiz — Ch 5-6 lab assign. 2	
WK 5		watercolor project due	preliminary bibliography	quiz — Ch 7-8	
WK 6	evaluation of trip to county jail			quiz — Ch 9-11 lab assign. 3	review *Emma*
WK 7	MIDTERM				
	test — Ch 1-11	NO MIDTERM	test — Ch 1-10	test — Ch 1-11	
WK 8	review of major sociology book		Outline of research paper	quiz — Ch 12 lab assign. 4	
WK 9		pastels project due		quiz — Ch 13-14	
WK 10	family history due			quiz — Ch 15-16; lab assign. 5	review *Sense and Sensibility*
WK 11		acrylic project due	annotated bibliography due	quiz — Ch 17-18	
WK 12	observation of political rally			quiz — Ch 19; lab assign. 6	
WK 13		oil painting due		quiz — Ch 20	review *Persuasion*
WK 14			research paper due	quiz — Ch 21; lab assign. 7	Final paper on Austin
FINALS WK	test — Ch 9-22	Final project due	test — Ch 11-18	test — Ch 12-21	NO FINAL

Figure 2: AN EXAMPLE OF A TYPICAL ASSIGNMENT SCHEDULE

It would also be helpful have a schedule of all of your assignments for the entire semester. Figure 2 illustrates this schedule; make one of your own by listing the courses across the top and the weeks of the semester down the side. Within the boxes, list tasks that must be completed for each class in a specific week. You can note tests, paper assignments, and other course work that has a deadline. This will help you plan how to divide your time among each course over the semester.

In addition to posting these semester-based schedules in a highly visible location like a bulletin board above your desk or inside your assignment book, get into the habit of using a daily schedule. This is a list of the day's tasks and the time frame in which you plan to accomplish each. A good time to make up this daily schedule is the evening before; spend a few minutes thinking about and then writing down all the things that you need to do the next day. This will free your mind of thinking about what lies ahead so that you will sleep more easily and when you get up in the morning, you will be prepared to begin the day and not waste time organizing at the last minute. Although this daily schedule reflects all the tasks that need to be done during the course of the day, some things are more important than others; get into the habit of prioritizing your list so that the most important are at the top and are guaranteed to get done first.

While making and using schedules is important to your success in college, so is learning to take advantage of spare moments in the day that are otherwise wasted; become aware of them so you can use them for impromptu study periods. Here are some ideas to consider:

✓ Most of us spend some time each day just waiting; for a bus or train, an appointment with a doctor or professor, or service in a bank or store. Bring something along to occupy yourself while you wait. It could be a book or article you have been assigned to read, a notebook with notes, or flash cards with formulas or vocabulary on them.
✓ While driving in the car, exercising, or cleaning house, listen to recorded tapes of important vocabulary, passages from text, or series of questions and answers on course material.
✓ Use the time immediately before class begins to recall main points from the previous class lecture, think about questions you have on the material that was covered in the last class or that will be covered in this class, or glance through notes.
✓ Keep a small notebook of ideas, questions, or thoughts you have about course material; whenever one of these comes into your mind, you can write it down and think about the answers later.

Finally, don't forget to devote some time each day to study breaks; rewards for hard work. Schedule them into your day and stick to them. They are not only something to look forward to as you studying hard, but they actually enhance your overall learning. After taking a jog or walk, having coffee with friends, watching a TV show, or reading the newspaper, you will return to the task of studying with a mind that is once again ready to tackle important course material.

Develop better concentration

Concentration is a skill that you need to develop to get the most out of your study periods. When you concentrate, focus all of your attention on the task in front of you. You will find this easier to do if you are able to eliminate distractions. How do you go about doing this? Begin by finding a space suitable for studying, one that you associate first and foremost with that activity and not some other. For instance, trying to study on your bed or in the snack bar of the student union is not a good idea because those areas are not associated primarily with studying.

Many students choose to study in their college library. There are a number of advantages to using the library; it is unlikely that you could find any quieter space in which to concentrate on your school work. The lighting in the library is designed for study, and you can usually claim adequate space in which to spread out your materials. It is also easier to eliminate visual and auditory distractions, as well as telephone and social interruptions at the library. Finally, many libraries have lounges for students to use for periodic breaks. Remember, while we can never completely eliminate all distractions in our world, finding a quiet place away from the hustle and bustle of our everyday lives will help enormously when it comes to studying.

Because concentration is enhanced when we are able to eliminate distractions, here are some additional measures you can take to achieve better concentration:

✓ **Use lists.** One list is a reminder of what you have to do during the study period; as you accomplish a task, check it off and move on to the next. A second list is for things you have to do later. You may find yourself preoccupied with some problem in your life and your mind continues to return to this problem time and time again. While you are trying to study, your concentration is broken by these other thoughts popping randomly into your mind; if you keep a second list, you can write these interrupting thoughts down on it, promising yourself that you will return to the list *after* you finish studying.

✓ **Take regular breaks.** Use a timer to keep track of your study time; when the alarm goes off, get up and take a break. This way, you will not be tempted to look at your watch every fifteen minutes, wondering how long you've studied and when your next break time is due.

✓ **Set a goal for each study session.** Decide how many pages to read or vocabulary words to be mastered during the time set aside for study. When you have reached the session goal, close your books and notes until the next time.

Achieve mastery over the material

In general, mastery is facilitated by good organization. Students who succeed are generally those who are able to stay on top of the course because they have developed a system for keeping track of all the materials. One suggestion is to purchase a loose-leaf notebook for each course, with the syllabus, handouts, assignments, and notes from your readings and lectures in separate tabbed sections.

Students often think sociology will not require much new learning; after all, they are part of society and thus intimately familiar with it. This is their first mistake; sociology, like every other discipline, has its own vocabulary that must be learned in order to be successful. Here are some ideas to help you:

✓ **Identify the concepts.** As you read the text, pay attention to the concepts that are in bold-face type. The definition is provided for you; refer back to it as you read.

✓ **Think of examples.** Try to think of some examples of your own; if you can relate the material to the world with which you are most familiar, you are more likely to remember it.

✓ **Make up flash cards.** Many times, it helps to make up flash cards, with the word on one side and the definition and an example on the other side. Keep these with you and review them while you are waiting in line or stopped at a red light.

All of these strategies will guarantee that you will incorporate new and unfamiliar concepts into your framework and remember them when the time comes for a test.

Achieving mastery over the material requires more than just learning key concepts. As a general rule, it is best to read the assigned material *prior* to class. As you read, get into the habit of taking notes. These should include summaries of the main points of the section you have read, connections between what you are reading now and what you read earlier in the semester, and examples to illustrate these ideas, as well as any questions that were raised in your mind in connection with the reading.

Sometimes it is easier to master new and unfamiliar material by drawing a concept map, which presents relationships between ideas and concepts in a visual format. Concept maps can be drawn for separate sections or topics found within a chapter and then combined into a map for each chapter. The key to mapping successfully is to identify the key concepts that relate to the section or topic and then link other concepts or ideas to each of these key concepts. Concept maps are helpful because they create a "picture" of the material that summarizes what must be mastered, showing the links between ideas.

If you have taken the time to read the material in advance, when you go to class, you should be prepared for what the professor is going to cover. If you have questions from the reading, now is the time to raise them. Before class begins, divide the pages of your notebook vertically into two columns: a narrower one to the left, about one-third the width of the page, and a wider one on the right, the remaining two-thirds of the page. As you take notes, use the wider column to record what the professor says. Later, as you review what you have written, use the narrower column in the same way that you would use the margins of your text — for making connections, writing down main ideas, and noting any questions you might have. You can also use this space to make reference to textbook pages that correspond to what the professor has said; this will come in handy when you are studying for exams.

Remember, if you miss a class for any reason, it is still your responsibility to find out what was covered. If you know in advance that you will be absent, make arrangements with another student to pick up any handouts that are distributed; make sure that you can get the class notes from the student. It is also a good idea to talk with the professor about making up any class assignments. If the absence is unexpected, you should make a point of getting the notes from another student and talk with the professor about any missed work; don't wait until the end of the semester to do this; do it as soon as you return to school.

Once you feel you have achieved some familiarity with the material, go back to the study guide and follow these steps:

✓ **Check the list of Key Terms.** Review the definition for each word and think of an example. If you need help thinking of an example, refer back to the textbook chapter.
✓ **Check the list of Key People.** See how many you know and whether or not you can identify their contribution to sociology. If you cannot, go back to the textbook and locate them within the chapter. (A quick way to do this is to refer to the Index at the back of the textbook and then go directly to the page listed.)
✓ **Take the Self-Test.** Mark those questions that you got wrong and go back to the text to find the correct answer. A few days later, try them again to see if you have now mastered the material. Use the Self-Test to review the material just before a test.

All of these tips aid in your review of the information. You might also want to review the chapter outline again. This provides you with a broad understanding of the ideas that were covered in the chapter. If there is information in the outline that is still unfamiliar to you, go back to the textbook and reread that section. The outline and the self-test can also be used when you are reviewing the material just before a test.

Here are some suggestions of books to help you make the most of your college experience. If you have trouble finding them in your college library, ask the bookstore to order them for you:

Lenier, Minnette and Janet Maker. *Keys to College Success: Reading and Study Improvement,* 4th edition. Upper Saddle River, NJ: Prentice-Hall, 1998.

Light, Richard J. *Making the Most of College: Students Speak Their Minds.* Boston, MA: Harvard University Press, 2001.

Pauk, Walter. *How to Study in College.* 7th edition. Boston, MA: Houghton Mifflin Company, 2000.

Reynolds, Jean. *Succeeding in College: Study Skills and Strategies.* Upper Saddle River, NJ: Prentice Hall, 2001.

Williamson, James C., Debra A. McCandrew and Charles T. Muse. *Roadways to Success for Community College Students.* 3rd edition. Upper Saddle River, NJ: Prentice Hall, 2003.

If you begin to incorporate some of the preceding tips into your regular study routines and use the resources in the Study Guide, you should finish the semester with good grades and a better understanding not only of sociology, but of yourself and your social world. I hope that you will enjoy your adventure and find that this subject opens new vistas of understanding to you. Good luck!

CHAPTER 1

THE SOCIOLOGICAL PERSPECTIVE

CHAPTER SUMMARY

- Sociology offers a perspective—a view of the world—that stresses the social experiences of people as the underlying cause of their behavior.

- The study of sociology emerged in the mid-1800s in Western Europe, during the upheavals of the Industrial Revolution. Early sociologists, who focused on the changes that were then occurring in Europe, were **Auguste Comte, Herbert Spencer, Karl Marx, Emile Durkheim,** and **Max Weber.**

- In the early years few women received the advanced education required to become a sociologist and the work of women like **Harriet Martineau**, who did become sociologists, was largely ignored.

- Sociology became established in North America by the end of the nineteenth century. In the United States there has always been a tension between basic sociology and attempts to reform society. Two early sociologists who combined sociology with social reform were **Jane Addams** and **W. E. B. Du Bois.**

- A **theory** is a statement about how facts are related to one another. Because no one theory encompasses all of reality, sociologists use three primary theoretical frameworks: (1) **symbolic interactionism**—which concentrates on the meanings that underlie people's lives—usually focuses on the **micro level**; (2) **functional analysis**—which stresses that society is made up of various parts that, when working properly, contribute to the stability of society—focuses on the **macro level**; and (3) **conflict theory**—which stresses inequalities and sees the basis of social life as a competitive struggle to gain control over scarce resources—also focuses on the **macro level**.

- Research and theory must work together because without theory research is of little value, and if theory is unconnected to research it is unlikely to represent the way life really is.

- Sociological research is needed because common sense is highly limited and often incorrect. Eight basic steps are included in scientific research: (1) **selecting a topic**, (2) **defining the problem**, (3) **reviewing the literature**, (4) **formulating a hypothesis**, (5) **choosing a research method**, (6) **collecting the data**, (7) **analyzing the results**, and (8) **sharing the results**.

- Sociologists use six research methods (or research designs) for gathering data: (1) **surveys**, (2) **participant observations**, (3) **secondary analysis**, (4) **documents**, (5) **experiments**, and (6) **unobtrusive measures**.

- Ethics are of concern to sociologists, who are committed to openness, honesty, truth, and protecting subjects. Sociologists agree that social research should be value-free, but recognize that, at any point in time, sociologists are members of a particular society and are infused with values of all sorts. One of the dilemmas for sociologists is deciding whether the goal of research should be only to advance understanding of human behavior or to also reform harmful social arrangements.

LEARNING OBJECTIVES

As you read Chapter 1, use these learning objectives to organize your notes. After completing your reading, you should be able to answer each of the objectives.

1. Understand what is meant by the broader social context that underlies human behavior, and how and why sociologists study these broader social contexts.
2. Know what is meant by social location and how it helps people define themselves and helps others define them.
3. Explain the sociological perspective: what it is, what it offers, and why C. Wright Mills referred to it as "the intersection of biography (the individual) and history (the social factors that influence the individual)."
4. Identify, understand, and make distinctions between tradition and science.
5. Discuss the social changes—and the changing social conditions—which fostered the development of sociology as a distinct academic discipline in the middle of the nineteenth century.
6. Identify and critique the sociological contributions of the following mid- to late-nineteenth and early twentieth century European sociologists: Auguste Comte, Herbert Spencer, Karl Marx, Emile Durkheim, Max Weber, and Harriet Martineau.
7. Understand how and why levels of social integration may affect rates of suicide and how Emile Durkheim's nineteenth century study of suicide helped demonstrate how social forces affect people's behaviors.
8. Discuss why there were so few women sociologists in the nineteenth and early twentieth century, and how the contributions of women sociologists during this time period were received and evaluated by their male counterparts.
9. Trace the history of sociology in North America from the late 1800s to the present time, identifying the specific sociological contributions of the following American sociologists: Jane Addams, W. E. B. Du Bois, Talcott Parsons, and C. Wright Mills.
10. Understand the historical tensions and ongoing debates in sociology in North America between social reform and social analysis, and how the sociological contributions of Jane Addams, W. E. B. Du Bois, Talcott Parsons, and C. Wright Mills fit into the tensions and debates.
11. Discuss the current state of sociology in America as it relates to the debate between social reform and social analysis and what role applied sociology plays in this debate.
12. Define what is meant by theory and explain why it is an important part of sociology.
13. Identify the three major theoretical perspectives in sociology—symbolic interactionism, functional analysis, and conflict theory—and describe the particular level of analysis, characteristics, viewpoints, and concerns associated with each.
14. Understand how to apply each level of analysis to various sociological topics, including divorce.
15. Explain what areas of human behavior and aspect of social life are valid topics for sociological research.
16. Explain why there is a need for sociological research.
17. List and describe the eight basic steps for conducting scientific research.
18. Define, describe, and discuss the significance of the following terms associated with the research process: hypothesis, variable, independent variable, dependent variable, operational definitions, validity, reliability, and replication.
19. Know and discuss the six research methods that sociologists use, the tools that they employ, and the strengths and limitations of each.
20. Define, describe, and discuss the significance of the following terms associated with the six research methods: survey, population, sample, random sample, stratified random sample, questionnaires, closed-ended questions, open-ended questions, rapport, participant observation, secondary analysis, documents, unobtrusive measures, experiment, experimental group, and control group.
21. Know the ethical guidelines that sociologists are expected to follow and talk about the ethical issues raised in Mario Brajuha's and Laud Humphreys research.

22. Discuss Max Weber's perspective on values in research.
23. Discuss the tension that remains between "pure" sociology and social reform.

CHAPTER OUTLINE

I. The Sociological Perspective

A. This perspective is important because it provides a different way of looking at life; and it contributes to our understanding of why people are the way they are.

B. Sociology stresses the broader social context of behavior.
1. At the center is the question of how people are influenced by their society.
2. Sociologists look at the social location–culture, social class, gender, race, religion, age, and education—of people.
3. Sociologists consider external influences—people's experiences—that are internalized and become part of a person's thinking and motivations.

II. Origins of Sociology

A. The study of sociology emerged as a result of the changes taking place in European societies at that time. These changes include: (1) the Industrial Revolution, in which traditional society and culture were transformed; (2) the American and French revolutions, out of which new ideas about the rights of individuals within society were accepted; and (3) the application of scientific methods to find answers for questions about the natural order and our social world.

B. **Auguste Comte** coined the term *sociology* and suggested the use of positivism—applying the scientific approach to the social world—but he did not utilize this approach himself.

C. **Herbert Spencer**, another social philosopher, viewed societies as evolutionary, coined the term *the survival of the fittest*, and became known for social Darwinism.

D. **Karl Marx**, founder of the conflict perspective, believed that class conflict—the struggle between the proletariat and the bourgeoisie—was the key to human history.

E. **Emile Durkheim** studied the social factors that underline suicide and found that the level of social integration, the degree to which people are tied to their social group, was a key social factor in suicide. Central to his studies was the idea that human behavior cannot be understood simply in individual terms, but must be understood within the larger social context in which it occurs.

F. **Max Weber** defined religion as a central force in social change, i.e., Protestantism encouraged greater economic development and was the central factor in the rise of capitalism in some countries.

III. Sexism in Early Sociology

A. In the 1800s women were assigned the roles of wife and mother. Few were able to acquire the education required to become sociologists and the work of those who did was ignored.

B. **Harriet Martineau** was exceptional. She studied social life in Great Britain and the United States and eventually published *Society in America* two to three decades before Max Weber or Emile Durkheim were even born.

IV.   Sociology in North America

A.   Sociology was transplanted to the United States in the late nineteenth century, first taking hold at the University of Chicago, the University of Kansas, and Atlanta University.

B.   **Jane Addams** was active in promoting social reform. In 1889 she founded Hull House, a settlement house that served the needs of Chicago's urban poor. Sociologists from the nearby University of Chicago were frequent visitors.

C.   **W. E. B. Du Bois** was the first African American to earn a doctorate at Harvard University. He spent most of his career at Atlanta University, where he conducted extensive research on race relations in the United States. He was committed to social action, helping to found the NAACP.

D.   During the 1940s, the focus shifted from reform to theory; **Talcott Parsons** developed abstract models of society to show how the parts of society harmoniously work together. In the 1950s, **C. Wright Mills** urged sociologists to get back to social reform. He saw imminent danger in the emergence of a power elite within the United States.

E.   Recently there have been attempts to blend sociological knowledge with practical results through the development of **applied sociology**.
  1.   Applied sociologists work in various social settings.
  2.   Applied sociology is not the same as social reform because the goal is not to rebuild society but to bring about change in a limited setting.

V.   Theoretical Perspectives in Sociology

A.   **Theory** is defined as a "general statement about how some parts of the world fit together and how they work." There are three major theoretical perspectives in sociology.

B.   **Symbolic interactionism** views society as composed of symbols that people use to establish meaning, define their relationship, develop their views of the world, and communicate with one another. A symbolic interactionist studying divorce would focus on the changing meanings of marriage, divorce, and family to explain the increase in divorce rates.

C.   **Functional analysis** sees society as composed of various parts, each with a function, which contributes to society's equilibrium. **Auguste Comte, Herbert Spencer**, and **Emile Durkheim** all contributed to the development of functionalism.
  1.   **Robert Merton** used the term *functions* to refer to the beneficial consequences of people's actions. There are both *manifest functions*—actions that are intended to help some part of the system—and *latent functions*—unintended consequences that help social systems adjust. There are also *latent dysfunctions*, unintended consequences that undermine a system's equilibrium.
  2.   In trying to explain divorce, a functionalist would look at how industrialization and urbanization both contributed to the changing function of marriage and the family.

D.   According to **conflict theory**, society is composed of groups competing for scarce resources. Divorce is seen as the outcome of the shifting balance of power within the family. As women have gained power and tried to address inequalities in the relationship, men have resisted.

E.   The perspectives differ in their level of analysis. *Macro-level analysis* an examination of large-scale patterns of society is the focus for functional and conflict analysis. Micro-level analysis—an examination of social interaction is the focus for symbolic interactionism.

F.   Each perspective provides a different and often sharply contrasting picture of the world. Sociologists use all three perspectives because no one theory or level of analysis encompasses all of reality.

G. Research without theory is of little value. It becomes a collection of meaningless *facts*. Theory that is unconnected to research is abstract and empty, unlikely to represent the way life really is. Theory is used to interpret research findings and research in turn helps to generate theory. Theory and research have a reciprocal relationship.

VI. Doing Sociological Research

A. Common sense cannot be relied on as a source of knowledge because it is highly limited and its insights often are incorrect. To move beyond common sense and understand what is really going on and why, it is necessary to do sociological research.

B. Scientific research follows eight basic steps.
1. Selecting a topic depends on what the researcher wants to know more about and explain.
2. Defining the problem involves specifying exactly what the researcher wants to learn about the topic.
3. Reviewing the literature uncovers existing knowledge about the problem.
4. Formulating a hypothesis involves stating the expected relationship between **variables**, based on a theory. Hypotheses need **operational definitions**—precise ways to measure the variables.
5. Choosing a research method is influenced by the research topic.
6. Collecting the data involves concerns over *validity*—the extent to which operational definitions measure what was intended—and *reliability*—the extent to which data produces consistent results.
7. Analyzing the results involves the use of a range of techniques—from statistical tests to content analysis—to analyze data. Computers have become powerful tools in data analysis because they reduce large amounts of data to basic patterns in much less time than it used to take.
8. Sharing the results by writing a report and publishing the results makes the findings available for replication and review by others.

VII. Research Methods

A. **Surveys** involve collecting data by having people answer a series of questions.
1. The first step is to determine a population—the target group to be studied—and selecting a sample—individuals from among the target population who are intended to represent the population to be studied.
2. In a **random sample** everyone in the target population has the same chance of being included in the study. A **stratified random sample** is a sample of specific subgroups (e.g. freshmen, sophomores, juniors) of the target population (a college or university) in which everyone in the subgroup has an equal chance of being included in the study. Because a random sample represents the target population, you can generalize your findings.
3. The **respondents** (people who respond to a survey) must be allowed to express their own ideas so that the findings will not be biased.
4. Sociologists must decide between asking **closed-ended questions** in which the respondent selects one from a list of possible answers and **open-ended questions** in which respondents answer the question in their own words.
5. It is important to establish **rapport**—a feeling of trust between researchers and subjects.

B. In **participant observation**, the researcher participates in a research setting while observing what is happening in that setting.

C. **Secondary analysis** is the analysis of data already collected by other researchers.

D.   **Documents**—written sources—may be obtained from many sources, including books, newspapers, police reports, and records kept by various organizations.

E.   **Experiments** are especially useful in determining causal relationships
   1.   Experiments require an **experimental group**—the group of subjects exposed to the independent variable—and a **control group**—the group of subjects not exposed to the independent variable.
   2.   Experiments involve **independent variables** (factors that cause a change in something) and **dependent variables** (factors that are changed).

F.   **Unobtrusive measures** involve observing social behavior of people who do not know they are being studied.

VIII.   Ethics In Sociological Research

A.   Ethics are of fundamental concern to sociologists when it comes to doing research.

B.   Ethical considerations include being open, honest, and truthful, not falsifying results or stealing someone else's work, not harming the subject in the course of conducting the research, protecting the anonymity of the research subjects, and not misrepresenting themselves to the research subjects.

C.   Efforts by **Mario Brajuha** to honor his research ethics reflect the seriousness with which sociologists view ethical considerations. Research by **Laud Humphreys** raised questions about how researchers represent themselves to subjects.

D.   **Weber** advocated that sociological research should be value-free—personal values or biases should not influence social research—and objective—totally neutral.
   1.   Sociologists agree that objectivity is a proper goal, but acknowledge that no one can escape values entirely.
   2.   **Replication**—repeating a study to see if the same results are found—is one means to avoid the distortions that differing values can cause.
   3.   This debate illustrates the continuing tensions over what should be the goal of sociological research. Some sociologists lean towards basic sociological research that has no goal beyond understanding social life and testing social theory, others feel that the knowledge should be used to reform society.

KEY TERMS

After studying the chapter, review each of the following terms.

applied sociology: the use of sociology to solve problems—from the micro level of family relationships to the macro level of crime and pollution (p. 12)

basic (or pure) sociology: sociological research whose purpose is to make discoveries about life in human groups, not to make changes in those groups (p. 12)

class conflict: Marx's term for the struggle between capitalists and workers (p. 7)

closed-ended questions: questions followed by a list of possible answers to be selected by the respondent (p. 25)

conflict theory: a theoretical framework in which society is viewed as being composed of groups competing for scarce resources (p. 18)

control group: the group of subjects not exposed to the independent variable (p. 28)

dependent variable: a factor that is changed by an independent variable (p. 28)

documents: in its narrow sense, written sources that provide data; in its extended sense, archival material of any sort, including photographs, movies, and so on (p. 28)

experiment: the use of control groups and experimental groups and dependent and independent variables to test causation (p. 28)

experimental group: the group of subjects exposed to the independent variable (p. 28)

functional analysis: a theoretical framework in which society is viewed as composed of various parts, each with a function that, when fulfilled, contributes to society's equilibrium; also known as *functionalism* and *structural functionalism* (p. 16)

hypothesis: a statement of the expected relationship between variables according to predictions from a theory (p. 20)

independent variable: a factor that causes a change in another variable, called the dependent variable (p. 28)

macro-level analysis: an examination of large-scale patterns of society (p. 18)

micro-level analysis: an examination of small-scale patterns of society (p. 19)

nonverbal interaction: communication without words through gestures, space, silence, and so on (p. 19)

open-ended questions: questions that respondents are able to answer in their own words (p. 25)

operational definitions: the ways in which variables in a hypothesis are measured (p. 20)

participant observation (or **fieldwork**): research in which the researcher participates in a research setting while observing what is happening in that setting (p. 28)

population: the target group to be studied (p. 24)

positivism: the application of the scientific method to the social world (p. 6)

random sample: a sample in which everyone in the target population has the same chance of being included in the study (p. 24)

reliability: the extent to which data produce consistent results (p. 21)

replication: repeating a study in order to test its findings (p. 30)

research method (or **research design**): one of six procedures sociologists use to collect data: surveys, participant observation, secondary analysis, documents, experiments, and unobtrusive measures (p. 21)

respondents: people who respond to a survey, either in interviews or by self-administered questionnaires (p. 25)

sample: the individuals intended to represent the population to be studied (p. 24)

science: requires the development of theories that can be tested by research (p.5)

secondary analysis: the analysis of data already collected by other researchers (p. 25)

social integration: the degree to which people feel a part of social groups (p. 8)

social interaction: what people do when they are in one another's presence (p. 19)

social location: the group memberships that people have because of their location in history and society (p. 4)

society: people who share a culture and a territory (p. 4)

sociological perspective: understanding human behavior by placing it within its broader social context (p. 4)

sociology: the scientific study of society and human behavior (p. 6)

survey: the collection of data by having people answer a series of questions (p. 22)

symbolic interactionism: a theoretical perspective in which society is viewed as composed of symbols that people use to establish meaning, develop their views of the world, and communicate with one another (p. 14)

theory: a general statement about how some parts of the world fit together and how they work; an explanation of how two or more facts are related to one another (p. 14)

unobtrusive measures: ways of observing people who do not know they are being studied (p. 29)

validity: the extent to which an operational definition measures what was intended (p. 21)

value free: the view that a sociologist's personal values or biases should not influence social research (p. 30)

values: the standards by which people define what is desirable or undesirable, good or bad, beautiful or ugly (p. 30)

variables: factors thought to be significant for behavior, which vary from one case to another (p. 20)

KEY PEOPLE

Review the major theoretical contributions or research findings of these theorists and thinkers.

Jane Addams: Addams was the founder of Hull House—a settlement house in the immigrant community of Chicago. She invited sociologists from nearby University of Chicago to visit. In 1931 she was a winner of the Nobel Peace Prize.

Mario Brajuha: During an investigation into a restaurant fire, officials subpoenaed notes taken by this sociologist in connection with his **participant observation research** on restaurant work. He was threatened with jail but would not turn over his notes.

Auguste Comte: Comte is often credited with being the founder of sociology, because he was the first to suggest that the scientific method be applied to the study of the social world.

Lewis Coser: Coser pointed out that conflict is likely to develop among people in close relationships because they are connected by a network of responsibilities, power, and rewards.

W. E. B. Du Bois: Du Bois was the first African American to earn a doctorate at Harvard University. For most of his career, he taught sociology at Atlanta University. He was concerned about social injustice, wrote about race relations, and was one of the founders of the National Association for the Advancement of Colored People.

Emile Durkheim: Durkheim was responsible for getting sociology recognized as a separate discipline. He was interested in studying how social forces shape individual behavior.

Laud Humphreys: The sociologist carried out doctoral research on homosexual activity. In order to obtain information, he misrepresented himself to his research subjects. When his methods became widely known, a debate developed over his use of questionable ethics.

Harriet Martineau: An Englishwoman who studied British and United States social life and published *Society in America* decades before either Durkheim or Weber was born.

Karl Marx: Marx believed that social development grew out of conflict between social classes; under capitalism, this conflict was between the *bourgeoisie*—those who own the means to produce wealth—and the *proletariat*—the mass of workers. His work is associated with the conflict perspective.

Robert Merton: Merton contributed the terms *manifest* and *latent functions* and *latent dysfunctions* to the functionalist perspective.

C. Wright Mills: Mills suggested that external influences—or a person's experiences—become part of his or her thinking and motivations and explain social behavior. In the 1950s he urged United States sociologists to get back to social reform. He argued that research without theory is of little value, simply a collection of unrelated *facts*, and theory that is unconnected to research is abstract and empty, unlikely to represent the way life really is.

Talcott Parsons: Parsons' work dominated sociology in the 1940s-1950s. He developed abstract models of how the parts of society harmoniously work together.

Herbert Spencer: Another early social philosopher, Spencer believed that societies evolve from barbarian to civilized forms. The first to use the expression "the survival of the fittest" to reflect his belief that social evolution depended on the survival of the most capable and intelligent and the extinction of the less capable. His views became known as *social Darwinism*.

Max Weber: Among Weber's many contributions to sociology were his study of the relationship between the emergence of the Protestant belief system and the rise of capitalism. He believed that sociologists should not allow their personal values to affect their social research and objectivity should become the hallmark of sociology.

SELF-TEST

After completing this self-test, check your answers in the Answer Key of this Study Guide.

MULTIPLE CHOICE QUESTIONS

1. The sociological perspective stresses the _____ in which people live.
   a. social contexts
   b. geographic location
   c. neighborhoods
   d. cities

2. Income, education, gender, and race all reflect a person's:
   a. personality.
   b. social placement.
   c. social location.
   d. perspective.

3. _____ requires the development of theories that can be tested by systematic research.
   a. Tradition
   b. Religion
   c. Science
   d. All of the above

4. Karl Marx did not develop the political system called:
   a. democracy.
   b. social integration.
   c. positivism.
   d. communism.

5. According to Karl Marx, capitalists, who own the means of production, exploit the:
   a. bourgeoisie.
   b. proletariat.
   c. masses.
   d. peasants.

6. According to Durkheim, the degree to which people are tied to their social group is:
   a. symbolic interaction.
   b. social integration.
   c. positivism.
   d. survival of the fittest

7. Weber concluded that the key factor in the rise of capitalism was:
   a. social upheaval.
   b. survival of the fittest.
   c. religion.
   d. technology.

8.   Despite writing an insightful examination of the United States, Harriet Martineau's work was ignored because she was:
    a.   not a real sociologist.
    b.   a theologian.
    c.   a woman.
    d.   working with Auguste Comte.

9.   During the 1940s, the emphasis in sociology shifted from _____ in the United States.
    a.   social reform to social theory
    b.   social theory to social reform
    c.   positivism to theory
    d.   theory to positivism

10.   The branch of sociology that focuses on using sociology to solve problems is:
    a.   social reform.
    b.   social activism.
    c.   applied sociology.
    d.   practical sociology.

11.   _____ study the symbols people use to establish meaning and communicate.
    a.   Functionalists
    b.   Symbolic interactionists
    c.   Dramaturgical theorists
    d.   Conflict theorists

12.   Society as a whole unit made up of interrelated parts that work together is the premise of:
    a.   symbolic interactionism.
    b.   functional analysis.
    c.   positivism.
    d.   conflict theory.

13.   The perspective that stresses society is composed of groups that engage in fierce competition for scarce resources is:
    a.   structural-functionalism.
    b.   conflict theory.
    c.   positivism.
    d.   symbolic interactionism.

14.   Conflict theorists might explain the high rate of divorce by looking at:
    a.   how men's and women's relationships have changed.
    b.   the role lawyers have played in society.
    c.   capitalism.
    d.   religion.

15.   The focus on large-scale patterns of society is:
    a.   the micro-level of analysis.
    b.   the social interaction-level of analysis.
    c.   the macro-level of analysis.
    d.   middle range.

16. Functionalists and conflict theorists focus on:
    a. the micro-level of analysis.
    b. the macro-level of analysis.
    c. middle-range analysis.
    d. feminism.

17. A precise way to measure a variable is:
    a. reliability.
    b. validity.
    c. an operational definition.
    d. not possible.

18. Reliability refers to:
    a. the extent to which operational definitions measure what they are intended to measure.
    b. the extent to which data produce consistent results.
    c. the integrity of the researcher.
    d. a measure of validity.

19. The method you choose when doing research depends on:
    a. the questions you want to answer.
    b. the time you have to do research.
    c. the amount of money you want to spend on the project.
    d. the number of people you expect to study.

20. Which of the following can be strongly influenced by extreme scores?
    a. The mode.
    b. The median.
    c. The mean.
    d. All of the above can be strongly influenced by extreme scores.

21. When everyone in your population has the same chance of being included in your research study, you are conducting:
    a. a random sample.
    b. a stratified random sample.
    c. a snowball sample.
    d. a biased sample.

22. If you ask respondents to choose—in regards to their level of education—between 1) high school diplomas; 2) some college but no degree; and 3) college degree, you would be using:
    a. an open-ended question.
    b. a closed-ended question.
    c. a neutral question.
    d. b and c only.

23. George is interested in doing research on autoworkers. He decides to move to a working class community and get a job on the assembly line of an auto plant so he can experience what it is like to be an autoworker while he is collecting his data. This type of research is referred to as:
    a. secondary analysis.
    b. a survey.
    c. an experiment.
    d. participant observation.

24.   The analysis of data already collected by other researchers is referred to as:
        a.   surveying the literature.
        b.   use of documents.
        c.   secondary analysis.
        d.   replication.

25.   Ethics in research condemns which of the following:
        a.   falsification of results.
        b.   plagiarism.
        c.   harming those being studied.
        d.   all of the above.

26.   Max Weber believed that sociology should be:
        a.   value laden.
        b.   value free.
        c.   religion based.
        d.   reliable.

27.   To overcome the distortions that values can cause, sociologists stress:
        a.   validity.
        b.   replication.
        c.   random samples.
        d.   analysis verification.

28.   Mario Brajuha refused to turn over his research notes to police because:
        a.   he did not want to get involved.
        b.   he was concerned about confidentiality and anonymity of those he studied.
        c.   he was afraid for his life.
        d.   none of the above.

29.   Laud Humphreys was criticized by many sociologists for being unethical because:
        a.   he did not identify himself as a researcher to those he studied.
        b.   the way he obtained addresses of those he studied.
        c.   of acting as a watchqueen.
        d.   he burning his notes.

30.   Research that has no goal beyond understanding social life and testing social theories is:
        a.   basic sociology.
        b.   applied sociology.
        c.   unobtrusive sociology.
        d.   none of the above.

TRUE-FALSE QUESTIONS

T F   1.   At the center of the sociological perspective is the question of how groups influence people.
T F   2.   C. Wright Mills stressed that the sociological perspective enables us to grasp the connection between history and biography.
T F   3.   Science requires the development of theories that can be tested by systematic research.

T F   4.   The scientific method uses subjective, systematic observations to test theories.
T F   5.   Herbert Spencer's ideas are known as social Darwinism.
T F   6.   Both Comte and Spencer were more social philosophers than sociologists.
T F   7.   Marxism is the same thing as communism.
T F   8.   People who are less socially integrated have high rates of suicide.
T F   9.   For Catholics, according to Weber, financial success was the major sign that God was on their side.
T F   10. Harriet Martineau is primarily known for her translations of Marx's work.
T F   11. Initially, the department of sociology at Chicago dominated sociology.
T F   12. Jane Addams was more of a basic sociologist than a social reformer.
T F   13. W. E. B. Du Bois was the first African American to earn a doctorate at Harvard.
T F   14. In everyday life we interpret what we observe by using common sense.
T F   15. Functionalists believe that society is composed of parts that work together.
T F   16. From the conflict perspective, the increase in divorce is a sign that marriage has weakened.
T F   17. Validity is the extent to which a researcher's operational definitions measure what they are intended to measure.
T F   18. If you wanted to know only about certain subgroups, in a research study, a stratified random sample should be used.
T F   19. Unobtrusive measures involve observing people who do not know they're being studied.
T F   20. In an experiment, the experimental group is not exposed to the independent variable in the study.

FILL-IN QUESTIONS

1.   The _____ stresses the social contexts in which people are immersed and that influence their lives.
2.   Comte believed that the _____ should be applied to social life.
3.   _____ is sometimes referred to as the second founder of sociology.
4.   Marx said that the _____ were the controlling class of capitalists.
5.   _____ came to eventually embrace revolutionary Marxism.
6.   Early sociologists envisioned the success of _____.
7.   A _____ is a general statement about how some parts of the world fit together and how they work.
8.   The theoretical perspective in which society is viewed as composed of symbols that people use to establish meaning, develop their views of the world, and communicate with one another is _____.
9.   _____ analysis is a theoretical framework in which society is viewed as composed of various parts, each with a function that contributes to society's equilibrium.
10. If an action is intended to help some part of a system, it is a _____ function.
11. Lewis Coser pointed out that conflict is most likely to develop among people who are in _____ relationships.
12. The means by which you collect your data is _____.
13. The individuals who are selected from a larger population to participate in a research study are called a _____.

14. To conduct an experiment, the researcher has two groups: 1) _____ and 2) _____

15. Personal beliefs should not affect research. Research should be _____.

MATCH THESE THEORISTS/PHILOSOPHERS WITH THEIR CONTRIBUTIONS

1.	Comte	a.	*The Protestant ethic*
2.	Spencer	b.	*Positivism*
3.	Marx	c.	*Social Darwinism*
4.	Durkheim	d.	*Class conflict*
5.	Weber	e.	*Social integration*

MATCH EACH CONCEPT WITH ITS DEFINITION

1.	Bourgeoisie	a.	*Use of sociology to solve problems*
2.	Protestant Ethic	b.	*Factors that change*
3.	Applied Sociology	c.	*Capitalists*
4.	Functional Analysis	d.	*Society is a whole unit*
5.	Variable	e.	*Self-denying approach to life.*

ESSAY QUESTIONS

1. Explain what the sociological perspective encompasses and then, using that perspective, discuss the forces that shaped the discipline of sociology.

2. Explain why there has been a continuing tension between analyzing society and working toward reforming society since the very beginning of society.

3. Explain each of the theoretical perspectives that are used in sociology and describe how a sociologist affiliated with one or another of the perspectives might undertake a study of gangs. Discuss how all three can be used in research.

4. Choose a topic and explain how you would go through the different steps in the research model.

5. The author of your text discusses six different research methods. Pick a research topic of interest to you and discuss how you might try to investigate this topic using these different methods. In your answer, consider how a particular method may or may not be suitable for the topic under consideration.

STUDENT PROJECTS

1. Observe three classes in which you are enrolled. How would you use symbolic interactionism to explain what happens (or does not happen) immediately before, during, and immediately after each class? How would you use functional theory? How would you use conflict theory? Explain.

2. Think back to the last time you participated in a survey (phone, web, or mail). Did you really want to participate in the survey? Why or why not? What problems did you notice with the survey? Do you think most people were compelled to give socially acceptable answers in the survey? Explain. Finally, discuss to what extent you think surveys are a good way to do research.

CHAPTER 2

CULTURE

CHAPTER SUMMARY

- **Culture** refers to the language, beliefs, values, norms, and material objects passed from one generation to the next. Culture is both **material** (buildings, clothing, tools) and **nonmaterial** (ways of thinking and patterns of behavior). **Ideal culture** refers to a group's values, norms, and goals. **Real culture** refers to its actual behavior. People are naturally **ethnocentric**, using their own culture to judge others; **cultural relativism** is the attempt to understand other cultures in their own terms.

- The central component of culture is symbols. Universally, the symbols of culture are language, gestures, values, norms, sanctions, folkways, and mores. Language is essential for culture because it allows us to move beyond the present, sharing with others our experiences and our future plans. According to the Sapir-Whorf hypothesis, language not only allows us to express our thinking and perceptions but it actually shapes them. All groups have **values**, standards by which they define what is desirable and undesirable, and **norms**, rules about appropriate behavior. Socially imposed sanctions maximize conformity to social norms.

- A **subculture** is a group whose values and related behaviors distinguish its members from the general culture. A **counterculture** is a subculture that subscribes to values that set its members in opposition to the dominant culture.

- Core values in U.S. society emphasize personal achievement and success, hard work, and moral orientation. **Value clusters** are interrelated individual values that together form a larger whole and sometimes individual values contradict one another. These contradictions reflect areas of social tension and potential points for social change. Values that are emerging as core values today within United States culture include leisure, physical fitness, self-fulfillment, and concern over the environment. Changes in a society's values often generate opposition.

- **Ogburn** used the term **cultural lag** to refer to situations in which a society's nonmaterial culture lags behind its changing technology. Today the technology in travel and communication makes **cultural diffusion** around the globe occur more rapidly than in the past, resulting in some degree of **cultural leveling**—a process by which cultures become similar to one another.

LEARNING OBJECTIVES

As you read Chapter 2, use these learning objectives to organize your notes. After completing your reading, you should be able to answer each of the objectives.

1. Define culture, discuss its effects, and differentiate between its material and nonmaterial components.
2. Know what is meant by culture shock, provide examples of situations that may result in culture shock, and explain how culture shock forces people to challenge their own cultural assumptions.
3. Define ethnocentrism and cultural relativism, offer examples of both concepts, and list the positive and negative consequences of each.
4. Define — and differentiate between — gestures and language.
5. Explain why language is the basis of culture, including why it is critical to human life and essential for cultural development.

6. Understand the Sapir-Whorf hypothesis and provide examples of how language not only reflects and expresses thinking, perceptions, and experiences, but also shapes and influences them.

7. Define values, norms, sanctions, folkways, mores, and taboos; provide examples of each; and discuss their sociological significance.

8. Compare, contrast, and offer examples of dominant cultures, subcultures, and countercultures.

9. List the core values in American society as identified by Robin Williams and supplemented by James Henslin.

10. Explain what is meant by value clusters and value contradictions, and offer examples of each in American society.

11. Understand how value contradictions can affect social change.

12. Define the five emerging values.

13. Discuss the differences between "ideal" and "real" culture.

14. List some current "new technologies" and talk about how they are changing social behaviors and relationships in the United States and around the world.

15. Define and discuss cultural lag, cultural diffusion, and cultural leveling.

CHAPTER OUTLINE

I. What Is Culture?

A. **Culture** is defined as the language, beliefs, values, norms, behaviors, and even material objects that are passed from one generation to the next.
1. **Material culture** includes things such as jewelry, art, buildings, weapons, machines, clothing, hairstyles, etc.
2. **Nonmaterial culture** is a group's ways of thinking (beliefs, values, and assumptions) and common patterns of behavior (language, gestures, and other forms of interaction.)

B. Culture provides a taken-for-granted orientation to life.
1. We assume that our own culture is normal or natural, but, in fact, it is not natural. Culture is learned. It penetrates our lives so deeply that it is taken for granted and provides the lens through which we perceive things.
2. It provides implicit instructions that tell us what we ought to do and a moral imperative that defines what we think is right and wrong.
3. Coming into contact with a radically different culture produces **culture shock**, challenging our basic assumptions about life.
4. A consequence of internalizing culture is **ethnocentrism**, using our own culture (and assuming it to be good, right, and superior) to judge other cultures. It is functional when it creates in-group solidarity, but can be dysfunctional if it leads to harmful discrimination.

C. **Cultural relativism** consists of trying to appreciate other groups' ways of life in the context in which they exist, without judging them as superior or inferior to our own.
1. This view attempts to refocus the lens in order to help us appreciate other cultures.
2. **Robert Edgerton** argues that we should develop a scale to evaluate cultures on their quality of life and that those cultural practices that result in exploitation should be judged morally inferior to those that enhance people's lives.

II. Components of Symbolic Culture

A. Sociologists sometimes refer to nonmaterial culture as symbolic culture because the central components are the symbols people use.

   1.   A **symbol** is something to which people attach meaning and for which people use to communicate with one another.
   2.   Symbols include language, gestures, values, norms, sanctions, folkways, and mores.

B.   **Gestures**, using one's body to communicate with others, are shorthand means of communication.
   1.   Gestures are used by people in every culture, although the gestures and the meanings differ; confusion or offense can result because of misunderstandings over the meaning of a gesture or it's misuse.
   2.   . Gestures, which vary remarkably around the world, can invoke strong emotions.

C.   **Language** consists of a system of symbols that can be put together in an infinite number of ways in order to communicate abstract thought. Each word is a symbol, a sound to which a culture attaches a particular meaning. Language is important because it is the primary means of communication between people.
   1.   It allows human experiences to be cumulative. Each generation builds on the body of significant experiences that is passed on to it by the previous generation, thus freeing people to move beyond their own immediate experiences.
   2.   It enables us to share our past experiences, and extend time into the future, allowing us to share our future plans. It expands connections beyond our immediate, face-to-face groups.
   3.   It allows shared perspectives or understandings and complex, goal-directed behavior.

D.   The **Sapir-Whorf hypothesis** states that our thinking and perception not only are expressed by language but are actually shaped by language because we are taught not only words but also a particular way of thinking and perceiving. Rather than objects and events forcing themselves onto our consciousness, our very language determines our consciousness.

E.   Values, norms, and sanctions are also components of culture.
   1.   **Values** are the standards by which people define good and bad, beautiful and ugly. Every group develops both values and expectations regarding the right way to reflect them.
   2.   **Norms** are expectations, or rules of behavior, that reflect a group's values.
   3.   **Sanctions** are the positive or negative reactions to the way in which people follow norms. **Positive sanctions** (a money reward, a prize, a smile, or even a handshake) are expressions of approval. **Negative sanctions** (a fine, a frown, or harsh words) denote disapproval for breaking a norm.
   4.   Norms can become rigorous, making people feel stifled. Moral holidays, like Mardi Gras, are specific times when people are allowed to break the norms.

F.   Folkways and mores are different types of norms.
   1.   **Folkways** are norms that are not strictly enforced, such as passing on the left side of the sidewalk. They may result in a person getting a dirty look.
   2.   **Mores** are norms that are believed to be essential to core values and we insist on conformity. A person who steals, rapes, or kills has violated some of society's most important mores and will be formally sanctioned.
   3.   One group's folkways may constitute another group's mores. A male walking down the street with the upper half of his body uncovered may be violating a folkway; a female doing the same thing may be violating accepted mores.
   4.   **Taboos** are norms so strongly ingrained that even the thought of them is greeted with revulsion. Eating human flesh and having sex with one's parents are examples of such behavior.

III. Many Cultural Worlds

A. **Subcultures** are groups whose values and related behaviors are so distinct that they set their members apart from the dominant culture.

1. Each subculture is a world within the larger world of the dominant culture. Each has a distinctive way of looking at life, but remains compatible with the dominant culture.

2. United States society contains tens of thousands of subcultures, some as broad as the way of life we associate with teenagers, others as narrow as that of body-builders or philosophers. Ethnic groups often form subcultures with their own language, distinctive food, religious practices, and other customs. Occupational groups also form subcultures.

B. **Countercultures** are groups whose values set their members in opposition to the dominant culture.

1. Countercultures challenge the culture's core values.

2. Countercultures are usually associated with negative behavior. For example, heavy metal music adherents who glorify Satanism, hatred, cruelty, rebellion, sexism, violence, and death, are an example of a counterculture.

3. Often threatened by a counterculture, members of the broader culture sometimes move against it in order to affirm their own values.

IV. Values in U.S. Society

A. Identifying core values in United States society is difficult due to the many different religious, racial, ethnic, and special interest groups that are found in this pluralistic society.

1. Sociologist **Robin Williams** identified the following as core values: achievement and success (especially doing better than others); individualism (success due to individual effort); activity and work; efficiency and practicality; science and technology (using science to control nature); progress; material comfort; humanitarianism (helpfulness, personal kindness, philanthropy); freedom; democracy; equality (especially of opportunity); and racism and group superiority.

2. Henslin updated Williams's list by adding education; religiosity (belief in a Supreme Being and following some set of matching precept); and romantic love (as the basis for marriage) and monogamy (no more than one spouse at a time.)

B. Values are not independent units. **Value clusters** are made up of related core values that come together to form a larger whole. In the value cluster surrounding success, for example, we find hard work, education, efficiency, material comfort, and individualism all bound together.

C. Some values conflict with each other. There cannot be full expressions of democracy, equality, racism, and sexism at the same time. These are **value contradictions** and as society changes, some values are challenged and undergo modification.

D. As society changes over time, new core values emerge that reflect changing social conditions. Examples of emerging values in the United States today are: leisure; physical fitness; self-fulfillment; and concern for the environment.

E. Core values do not change without meeting strong resistance. Today's clash in values is so severe that it is referred to a culture war.

F. Values and their supporting beliefs may blind people to other social circumstances. The emphasis on individualism is so high that many people in the United States believe that everyone is free to pursue the goal of success, thereby blinding them to the dire consequences of family poverty, lack of education, and dead-end jobs.

G. **Ideal culture** refers to the ideal values and norms of a group. What people actually do usually falls short of this ideal, and sociologists refer to the norms and values that people actually follow as **real culture**.

V. Technology in the Global Village

A. Central to a group's material culture is its technology. In its simplest sense, technology refers to tools, in its broadest sense it includes the skills or procedures to make and use those tools.
1. **New technologies** refer to the emerging technologies that have a major impact on human life during a particular era.
2. Technology sets a framework for a group's nonmaterial culture.

B. **William Ogburn** first used the term **cultural lag** to refer to situations where not all parts of a culture change at the same pace: when some part of culture changes, other parts lag behind.
1. A group's material culture usually changes first, with the nonmaterial culture lagging behind.
2. Sometimes nonmaterial culture never catches up to the changes. We hold on to some outdated form that was once needed but now has been bypassed by new technology.

C. Most human cultures throughout history had little contact with one another. However, there was always some contact with other groups, resulting in groups learning from one another.
1. Social scientists refer to this transmission of cultural characteristics as **cultural diffusion**.
2. Material culture is more likely than the nonmaterial culture to change because of cultural diffusion.
3. Cultural diffusion occurs more rapidly today, given the changes in travel and communications that unite the world to such an extent that there is almost no "other side of the world."
4. One consequence of cultural diffusion is **cultural leveling**, the process in which cultures become similar to one another. Japan, for example, no longer is a purely Eastern culture, having adopted not only Western economic production, but also Western forms of dress, music, and so on.

KEY TERMS
After studying the chapter, review each of the following terms.

counterculture: a group whose values, beliefs, and related behaviors place its members in opposition to the broader culture (p. 47)

cultural diffusion: the spread of cultural characteristics from one group to another (p. 55)

cultural lag: Ogburn's term for human behavior lagging behind technological innovations (p. 54)

cultural leveling: the process by which cultures become similar to one another; especially refers to the process by which U.S. culture is being imported and diffused into other nations (p. 55)

cultural relativism: not judging a culture but trying to understand it on its own terms (p. 38)

culture: the language, beliefs, values, norms, behaviors, and even material objects that are passed from one generation to the next (p. 36)

culture shock: the disorientation that people experience when they come in contact with a fundamentally different culture and can no longer depend on their taken-for-granted assumptions about life (p. 37)

ethnocentrism: the use of one's own culture as a yardstick for judging the ways of other individuals or societies, generally leading to a negative evaluation of their values, norms, and behaviors (p. 37)

folkways: norms that are not strictly enforced (p. 46)

gestures: the ways in which people use their bodies to communicate with one another (p. 40)

ideal culture: the ideal values and norms of a people; the goals held out for them (as opposed to *real culture)* (p. 54)

language: a system of symbols that can be combined in an infinite number of ways and can represent not only objects but also abstract thought (p. 42)

material culture: the material objects that distinguish a group of people, such as their art, buildings, weapons, utensils, machines, hairstyles, clothing, and jewelry (p. 36)

mores: norms that are strictly enforced because they are thought essential to core values (p. 46)

negative sanction: an expression of disapproval for breaking a norm, ranging from a mild, informal reaction such as a frown to a formal reaction such as a prison sentence or an execution (p. 46)

new technology: an emerging technology that has a significant impact on social life (p. 54)

nonmaterial culture (also called *symbolic culture*): a group's ways of thinking (including its beliefs, values, and other assumptions about the world) and doing (its common patterns of behavior, including language and other forms of interaction) (p. 36)

norms: the expectations, or rules of behavior, that develops to reflect and enforce values (p. 46)

pluralistic society: a society made up of many different groups (p. 50)

positive sanction: a reward or positive reaction for following norms (p. 46)

sanctions: expressions of approval or disapproval given to people for upholding or violating norms (p. 46)

Sapir-Whorf hypothesis: Edward Sapir's and Benjamin Whorf's hypothesis that language creates ways of thinking and perceiving (p. 45)

subculture: the values and related behaviors of a group that distinguish its members from the larger culture; a world within a world (p. 47)

symbol: something to which people attach meanings and then use to communicate with others   (p. 39)

symbolic culture: another term for nonmaterial culture (p. 39)

taboo: a norm thought essential for society's welfare, one so strong that it brings revulsion if violated (p. 47)

technology: in its narrow sense, tools; its broader sense includes the skills or procedures necessary to make and use those tools (p. 54)

value cluster: a series of interrelated values that together form a larger whole (p. 52)

value contradiction: values that contradict one another; to follow the one means to come into conflict with the other (p. 52)

values: the standards by which people define what is desirable or undesirable, good or bad, beautiful or ugly (p. 46)

KEY PEOPLE
Review the major theoretical contributions or research findings of these theorists and thinkers.

Robert Edgerton: Edgerton attacks the concept of cultural relativism, suggesting that because some cultures endanger their people's health, happiness, or survival, there should be a scale to evaluate cultures on their quality of life.

Douglas Massey: This sociologist has studied what happens in urban areas when immigration rates exceed the speed with which new residents can learn English and the proportion of non-English speakers increases.

William Ogburn: Ogburn coined the term cultural lag.

Edward Sapir and Benjamin Whorf: These anthropologists argued that language not only reflects thoughts and perceptions, but that it actually shapes the way a people perceive the world.

JoEllen Shively: Shively researched the reasons why both Anglo and Native American moviegoers identify more with the cowboys than the Indians.

William Sumner: Sumner developed the concept of ethnocentrism.

Robin Williams: He identified twelve core values in United States society.

SELF-TEST
After completing this self-test, check your answers in the Answer Key of this Study Guide.

MULTIPLE CHOICE

1.   Culture includes:
        a.   language.
        b.   beliefs.
        c.   values.
        d.   buildings.
        e.   all of the above.

2.   A group's way of thinking and doing, including language and other forms of interaction, is:
      a.   material culture.
      b.   nonmaterial culture.
      c.   ideological culture.
      d.   values.

3.   Learned and shared ways of believing and of doing penetrate our being at an early age. We take for granted what is "normal" behavior. This is the concept of:
      a.   culture shock.
      b.   culture within us.
      c.   culture lag.
      d.   cultural pluralism.

4.   The disorientation people experience when coming into contact with a radically different culture and when no longer able to depend on their taken-for-granted assumptions about life is known as:
      a.   cultural diffusion.
      b.   cultural leveling.
      c.   cultural relativism.
      d.   culture shock.

5.   Using one's culture as a yardstick to judge other cultures is known as practicing:
      a.   material culture.
      b.   culture shock.
      c.   cultural pluralism.
      d.   ethnocentrism.

6.   Gestures:
      a.   are studied by anthropologists but not sociologists.
      b.   are universal.
      c.   always facilitate communication between people.
      d.   can lead to misunderstandings and embarrassment.

7.   Symbols are the basis of:
      a.   material culture.
      b.   non-material culture.
      c.   sociobiology.

8.   The sociological theory that language creates a particular way of thinking and perceiving is:
      a.   sociobiology.
      b.   the Davis-Moore theory.
      c.   the Sapir-Whorf hypothesis.
      d.   the language theory.

9.   Every group develops expectations concerning the right way to reflect its values. The group's expectations are called:
      a.   pluralism.
      b.   norms.
      c.   universals.
      d.   leveling.

10.   Norms that are not strictly enforced are called:
      a.   values.
      b.   folkways.
      c.   mores.
      d.   taboo.

11.   Mores:
      a.   are essential to our core values and require conformity.
      b.   are norms that are not strictly enforced.
      c.   state that a person should not try to pass you on the left side of the sidewalk.
      d.   are less important in contemporary societies.

12.   In American culture, if a person intentionally kills another person, the behavior violates:
      a.   a folkway.
      b.   a more.
      c.   neither "a" nor "b."

13.   In American culture, eating human flesh is a violation of a:
      a.   universal.
      b.   more.
      c.   folkway.
      d.   taboo.

14.   Subcultures:
      a.   are a world within a world.
      b.   have values and related behaviors that set its members apart from the larger culture.
      c.   include ethnic groups.
      d.   all of the above.

15.   In general, physicians in the United States society are:
      a.   a subculture.
      b.   a counterculture.
      c.   not ethnocentric.
      d.   a value cluster.

16.   The Ku Klux Klan is a:
      a.   counterculture.
      b.   subculture.
      c.   cultural universal.
      d.   pluralistic group.

17.   A pluralistic society:
      a.   is made up of many different groups.
      b.   tends to discourage subcultures.
      c.   does not share core values.
      d.   no longer exists in the world.

18. Value contradictions occur when:
    a. a value, such as one that stresses group superiority, comes into direct conflict with other values, such as democracy and equality.
    b. societies have very little social change.
    c. a series of interrelated values bind together to form a larger whole.
    d. none of the above.

19. Which of the following is not one of the underlying core values of U.S. society as identified by sociologist Robin Williams?
    a. success
    b. community
    c. progress
    d. freedom

20. Which of the following is not of the three core values added by your textbook author? James Henslin?
    a. education
    b. religiosity
    c. romantic love
    d. happiness

21. Which of the following is not one of the five emerging values in the United States?
    a. leisure.
    b. security.
    c. physical fitness.
    d. youthfulness.

22. The valuing of youth and the disparagement of old age seems to be more urgent because of:
    a. the elderly.
    b. young children.
    c. the baby boomers.
    d. teenagers.

23. In U.S. society, efforts to legalize same-sex marriages, and the reactions to such marriages by traditionalists, are an example of:
    a. cultural leveling.
    b. cultural diffusion.
    c. cultural war.
    d. the universality of culture.

24. Ideal culture is:
    a. a value, norm, or other cultural trait that is found in every group.
    b. the ideal values and norms of a people and the goals held out for them.
    c. the norms and values that people follow when they know they are being watched.
    d. not a sociological concept.

25. Sociologists call the norms and values that people actually follow_____.
    a. real culture.
    b. normal culture.
    c. ideal culture.
    d. none of the above.

26.   Sociologists use the term _____ to refer to an emerging technology that has significant impact on social life.
    a.   emergent technology
    b.   revolutionary technology
    c.   new technology
    d.   changing technology

27.   William Ogburn pointed out that a group's _____ culture usually changes first, with the _____ culture lagging behind.
    a.   ideal; real
    b.   old; new
    c.   material; nonmaterial
    d.   nonmaterial; material

28.   In our society, it is the custom for the school year to be nine months long, with students having a three-month summer break. Today, this pattern would be an example of:
    a.   a core value.
    b.   real culture.
    c.   cultural lag.
    d.   value contradiction.

29.   The worldwide emergence of the computer as a source of communication is an example of:
    a.   cultural ethnocentrism
    b.   cultural diffusion.
    c.   cultural filching.
    d.   cultural taboos.

30.   The golden arches of McDonald's in Tokyo, Paris, and London are examples of:
    a.   culture shock.
    b.   cultural contradictions.
    c.   cultural universals.
    d.   cultural leveling.

TRUE-FALSE QUESTIONS

T F   1.   Nonmaterial culture includes beliefs, values, gestures, and machines.
T F   2.   No one can be entirely successful at practicing cultural relativism.
T F   3.   Ethnocentrism has positive and negative consequences.
T F   4.   Everyone in the world is influenced by culture.
T F   5.   Trying to understand a culture on its own terms is cultural relativism.
T F   6.   Gestures are ways in which people use their bodies to communicate with others.
T F   7.   Language allows human experience to be cumulative.
T. F.   8.   Mores are essential to our core values.
T F   9.   Subcultures remain compatible with the dominant culture while countercultures are in opposition to the dominant culture.
T F   10.   A pluralistic society is made up of many different groups.
T F   11.   Racism and group superiority are core values in United States society.
T F   12.   Core values may contradict one another.

T F 13. An emerging core value in the United States is *youthfulness*.
T F 14. Core values do not change without meeting strong resistance.
T F 15. Ideal values can blind people to real culture.
T F 16. Technology sets a framework for a group's nonmaterial culture.
T F 17. Ogburn referred to the condition of uneven cultural change as *cultural lag*.
T F 18. Ogburn pointed out that a group's nonmaterial culture generally changes first, with the material culture lagging behind.
T F 19. Globalization of capitalism is producing cultural leveling.
T F 20. Cultural leveling inevitably increases cultural distinctiveness.

FILL-IN QUESTIONS

1. The material objects that distinguish a group of people, such as their art, building, weapons, utensils, machines, hairstyles, clothing, and jewelry are known as _____.

2. _____ is the tendency to use our own group's way of doing things as a yardstick for judging others.

3. Trying to understand a culture on its own terms is the concept of _____.

4. A _____ is something to which people attach meaning and then use to communicate with others.

5. _____ is a system of symbols that can be combined in an infinite number of ways and can represent not only objects but also abstract thought.

6. The Sapir-Whorf hypothesis indicates that our _____ determines our consciousness.

7. Expectations, or rules of behavior, that develop out of a group's values, are _____.

8. Norms that are not strictly enforced are _____.

9. Various occupational groups form _____.

10. _____ are a series of interrelated values that together form a larger whole.

11. When values clash in a society, sociologists refer to this as _____.

12. Sociologists call the norms and values that people actually follow _____.

13. Emerging technologies that have a significant impact on social life are referred to as _____.

14. William Ogburn used the term_____ to refer to a situation in which nonmaterial culture takes a period of time to adjust to changes in the material culture.

15. The process in which cultures become similar to one another is _____.

MATCH THESE THEORISTS/PHILOSOPHERS WITH THEIR CONTRIBUTIONS

1. Edgerton
2. Henslin
3. Sapir-Whorf
4. Williams
5. Ogburn

a. *concept of "sick societies"*
b. *thinking and perception are shaped by language*
c. *culture lag*
d. *identified core values of the U.S*
e. *experienced culture shock in Africa*

MATCH EACH CONCEPT WITH ITS MEANING

1. Nonmaterial Culture.
2. Ethnocentrism
3. Ideal Culture
4. Culture lag
5. Counterculture

a. *"Our way is the best way."*
b. *a group's way of thinking*
c. *human behavior lagging behind technological change*
d. *norms worth aspiring to*
e. *in opposition to the dominant culture*

ESSAY QUESTIONS

1. Explain cultural relativism and discuss both the advantages and disadvantages of practicing it.
2. As the author points out, the United States is a pluralistic society, made up of many different groups. Discuss some of the things that are gained by living in such a society, as well as some of the problems that are created.
3. Consider the degree to which the real culture of the United States falls short of the ideal culture. Provide concrete examples to support your essay.
4. Evaluate what is gained and lost as technology advances in society.
5. Discuss whether cultural leveling is a positive or negative process.

STUDENT PROJECTS

1. Over a period of two or three days observe various gestures that people use to communicate. List the various gestures. Are these gestures confusing to people as they try to communicate with one another? Do they have easily shared meanings?

2. As noted in the text, as new technologies emerge, they have a significant impact on our culture and our lives. Choose two new technologies that you currently use and explore the positive and negative effects these technologies have on society. For each technology, list three positive and three negative effects. Overall, do you think culture will "catch up" to the newest technological developments? Explain your answer.

CHAPTER 3

SOCIALIZATION

CHAPTER SUMMARY

- Scientists have attempted to determine how much of people's characteristics come from heredity and how much from the social environment. Observations of isolated and institutionalized children help to answer this question. These studies have concluded that language and intimate interaction are essential to the development of human characteristics.
- **Charles Horton Cooley, George Herbert Mead, Jean Piaget,** and **Sigmund Freud** provide insights into the social development of human beings. Cooley and Mead demonstrated that the self is created through our interactions with others. Piaget identified four stages in the development of our ability to reason: (1) sensorimotor; (2) preoperational; (3) concrete operational; and (4) formal operational. Freud defined the personality in terms of the id, ego, and superego. Personality developed as the inborn desires (id) clashed with social constraints (superego). Socialization into emotions is one way societies produce conformity; not only do we learn how to express our emotions, but also what emotions to feel.
- **Gender socialization** is a primary means of controlling human behavior, and a society's ideals of sex-linked behaviors are reinforced by its social institutions.
- The main **agents of socialization**—the mass media, the family, the neighborhood, religion, day care, school, peer groups, sports, and the workplace—each contribute to the socialization of people to become full-fledged members of society.
- **Resocialization** is the process of learning new norms, values, attitudes, and behaviors. Intense resocialization takes place in total institutions. Most resocialization is voluntary, but some is involuntary.
- **Socialization**, which begins at birth, continues throughout the life course. At each stage the individual must adjust to a new set of social expectations. **Life course** patterns vary by social location, such as history, gender, race-ethnicity, and social class.
- Although socialization lays down the basic self and is modified by our social location, humans are not robots but rational beings who consider options and make choices.

LEARNING OBJECTIVES
As you read Chapter 3, use these learning objectives to organize your notes. After completing your reading, you should be able to answer each of the objectives.

1. Discuss the ongoing debate over what most determines human behavior: "nature" (heredity) or "nurture" (social environment), and cite the evidence that best supports one position or the other.
2. Explain the statement: "It is society that makes people human."
3. Discuss how studies of feral, isolated, and institutionalized children prove that social contact and interaction is essential for healthy human development.
4. Understand, distinguish between, and state the respective strengths and limitations of the following theorists' insights into human development: Charles Horton Cooley, George Herbert Mead, Jean Piaget, Sigmund Freud, Lawrence Kohlberg, and Carol Gilligan.
5. Talk about how socialization is not only critical to the development of the mind, but to the development of emotions as well— affecting not only how people express their emotions, but also what particular emotions they may feel.

6. Know what is meant by gender socialization and how the family, media, and other agents of socialization teach children, from the time of their birth, to act masculine or feminine based on their gender.

7. Describe some of the "gender messages" in the family and mass media and discuss how these messages may contribute to social inequality between men and women.

8. List the major agents of socialization in American society, and talk about how each of these teach —and influence—people's attitudes, behaviors, and other orientations toward life.

9. Define the term resocialization and provide examples of situations that may necessitate resocialization.

10. Discuss how different settings, including total institutions, may go about the task of resocializing individuals.

11. Understand why socialization is a lifelong process and summarize the needs, expectations, and responsibilities that typically accompany different stages of life.

12. Discuss why human beings are not prisoners of socialization while providing examples of how people can—and do—exercise a considerable degree of freedom over which agents of socialization to follow and which cultural messages to accept—or not accept—from those agents of socialization.

CHAPTER OUTLINE

I.   What Is Human Nature?

A. Examples like Isabelle show how humans would be if they were isolated from society at an early age. Isabelle, raised in isolation, appeared severely retarded. Without companionship, she had been unable to develop into an intelligent human. Subsequent interaction with others, at an early age, allowed her to reach normal intellectual levels.

B. Studies of institutionalized children show that characteristics we think of as human traits (intelligence, cooperative behavior, and friendliness) result from early close relations with other humans.

    1. When infants in orphanages received little adult interaction, they appeared mentally retarded. When some were placed in the care of adult women—even though the women were mentally retarded—one-on-one relationships developed and the infants gained intelligence. As adults, these individuals had, on average, achieved a high school education, married, and were self-supporting.

    2. A control group of infants remained in the orphanage. A follow-up investigation found that they actually lost intelligence. As adults, this group averaged less than a third grade education. A few had remained in the institution, while the others had low-level employment.

    3. Genie, who was locked in a small room from infancy until she was found at age 13, demonstrates the importance of early interaction. Intensive training was required for her to learn to walk, speak simple sentences, and chew correctly. Yet even so, she remained severely retarded.

C. Studies of monkeys raised in isolation have shown similar results. The longer and more severe the isolation, the more difficult later adjustment becomes.

D. Babies do not *naturally* develop into human adults; although their bodies grow, human interaction is required for them to acquire the traits considered normal for human beings.

II. Socialization into the Self and Mind

A. Charles Horton Cooley (1864-1929) concluded that human development is socially created—that our sense of self develops from interaction with others. He coined the term *looking-glass self* to describe this process.

    1. The process contains three steps: (1) we imagine how we look to others; (2) we interpret others' reactions to us; and (3) we develop a self-concept.

    2. A favorable reflection in the *social mirror* leads to a positive self-concept, while a negative reflection leads to a negative self-concept.

    3. Even the misjudgments of others' reactions become part of our self-concept.

    4. This development process is an ongoing, lifelong process.

B. George Herbert Mead (1863-1931) agreed with Cooley, but added that play is critical to the development of a self. In play, we learn to take the role of the other: to understand and anticipate how others feel and think.

    1. Mead concluded that children first take only the role of significant others (parents or siblings, for example). As the self develops, children internalize first the expectations of significant others, and then eventually the entire group. The norms, values, attitudes and expectations of people *in general* are the generalized other.

    2. According to Mead, the development of the self goes through three stages.

        a. Imitation: Children initially can only mimic the gestures and words of others.

        b. Play: Beginning at age three, children play the roles of specific people, such as a firefighter or the Lone Ranger.

        c. Games: In the first years of school, children become involved in organized team games and must learn the role of each member of the team.

    3. He distinguished between the *I* and the *me* in development of the self. The *I* component is the subjective, active, spontaneous, creative part of the social self; for instance, "I shoved him.*"* The *me* component is the objective part—internalized from interactions with others; for instance, "He shoved me."

    4. Mead argued that we are not passive participants in this process, but actively evaluate the reactions of others and organize them into a unified whole.

    5. Mead concluded that not only the self but also the human mind is a social product. The symbols that we use in thinking originate in the language of our society.

C. Jean Piaget (1896-1980) noticed that when young children take intelligence tests, they consistently give similar wrong answers while older children are able to give the expected answer. To understand why, he studied the states a child goes through in learning to reason.

    1. The sensorimotor stage (ages 0-2): Understanding is limited to direct contact with the environment (touching, listening, seeing.)

    2. The preoperational stage (ages 2-7): Children develop the ability to use symbols that allows them to experience things without direct contact.

    3. The concrete operational stage (ages 7-12): Reasoning abilities become much more developed. Children now can understand numbers, causation, and speed, but have difficulty with abstract concepts such as truth.

    4. The formal operational stage (ages 12+): Children become capable of abstract thinking, and can use rules to solve abstract problems (If X is true, why doesn't Y follow?)

D.   While the work of Cooley and Mead appears to have universal application, there is less agreement that Piaget's four stages are globally true.
           1.   Child development specialists suggest that the stages are less distinct and that children develop reasoning skills more gradually than Piaget outline.
           2.   The content of what children learn varies from one culture to the next. Because childhood activities are different, the development of thinking processes will be different.

E.   Sigmund Freud (1856-1939) believed that personality consists of three elements.
           1.   The id (inherited drives for self-gratification) demands fulfillment of basic needs such as attention, safety, food, and sex. The id's drive for immediate and complete satisfaction often conflicts with the needs of others.
           2.   The ego balances between the needs of the id and the demands of society.
           3.   The **superego** (the social conscience we have internalized from social groups) gives us feelings of guilt or shame when we break rules, and feelings of pride and self-satisfaction when we follow them.
           4.   Sociologists object to Freud's view that inborn and unconscious motivations are the primary reasons for human behavior, for this view denies the central tenet of sociology that social factors shape people's behavior.

F.   Most socialization is meant to turn us into conforming members of society. We do some things and not others a result of socialization. Our social mirror—the result of being socialized into self and emotions—sets up effective controls over our behavior.

III.   Socialization into Gender

A.   Society also channels our behavior through **gender socialization**. By expecting different behaviors from people because they are male or female, society nudges boys and girls in separate directions from an early age, and this foundation carries over into adulthood.

B.   Parents begin the process.
           1.   Studies conclude that in U.S. society, mothers unconsciously reward female children for being passive and dependent and male children for being active and independent.
           2.   In general, parents teach their children gender roles in subtle ways—with the toys they buy, the rules they set, and the expectations they have.

C.   Peer groups also play an important role in gender socialization.

D.   The **mass media** reinforce society's expectations of gender in many ways.
           1.   On TV, male characters outnumber females two to one and are more likely to be portrayed in higher status positions.
           2.   There are some notable exceptions to these stereotypes, which are a sign that things are changing.
           3.   Although young people spend countless hours playing video games, there are no studies yet showing how these games affect players' ideas of gender.

IV.   Agents of Socialization

A.   People and groups that influence our self-concept, emotions, attitudes, and behavior are called **agents of socialization**.

B.   Our socialization experiences in the family are influenced by social class.
           1.   Research by **Melvin Kohn** suggests social class differences in child-rearing. Often the main concern of working-class parents is their children's outward conformity (be neat and clean, and follow the rules), and they are more likely to use physical punishment to encourage conformity. Middle-class parents show

greater concern for the motivations for their children's behavior, and are more likely to punish by withdrawing privileges and affection.

2. Kohn found that over and above social class, the type of job held by the parent is a factor. The more closely supervised the job is, the more likely the parent is to insist on outward conformity.

C. Some neighborhoods are better for children than others. Research shows that children from poor neighborhoods are more likely to get into trouble with the law, to get pregnant, to drop out of school, and to end up disadvantaged.

D. Religion plays a major role in the socialization of most Americans; 70 percent of Americans belong to a local congregation, and two in every five Americans attend a religious service weekly. Religion especially influences morality, but also ideas about dress, speech, and manners that are appropriate.

E. With more mothers working outside the home today, day care has become a significant **agent of socialization**.

1. Researchers found the effects of day care largely depend on the child's background and the quality of care. Children from poor households or dysfunctional families appear to benefit from day care. Researchers studied 120 day care centers and found that children in higher quality day care interact better with other children and have fewer behavioral problems.

2. One national study involved following 1300 children from infancy into preschool, with researchers observing them at home and at day care. The results indicated that the more hours per week children spend in day care, the weaker the bonds between mothers and children and the more negative their interactions. Researchers conclude that mothers who spend more time with their infants become more familiar and responsive to their signaling system.

F. In school, children are placed outside the direct control of the family and learn to be part of a large group of people of similar age—a **peer group**. Peer groups, linked by common interests, are a powerful socializing force.

1. Research by **Patricia and Peter Adler** demonstrates how peer groups influence behavior. For boys, the norms that make them popular are athletic ability, coolness, and toughness. For girls, the norms are family background, physical appearance, and interest in more mature concerns such as the ability to attract boys.

2. It is almost impossible to go against peer groups; those who do become labeled as *outsiders*, *nonmembers*, or *outcasts*.

G. Sports are another powerful socializing agent, teaching skills as well as values.

H. The workplace is a significant agent of socialization in later life.

1. The part-time jobs we fill during high school and college provide opportunities for **anticipatory socialization**—learning to play an occupational role before actually entering it.

2. There is a tendency for the work that we do to become part of our self-image; we often identify ourselves in terms of our occupation.

V. Resocialization

A. **Resocialization** refers to the process of learning new norms, values, attitudes, and behaviors to match new situations in life.

1. Resocialization, in its most common form, occurs each time we learn something contrary to our previous experiences, such as going to work in a new job with a boss who wants things done differently than we've done before.

2. Most resocialization is mild, but it can be intense.

    B.   **Erving Goffman** coined the term **total institution** to refer to a place—such as boot camp, prison, a concentration camp, or some mental hospitals, religious cults, and boarding schools—where people are cut off from the rest of society and are under almost total control of agents of the institution.

        1.   A person entering the institution is greeted with a **degradation ceremony** through which current identity is stripped away and replaced (e.g. fingerprinting, shaving the head, banning personal items, and being forced to strip and wear a uniform.)

        2.   Total institutions are quite effective because they isolate people from outside influences and information, supervise their activities, suppress previous roles, statuses, and norms, and replace them with new rules and values, controlling rewards and punishments.

VI.   Socialization Through the Life Course

    A.   Socialization occurs throughout a person's entire lifetime. As we pass through the different stages our behaviors and attitudes change in ways that reflect the social expectations of that stage. An individual's life course is also influenced by social location.

    B.   A general outline of the different stages in the life course includes:

        1.   Childhood (birth to age 12): In earlier times, children were considered miniature adults who served an apprenticeship in which they learned and performed tasks. To keep them in line, they were beaten and subjected to psychological torture. The current view is that children are tender and innocent, and parents should guide the physical, emotional, and social development of their children, while providing them with care, comfort, and protection.

        2.   Adolescence (ages 13 to 17): Economic changes resulting from the Industrial Revolution brought about material surpluses that allowed millions of teenagers to remain outside the labor force, while at the same time the demand for education increased. Biologically equipped for both work and marriage but denied both, adolescents suffer inner turmoil and develop their own standards of clothing, hairstyles, language, music, and other claims to separate identities.

        3.   Young adulthood (ages 18-29): Adult responsibilities are postponed through extended education. At some point during this period, young adults gradually ease into adult responsibilities—finishing school, getting a job, getting married.

        4.   Middle years (ages 30-65): People are more sure of themselves and their goals in life than before, but severe jolts such as divorce or being fired can occur. For women in the United States, it can be a difficult period due to trying to *have it all*—job, family, and everything. Later adulthood results in a different view of life—trying to evaluate the past and come to terms with what lies ahead. Individuals may feel they are not likely to get much farther in life, while health and mortality become concerns. However, for most people it is the most comfortable period in their entire lives.

        5.   Older years (age 65 and beyond): People today live longer and there has been an improvement in general health. At the same time, people in this stage become more concerned with death—feeling that their time is *closing in* on them.

VII.   Are We Prisoners of Socialization?

    A.   Sociologists do not think of people as little robots who simply are the result of their exposure to socializing agents. Although socialization is powerful, and profoundly affects us all, we have a self and the self is dynamic. Each of us uses his or her own mind to reason and make choices.

B.   In this way, each of us is actively involved in the social construction of the self. Our experiences have an impact on us, but we are not doomed by them if we do not like them.

KEY TERMS

After studying the chapter, review each of the following terms.

agents of socialization: people or groups that affect our self-concept, attitudes, behaviors, or other orientations toward life (p. 71)

anticipatory socialization: because one anticipates a future role, one learns parts of it now (p. 75)

degradation ceremony: a term coined by Harold Garfinkel to describe an attempt to remake the self by stripping away an individual's self–identity and stamping a new identity in its place (p. 75)

ego: Freud's term for a force that balances the id and the demands of society (p. 66)

gender socialization: the ways in which society sets children onto different courses in life *because* they are male or female (p. 69)

generalized other: the norms, values, attitudes, and expectations of people "in general"; the child's ability to take the role of the generalized other is a significant step in the development of a self (p. 64)

I: Mead's term for the self as subject, the active, spontaneous, creative part of the self (p. 65)

id: Freud's term for the individual's inborn basic drives (p. 66)

life course: the stages of our life as we go from birth to death (p. 77)

looking-glass self: a term coined by Charles Horton Cooley to refer to the process by which our sense of self develops through internalizing other's reactions to us (p. 63)

mass media: forms of communication, such as radio, newspapers, movies, and television that are directed to mass audiences (p. 70)

resocialization: the process of learning new norms, values, attitudes, and behaviors (p. 75)

self: the uniquely human capacity of being able to see ourselves "from the outside"; the picture we gain of how others see us (p. 63)

significant other: an individual who significantly influences someone else's life (p. 64)

social environment: the entire human environment, including direct contact with others (p. 60)

social inequality: giving privileges and obligations to one group of people while denying them to another (p. 71)

socialization: the process by which people learn the characteristics of their group—the knowledge, skills, attitudes, values, and actions thought appropriate for them (p. 63)

superego: Freud's term for the conscience, the internalized norms and values of our social groups (p. 66)

take the role of the other: putting oneself in someone else's shoes; understanding how someone else feels and thinks and thus anticipating how that person will act (p. 64)

total institution: a place in which people are cut off from the rest of society and are almost totally controlled by the officials who run the place (p. 75)

transitional adulthood: a period of extended youth during which young people gradually ease into adult responsibilities (p.79)

KEY PEOPLE

Review the major theoretical contributions or research findings of these theorists and thinkers.

Patricia and Peter Adler: These sociologists have documented how peer groups socialize children into gender-appropriate behavior.

Philippe Ariés: Ariés studied paintings from the Middle Ages to learn more about past notions of childhood.

Charles H. Cooley: Cooley studied the development of the self, coining the term the *looking-glass self.*

Sigmund Freud: Freud developed a theory of personality development that took into consideration inborn drives (id), the internalized norms and values of one's society (superego), and the individual's ability to balance the two competing forces (ego).

Erving Goffman: Goffman studied the process of resocialization within total institutions.

Susan Goldberg and Michael Lewis: Two psychologists who studied how parents' unconscious expectations about gender behavior are communicated to their young children.

Harry and Margaret Harlow: These psychologists studied the behavior of monkeys raised in isolation and found that the length of time they were in isolation affected their ability to overcome the effects of isolation.

Kenneth Keniston: Keniston noted that industrial societies seem to be adding a period of prolonged youth to the life course, in which adult responsibilities are postponed.

Melvin Kohn: Kohn has done extensive research on the social class differences in child-rearing patterns.

George Herbert Mead: Mead emphasized the importance of play in the development of self-esteem in men.

Jean Piaget: Piaget studied the development of reasoning skills in children.

H.M. Skeels and H.B. Dye: These two psychologists studied the impact that close social interaction had on the social and intellectual development of institutionalized children.

SELF-TEST

After completing this self-test, check your answers in the Answer Key of this Study Guide.

MULTIPLE CHOICE

1. From the cases of institutionalized children, it is possible to conclude that:
   a. humans have no natural language.
   b. social interaction is important for humans to establish close bonds with others.
   c. it is impossible for a person who has been isolated to progress through normal learning stages.
   d. all of the above.

2. The *looking-glass self* includes:
   a. imagining how we appear to those around us.
   b. interpreting others' reaction to us.
   c. developing a self-concept.
   d. all of the above.

3. All of the following statements about Cooley's theory of the development of self are correct *except*:
   a. the development of self is an ongoing, lifelong process.
   b. we move beyond the looking-glass self as we mature.
   c. the process of the looking-glass self applies to old age.
   d. the self is always in process.

4. Taking the role of the other means to:
   a. put ourselves in someone else's shoes.
   b. take a role away from someone.
   c. develop self-esteem
   d. reach the *play* stage.

5. According to George Herbert Mead which of the following is not one of the three stages in learning to take the role of the generalized other?
   a. imitation
   b. transition
   c. play
   d. game

6. The *stage* of learning to take the role of the other, which generally takes place from three to six years of age, is:
   a. the *play* stage.
   b. the *games* stage.
   c. The *imitation* stage.

7. According to Jean Piaget, children develop the ability to use symbols during the
   _____ stage.
   a. sensorimotor

      b.   preoperational

      c.   concrete operational

      d.   formal operational

8.   In Piaget's *formal operational stage* children are:
   a.   capable of abstract thinking.
   b.   capable of only taking the role of the other.
   c.   capable of only using symbols.

9.   Freud's term for a balancing force between the inborn drives for self-gratification and the demands of society is the:
   a.   id.
   b.   superego.
   c.   ego.
   d.   libido.

10.   Paul Elkman found that everyone in the world experiences six basic:
   a.   beliefs.
   b.   values.
   c.   emotions.
   d.   folkways.

11.   _____ not only leads to different ways of expressing emotions, but even affects what we feel.
   a.   Language
   b.   Socialization
   c.   Culture
   d.   Religion

12.   The result of being socialized into a self and emotions sets up effective _____ over our behavior.
   a.   controls
   b.   laws
   c.   agents
   d.   customs

13.   Usually, the significant others who first teach us our part in the gender-division of the world are:
   a.   our peers.
   b.   our parents.
   c.   our teachers.
   d.   our televisions.

14.   People and groups that influence our self-concept, emotions, attitudes and behavior are:
   a.   likely to be in single-parent households.
   b.   generalized others.
   c.   agents of socialization.
   e.   primarily passive influences.

15.   According to sociologist Melvin Kohn, middle-class parents try to develop their children's:
   a.   outward conformity.

b.   level of obedience, neatness, and cleanliness.
c.   curiosity, self-expression, and self-control.
d.   all of the above.

16.   When we examine influences of religion, how many Americans belong to a local congregation?
a.   Ten percent
b.   Sixty-five percent
c.   One-hundred percent
d.   Thirty percent

17.   According to researchers, which children seem to benefit most from day care?
a.   Middle-class children
b.   Poor children
c.   Children from dysfunctional families
d.   Both "b" and "c" above

18.   According to a study by Adler & Adler, the norms that made boys popular in elementary school include all *except*:
a.   athletic ability.
b.   family background.
c.   coolness.
d.   toughness.

19.   _____ socialization is learning to play a role before entering it.
a.   Total
b.   Childhood
c.   Workplace
d.   Anticipatory

20.   Concern about what answers to give during a job interview reflects:
a.   resocialization.
b.   anticipatory socialization.
c.   desocialization.
d.   mature socialization.

21.   Total institutions:
a.   is a term coined by Harold Garfinkel.
b.   exist primarily in societies with totalitarian governments.
c.   are places in which people are cut off from the rest of society and are almost totally controlled by the officials who run the place.
d.   all of the above.

22.   The stages that we all go through in life are called the:
a.   birth to death sequence.
b.   life course.
c.   life stages.
d.   birth to death stages.

23.   Everyone's childhood occurs at some point in history, and is embedded in:
a.   particular social locations.
b.   social class.

c.   gender.
d.   all of the above.

24.   The *sandwich generation* experience is most likely to occur in the United States during:
a.   the early middle years.
b.   the older years.
c.   young adulthood.
d.   the late middle years.

25.   Given recent social changes that have taken place within the United States, which of the following groups are particularly challenged by the early middle years stage of the life course?
a.   Generation X
b.   Women
c.   Baby boomers
d.   Men

26.   For many aging people, the most comfortable period in their lives is:
a.   the older years.
b.   the later middle years.
c.   young adulthood.
d.   the early middle years.

27.   Most men and women in their 60s and 70s are _____ active.
a.   sexually
b.   physically
c.   mentally
d.   all of the above

28.   Increasingly during the last stage of life, people begin to contemplate:
a.   death.
b.   retirement.
c.   taking care of grandchildren.
d.   loss of physical ability.

29.   What is it that prevents us from being prisoners of socialization?
a.   Our culture
b.   Our education
c.   Our self
d.   Our families

30.   Each of us is actively involved in the construction of the:
a.   mind.
b.   self.
c.   norms of society.
d.   id and the ego.

TRUE-FALSE QUESTIONS

T F   1.   Studies of both isolated and institutionalized children demonstrate that some of the characteristics that we take for granted as being "human" traits result from our basic instincts.

T F   2.   Studies of monkeys suggest that animals do not react in similar ways to humans when isolated.

T F   3.   Socialization is the process by which we learn the ways of society, or all particular groups.

T F   4.   George H. Mead introduced the concept of the *generalized other* to sociology.

T F   5.   According to Cooley, the development of the self is essentially completed by adolescence.

T F   6.   Mead thought that *play* is crucial to the development of the self.

T F   7.   According to Mead, from the ages of about three to six, children can only mimic others.

T F   8.   The *I* is the self as subject.

T F   9.   Piaget used the term "operational" to mean the ability to reason.

T F   10.   During Piaget's *preoperational stage,* a child's understanding is limited to direct contact with the environment.

T F   11.   The technique of *psychoanalysis* was founded by Piaget and Freud.

T F   12.   Freud assumed that to be *male* is normal.

T F   13   Each culture has *norms of emotion* that demand conformity.

T F   14.   Our social mirror sets up effective controls over our behavior.

T F   15.   Sociologists Melvin Kohn found that the main concern of middle-class parents is their children's outward conformity.

T F   16.   The Adler study found that athletic ability helped make boys popular.

T F   17.   Anticipatory socialization involves learning to play a role before actually taking on that role.

T F   18.   A person, who was married but is now divorced and single will experience the process of resocialization.

T F   19.   Total institutions rarely encourage degradation ceremonies.

T F   20.   Industrialization brought with it a delay in the onset of old age.

FILL-IN QUESTIONS

1.   In the case of Isabelle, the debate about _____ became important again.

2.   In a series of experiments with rhesus monkeys, the researchers Harlow & Harlow demonstrated the importance of _____.

3.   Charles H. Cooley coined the term _____ to describe the process by which a sense of self develops.

4.   To put yourself in someone else's shoes is to learn how to _____.

5.   The ability to understand how the group as a whole feels and thinks is to perceive the

     _____.

6.   _____ is the term used to describe someone, such as a parent and/or a sibling, who plays a major role in our social development.

7.   The ego develops to balance the _____.

8. In their studies of young children, Goldberg and Lewis concluded that mothers unconsciously reward their daughters for being _____.

9. One of the main findings of the sociologist Kohn was that socialization depends on a family's _____.

10. The process of learning new norms, values, attitudes, and behaviors to match new life situations is _____.

11. An attempt to remake the self by stripping away the individual's current identity and stamping a new one in its place is a _____.

12. Stages, from birth to death, are called _____.

13. The life course *stage* between childhood and adulthood is _____.

14. The stage of the life course that poses a special challenge for women in the United States is _____.

15. In pre-industrial societies, *old age* was thought to begin around age _____.

MATCH THESE THEORISTS/PHILOSOPHERS WITH THEIR CONTRIBUTIONS

1. Cooley
2. Freud
3. Mead
4. Kohn
5. Piaget

a. *coined the term "generalized other"*
b. *coined the term "looking-glass self"*
c. *id, ego, and superego*
d. *studied social class differences in child-rearing*
e. *concluded that children experience four stages of development.*

MATCH EACH CONCEPT WITH ITS MEANING

1. looking glass self
2. resocialization
3. significant other
4. gender socialization
5. peer group

a. *process of learning new norms*
b. *developed by Charles Cooley.*
c. *an individual who significantly impacts a person's life*
d. *learning to be "male" or "female"*
e. *groups of individuals approximately the same age*

ESSAY QUESTIONS

1. Explain what is necessary in order for us to develop into full human beings.
2. Why do sociologists argue that socialization is a process and not a product?
3. Having read about how the family, the media, and peers all influence our gender socialization, discuss why gender roles tend to remain unchanged from one generation to the next.

4.   As the text points out, the stages of the life course are influenced by the biological clock, but they also reflect broader social factors. Identify the stages of the life course and indicate how social factors have contributed to the definition of each of these stages.

5.   How would you answer the question, "Are We Prisoners of Socialization?"

STUDENT PROJECTS

1.   Watch one afternoon and one evening of television. (Some people might say you ought not to be encouraged to do this!) Note the time of the day or evening, what day or night of the week it is, and the type of program (soap opera, or sit-com, etc.). What images of men and women are on the programs? Refer to gender, age/aging, and social class. Log your observations, and relate them to your text's discussions of socialization.

2.   Think about the agents of socialization that you have experienced in your life. Which one has been the most influential? Explain why? Which agent do you think was more important for your parents? Explain why?

CHAPTER 4

SOCIAL STRUCTURE AND SOCIAL INTERACTION

CHAPTER SUMMARY

- There are two levels of sociological analysis: *macrosociology* investigates the large-scale features of social structure, while *microsociology* focuses on social interaction. Functional and conflict theorists tend to use a macrosociological approach while symbolic interactionists are more likely to use a macrosociological approach.

- The term *social structure* refers to a society's framework. Culture, social class, social status, roles, groups, and institutions are the major components of the social structure. The individual's location in the social structure affects his or her perceptions, attitudes, and behaviors.

- Social institutions are the organized and standard means that a society develops to meet its basic needs. Sociologists have identified nine such institutions—the family, religion, law, politics, economics, education, medicine, science, and the military. A tenth—the mass media—is emerging.

- Over time, social structure undergoes changes; sweeping changes have followed each of the four social revolutions—the *first* is associated with the domestication of animals and plants, the *second* the invention of the plow, the *third* the invention of the steam engine, and the *fourth* the invention of the microchip. Both Durkheim's concepts of mechanical and organic solidarity and Tönnies' constructs of *Gemeinschaft* and *Gesellschaft* focus on the social transformations of agricultural societies to industrial societies.

- Symbolic interactionists examine how people use physical space, noting that a "personal bubble," which we carefully protect, surrounds each of us. The dramaturgical analysis provided by Erving Goffman analyzes everyday life in terms of the roles we play; at the core of this analysis is impression management, or our attempts to control the impressions we make on others. The social construction of reality refers to the ways in which we construct our view of the world. Ethnomethodology is the study of the background assumptions people have to help them make sense of their everyday lives.

- While it is too soon for us to know the full effect that the Internet may have on human relationships, there is concern that virtual relationships could drive a wedge between some Internet users and their real-life relationships.

- Both macrosociology and microsociology are needed to understand human behavior because we must grasp both social structure and social interaction.

LEARNING OBJECTIVES

As you read Chapter 4, use these learning objectives to organize your notes. After completing your reading, you should be able to answer each of the objectives.

1. Differentiate between the macrosociological and microsociological approach to studying social life, and indicate which of the approaches is most likely to be used by functionalists, conflict theorists, and symbolic interactionists.

2. Define social structure, list its major components, and discuss how it guides people's behaviors.

3. Understand the concepts of culture, social class, social status, roles, groups, and social institutions.
4. Identify the various types of societies including hunting and gathering, pastoral and horticultural, agricultural, industrial, postindustrial and bioeconomic societies.
5. Differentiate between Emile Durkheim's concepts of mechanical and organic solidarity and Ferdinand Tönnies' constructs of *Gemeinschaft* and *Gesellschaft*, and discuss why they continue to be relevant.
6. Define stereotypes and explain their significance.
7. Talk about the various ways people in different cultures perceive and use personal space, touching, and eye contact.
8. Know the key components of dramaturgy and discuss how people try to control other people's impressions of them through assigned roles, teamwork, and face-saving behavior.
9. Differentiate between role conflict, role exit and role strain, and provide examples of each.
10. Understand how and why ethnomethodologists examine the different ways people use background assumptions to make sense out of everyday life.
11. Explain what is meant by the "social construction of reality" and how it is related to the "Thomas theorem."
12. Know why both macrosociology and microsociology are essential to understanding social life.

CHAPTER OUTLINE

I. Levels of Sociological Analysis

    A. **Macrosociology** places the focus on large-scale features of social structure. It investigates large-scale social forces and the effects they have on entire societies and the groups within them. It is utilized by **functionalist** and **conflict theorists**.

    B. **Microsociology** places the emphasis on social interaction, or what people do when they come together. Symbolic interaction is an example.

    C. While each has a different focus, together these two levels of analysis provide a fuller picture of social life.

II. The Macrosociological Perspective: Social Structure

    A. **Social structure** is defined as the patterned relationships between people that persist over time; it is sociologically significant because it guides our behavior.

        1. Personal feelings and desires tend to be overridden by social structure. An individual's behaviors and attitudes are determined by that person's location in the social structure.

        2. Major components of social structure are culture, social class, social status, roles, groups, social institutions, and societies.

    B. **Culture** refers to a group's language, beliefs, values, behaviors, gestures, and the material objects used by a group. It determines what kind of people we will become.

    C. **Social class** in U.S. society is generally based on income, education, and occupational prestige. A large number of people who have similar amounts of income and education and who work at jobs that are roughly comparable in prestige make up a social class.

    D. **Social status** refers to the positions that an individual occupies. Each status provides guidelines for how people are to act and to feel.

        1. **Status set** refers to all the statuses or positions that an individual occupies.

        2. **Ascribed statuses** are positions an individual either inherits at birth or receives involuntarily later in life. **Achieved statuses** are positions that are earned, accomplished, or involve at least some effort or activity on the individual's part.

3.   **Status symbols** are signs that identify a status.
4.   A **master status**—such as being male or female—cuts across the other statuses that an individual occupies. Status inconsistency is a contradiction or mismatch between statuses.

E.   **Roles** are the behaviors, obligations, and privileges attached to a status.
    1.   The individual occupies a status, but plays a role.
    2.   Roles are an essential component of culture because they lay out what is expected of people, and as individuals perform their roles, those roles mesh to form the society.

F.   A **group** consists of people who regularly and consciously interact with one another and typically share similar values, norms, and expectations. The groups to which we belong are powerful forces in our lives. Belonging to a group means that we yield to others the right to make certain decisions about our behavior.

G.   **Social institutions** are society's organized means of meeting its basic needs.
    1.   The family, religion, law, politics, economics, education, science, medicine, and the military all are social institutions.
    2.   Each institution has its own set of roles, values, and norms that set limits and provide guidelines for behavior.
    3.   In industrialized societies, social institutions tend to be more formal, while they are more informal in tribal societies.

H.   **Society**, which consists of people who share a culture and a territory, is the largest and most complex group that sociologists study.
    1.   The first societies were **hunting and gathering societies,** which were small and nomadic; the group moved when the supply of food ran out. There were no opportunities to accumulate possessions; therefore, these were the most **egalitarian** of all societies, with social divisions based primarily on the family.
    2.   As a result of the **domestication revolution**, which was called the first social revolution, hunting and gathering societies were transformed into **pastoral**—characterized by the pasturing of animals—and **horticultural**—characterized by the growing of plants—societies. Food surpluses emerged, which led to larger populations and some specialized division of labor. As trade developed, people began to accumulate objects they considered valuable, with leaders accumulating more of these possessions than others. Simple equality began to give way to inequality.
    3.   The **agricultural revolution** (the second social revolution) occurred with the invention of the plow; pastoral and horticultural societies were transformed. A much larger food surplus was produced and more people engaged in activities other than farming. Sometimes referred to as the dawn of civilization, this period also produced the wheel, writing, and numbers. Cities developed and groups began to be distinguished by their greater or lesser possessions. An elite gained control of the surplus resources. Social inequalities became more complex, and females became subjugated to males.
    4.   **The Industrial Revolution** (the third social revolution) began in 1765 when the steam engine was first used to run machinery. Agricultural society gave way to industrial society. Initially, social inequality increased greatly as the individuals who first utilized the new technology accumulated great wealth, controlling the means of production and dictating the conditions under which people could work for them. A huge surplus of labor developed as masses of people were thrown off the land their ancestors had farmed and these new industrial workers eventually won their demands for better living conditions. The consequence was that wealth

spread to larger segments of society. As industrialization continued, the pattern of growing inequality was reversed.

     5.   Industrial societies are being transformed into postindustrial societies, suggesting a fourth social revolution, **the information revolution**. The basic component of this society is information and the primary technological change involved is the microchip. Postindustrial societies are moving away from production and manufacturing to service industries. The United States was the first country to have more than fifty percent of its work force employed in service industries. Australia, New Zealand, western Europe, and Japan soon followed.

     6.   Some social analysts think that we are seeing the birth of a biotech society. The chief distinguishing characteristic of the society will be an economy that centers on the application of genetics. However, the wedding of genetics and economics may turn out to be simply one more aspect of the information (post industrial) society.

  I.   Sociologists have tried to find an answer to the question of what holds society together.

     1.   For Durkheim, **mechanical solidarity**—based on a collective consciousness that people experience as a result of performing the same or similar tasks—and **organic solidarity**—a collective consciousness based on the interdependence brought about by how tasks are divided among a populace—explained **social cohesion**, or the degree to which members of a society feel united by shared values and other social bonds.

     2.   For Tönnies, the answer lay in the type of society that existed. *Gemeinschaft* is a society in which life is intimate; a community in which everyone knows everyone else and people share a sense of togetherness; *Gesellschaft* is a society dominated by impersonal relationships, individual accomplishments, and self-interest.

III.   The Microsociological Perspective: Social Interaction in Everyday Life

  A.   The **microsociological approach** places emphasis on face-to-face social interaction, or what people do when they are in the presence of one another.

  B.   **Symbolic interactionists** study personal space and how people surround themselves with a *personal bubble*, regulating who they let in (intimates) and who they keep out (strangers).

     1.   The amount of personal space people prefer varies from one culture to another.

     2.   Anthropologist Edward Hall found that Americans use four different distance zones: (1) **Intimate distance**—about 18 inches from the body—for lovemaking, wrestling, comforting, and protecting. (2) **Personal distance**—from 18 inches to 4 feet—for friends, acquaintances, and ordinary conversations. (3) **Social distance**—from 4 feet to 12 feet—for impersonal or formal relationships such as job interviews. (4) **Public distance**—beyond 12 feet—for even more formal relationships such as separating dignitaries and public speakers from the general public.

  C.   **Dramaturgy** is an analysis of how we present ourselves in everyday life. Dramaturgy is the name given to an approach, pioneered by Erving Goffman, for analyzing social life in terms of drama or the stage.

     1.   According to Goffman, people learn to perform on the stage of everyday life through **socialization**.

     2.   **Impression management** is the person's efforts to manage the impressions that others receive of her or him.

3. **Front stage** is when performances are given (wherever a person delivers his or her lines). **Back stage** is when people rest from their performances, discuss their presentations, and plan future performances.

4. **Role performance** is the particular emphasis or interpretation that an individual gives a role; or the person's *style*. **Role conflict** occurs when the expectations of one role are incompatible with those of another role; in other words, conflict between roles. **Role strain** refers to conflicts that someone feels within a role.

5. Teamwork, when two or more players work together to make sure a performance happens as planned, shows that we are adept players.

6. When a performance does not happen as planned, we engage in **face-saving behavior**—ignoring the flaws in someone's performance. These include the use of tact and studied nonobservance.

D. **Ethnomethodology** involves the discovery of basic rules concerning our views of the world and how people ought to act.

1. Ethnomethodologists try to undercover people's background assumptions, which form the basic core of one's reality, and provide basic rules concerning our view of the world and of how people ought to act.

2. Harold Garfinkel founded the ethnomethodological approach.

E. The **social construction of reality** refers to what people define as real based on their background assumptions and life experiences.

1. The Thomas theorem (by sociologist W. I. Thomas) states, "If people define situations as real, they are real in their consequences."

2. **Symbolic interactionists** believe that people define their own reality and then live within those definitions.

F. Microsociologists are also interested in social interactions over the Internet, or computer-mediated face-to-face interaction. A major concern is that virtual relationships may actually replace the real-life relationships we have with family and friends.

IV. The Need for Both Macrosociology and Microsociology

A. To understand human behavior, it is necessary to grasp both **social structure** (macrosociology) and **social interaction** (microsociology).

B. Both are necessary for us to understand social life fully because each, in its own, way adds to our knowledge of human experience.

KEY TERMS

After studying the chapter, review each of the following terms.

achieved statuses: positions that are earned or accomplished, or that involve at least some effort or activity on the individual's part (p. 87)

agricultural society: those who were able to accumulate a huge food surplus after the invention of the plow (p. 92)

ascribed statuses: positions an individual either inherits at birth or receives involuntarily later in life (p. 87)

background assumptions: deeply embedded common understandings, or basic rules, concerning our view of the world and how people ought to act (p. 104)

biotech society: where the economy centers on applying and altering genetic structures to produce food, medicine, and materials (p. 93)

division of labor: the splitting of a group's or a society's tasks into specialties (p. 94)

dramaturgy: an approach, pioneered by Erving Goffman, in which social life is analyzed in terms of drama or the stage; also called *dramaturgical analysis* (p. 100)

ethnomethodology: the study of how people use background assumptions to make sense of life (p. 103)

face-saving behavior: techniques people use to salvage a performance that is going sour (p. 101)

Gemeinschaft: a type of society in which life is intimate; a community in which everyone knows everyone else and people share a sense of togetherness (p. 94)

Gesellschaft: a type of society that is dominated by impersonal relationships, individual accomplishments, and self-interest (p. 94)

group: people who have something in common and who believe that what they have in common is important; also called a social group (p. 89)

horticultural society: a society based on cultivating plants by the use of tools (p. 91)

hunting and gathering society: a human group dependent on hunting and gathering for survival (p. 89)

impression management: people's efforts to control the impressions that others receive of them (p. 100)

Industrial Revolution: the third social revolution occurring when machines powered by fuels replaced most animal and human power (p. 92)

Industrial society: an efficient society with greater surplus and inequality (p. 92)

macrosociology: analysis of social life that focuses on broad features of social structure, such as social class and the relationships of groups to one another; an approach usually used by functionalists and conflict theorists (p. 84)

master status: a status that cuts across the other statuses that an individual occupies (p. 88)

mechanical solidarity: Durkheim's term for the unity (a shared consciousness) that people feel as a result of performing the same or similar tasks (p. 94)

microsociology: analysis of social life that focuses on social interaction; an approach usually used by symbolic interactionists (p. 85)

organic solidarity: solidarity based on the interdependence that results from the division of labor; people needing others to fulfill their jobs (p. 94)

pastoral society: a society based on the pasturing of animals (p. 91)

postindustrial society: a new type of society based on information, services, and the latest technology rather than on raw materials and manufacturing (p.93)

role: the behaviors, obligations, and privileges attached to a status (p. 89)

role conflict: conflicts that someone feels *between* roles because the expectations attached to one role are incompatible with the expectations of another role (p. 100)

role performance: the particular emphasis or interpretation that we give to a role (p. 100)

role strain: conflicts that someone feels *within* a role (p. 101)

social class: according to Weber, a large number of people who rank close to one another in wealth, power, and prestige; according to Marx, one of two groups: capitalists who own the means of production or workers who sell their labor (p. 87)

social construction of reality: the use of background assumptions and life experiences to define what is real (p. 105)

social institution: the organized, usual, or standard ways by which society meets its basic needs   (p. 89)

social integration: the degree to which members of a society are united by shared values and other social bonds (p.94)

social interaction: what people do when they are in one another's presence (p. 85)

social structure: the framework that surrounds us, consisting of the relationship of people and groups to one another , which give direction to and set limits on behavior (p. 85)

society: people who share a culture and a territory (p. 89)

status: social ranking; the position that someone occupies in society or a social group (p. 87)

status inconsistency: a contradiction or mismatch between statuses; a condition in which a person ranks high on some dimensions of social class and low on others (p. 88)

status set: all the statuses or positions that an individual occupies (p. 87)

status symbols: items used to identify a status (p. 87)

teamwork: the collaboration of two or more people to manage impressions jointly (p. 101)

Thomas theorem: William I. And Dorothy S. Thomas' classic formulation of the definition of the situation: "If people define situations as real, they are real in their consequences." (p. 105)

KEY PEOPLE
Review the major theoretical contributions or research findings of these theorists and thinkers.

William Chambliss: Chambliss used macro- and microsociology to study high school gangs and found that social structure and interaction explained the patterns of behavior in these groups.

Emile Durkheim: Durkheim identified mechanical and organic solidarity as the keys to social cohesion.

Harold Garfinkel: Garfinkel is the founder of ethnomethodology; he conducted experiments in order to uncover people's background assumptions.

Erving Goffman: Goffman developed dramaturgy, the perspective within symbolic interactionism that views social life as a drama on the stage.

Edward Hall: This anthropologist found that personal space varied from one culture to another and that North Americans use four different *distance zones*.

W. I. Thomas: This sociologist was known for his statement, "If people define situations as real, they are real in their consequences."

Ferdinand Tönnies: Tönnies analyzed different types of societies that existed before and after industrialization. He used the terms *Gemeinschaft* and *Gesellschaft* to describe the two types of societies.

SELF-TEST
After completing this self-test, check your answers in the Answer Key of this Study Guide.

MULTIPLE CHOICE QUESTIONS

1. On which of the following does microsociology focus?
   a. Structural functionalism
   b. Conflict theory
   c. Broad features of social structure
   d. Social interaction

2. If a sociologist decided to research the perceptions that different social classes have of each other in the United States, which level of analysis would be appropriate?
   a. Macrosociology
   b. Microsociology
   c. Middle range sociology
   d. None of the above

3. The framework of a society that was already laid out before you were born is:
   a. social structure.
   b. your master status.
   c. social process.
   d. none of the above.

4. According to sociologists, differences among individuals in behavior and attitude is due to:
   a. biology.
   b. location in the social structure.
   c. conceptions of personal space.
   d. different styles of impression management.

5.   A group's language, beliefs, values, and behaviors is known as:
     a.   master status.
     b.   status inconsistency.
     c.   culture.
     d.   role behavior.

6.   Social class is based on all the following except:
     a.   income.
     b.   age.
     c.   occupational prestige.
     d.   education.

7.   You are a student, a friend, a son or a daughter, a sister or a brother. These characteristics are known as your:
     a.   social structure.
     b.   social class.
     c.   status set
     d.   prestige.

8.   All of the following are **achieved statuses** *except*:
     a.   sex.
     b.   friend.
     c.   student.
     d.   married.

9.   All of the following are correct statements regarding status symbols, *except*:
     a.   Status symbols are signs that identify a status.
     b.   Status symbols often are used to show that people have "made it."
     c.   Status symbols are always positive signs or people would not wear them.
     d.   Status symbols are used by people to announce their statuses to others.

10. In contemporary America, which of the following status sets would very likely be your **master status**?
     a.   Close friend
     b.   Student
     c.   AIDS victim
     d.   Sibling

11. Which one of the following is a **status inconsistency**?
     a.   A 21-year-old college student
     b.   A 35-year-old mother
     c.   A male elementary school teacher
     d.   A lower social class, short-order cook

12. The behaviors, obligations, and privileges attached to statuses are called:
     a.   status sets.
     b.   master statuses.
     c.   status differentiations.
     d.   roles.

13. The means that each society develops to meet its needs are:
   a. your status sets.
   b. social institutions.
   c. social roles.
   d. stereotypes.

14. A society that is egalitarian, small, and nomadic is a:
   a. bioeconomic society.
   b. hunting and gathering society.
   c. horticultural society.
   d. pastoral society

15. The use of the steam engine to run machinery ushered in:
   a. the industrial revolution.
   b. the postindustrial revolution.
   c. the "dawn of civilization."
   d. the increased growth of egalitarianism.

16. The societies in which groups first developed permanent settlements were:
   a. the hunting and gathering societies.
   b. the industrial societies.
   c. the horticultural societies.
   d. biotech society.

17. The industrial revolution is associated with the invention of the:
   a. the cotton gin
   b. steam engine.
   c. plow
   d. computer

18. A society whose chief distinguishing characteristic is an economy centered on the application of genetics is:
   a. an industrial society.
   b. a horticultural society.
   c. a postindustrial society.
   d. a biotech society.

19. Workers in service industries do all the following *except*:
   a. provide information.
   b. apply information.
   c. produce material goods.
   e. sell their specialized knowledge.

20. The basic component of the postindustrial society is:
   a. information.
   b. technology.
   c. assembly line work.
   d. outsourcing.

21.   As societies get larger, their_____ becomes more specialized.
        a.   division of labor
        b.   communities
        c.   religions
        d.   cities

22.   Organic solidarity refers to a society:
        a.   with a highly specialized division of labor.
        b.   whose members are interdependent on one another.
        c.   with a high degree of impersonal relationships.
        d.   all of the above.

23.   A society in which contracts replace handshakes and work centers on strangers and short-term
        acquaintances is a:
        a.   Gesellschaft society.
        b.   Gemeinschaft society.
        c.   mechanical solidarity
        d.   organic solidarity

24.   Hall observed that North Americans used different "distance zones." The "zone" that marks
        impersonal or formal relationships is:
        a.   the social distance zone.
        b.   the intimate zone.
        c.   the personal distance zone.
        d.   the public distance zone.

25.   _____ is the term used to describe Goffman's perspective that life is like a stage play.
        a.   Ethnomethodology
        b.   Dramaturgy
        c.   Thomas theorem
        d.   None of the above

26.   You have an Introduction to Sociology exam to take tomorrow, but you also have need to visit
        your mother who is in the hospital. What might you experience?
        a.   role strain.
        b.   role conflict.
        c.   role anomie.
        d.   role challenge

27.   When performances do not go off as planned, we often have to engage in _____ behavior.
        a.   corrective
        b.   face-saving
        c.   studied nonobservance
        d.   conflictual

28.   The study of how people use common sense understandings to get through everyday life is:
        a.   ethnomethodology research.
        b.   survey research.
        c.   experimental laboratory research.
        d.   dramaturgy

29.   The Thomas theorem is based on:
        a.   functionalism.
        b.   conflict theory.
        c.   symbolic interactionism.
        d.   exchange theory.

30.   Whereas macrosociology stresses the importance of social structure, microsociology helps us understand the role _____ plays in our everyday lives.
        a.   social interaction
        b.   impression management
        c.   dramaturgy
        d.   role conflict

TRUE-FALSE QUESTIONS

T F   1.   Conflict theory and functionalism both focus on the macrosociological   perspective.
T F   2.   Macrosociology focuses on the broad features of society.
T F   3.   Culture is the broadest framework that determines what kind of people we become.
T F   4.   Social status refers to the position that someone occupies.
T F   5.   Student is an example of an ascribed status.
T F   6.   Master statuses can be ascribed, or achieved, statuses.
T F   7.   Belonging to a group means that we yield to others the right to make certain decisions about our behavior.
T F   8.   Hunting and gathering societies have been called the "*dawn of civilization.*"
T F   9.   Medicine is a social institution.
T F   10.   The industrial revolution began in Great Britain.
T F   11.   The postindustrial society's main component is information.
T F   12.   The bioeconomic society is centered around the application of genetic structures.
T F   13.   According to Emile Durkheim, with industrialization as a basis, social cohesion shifts from organic to mechanical solidarity.
T F   14.   *Gemeinschaft* society is characterized by impersonal, short-term relationships.
T F   15.   Microsociologists examine face-to-face interaction.
T F   16.   *Personal distance* is space reserved for impersonal or formal relationships.
T F   17.   Role conflict is a conflict that someone feels within a role.
T F   18.   *Studied nonobservance* is a form of face-saving.
T F   19.   Symbolic interactionists assume that reality has an objective existence, and people must deal with it.
T F   20.   The social construction of reality involves subjective interpretation.

FILL-IN QUESTIONS

1.   _____ places the focus on broad features of society.
2.   _____ is what people do when they are in the presence of one another.
3.   The Down-to-Earth sociology box on football mirrors social _____.
4.   Income, education, and occupational prestige indicate_____.
5.   A _____ is one that cuts across the other statuses you hold.
6.   _____ are the behaviors, obligations, and privileges attached to a status.

7. _____ work together to meet universal needs.

8. _____ is the degree to which members of a society feel united by shared values and other bonds.

9. As societies get larger, their _____ becomes more specialized.

10. Ferdinand Tönnies used the term _____ to refer to societies dominated by impersonal relations, individual accomplishments, and self interest.

11. _____ is the conflict one feels within a role.

12. When two or more people collaborate to manage impressions jointly, this is referred to as _____.

13. Goffman called the techniques that we use to salvage a performance that is going bad as _____.

14. Ethnomethodologists explore _____ assumptions.

15. What people define as real because of their background assumptions and life experiences is the _____.

MATCH THESE THEORISTS/PHILOSOPHERS WITH THEIR CONTRIBUTIONS

1. Emile Durkheim
2. Ferdinand Tönnies
3. Edward Hall
4. Erving Goffman
5. W. I. Thomas

a. *described **Gemeinschaft** and **Gesellschaft** societies*
b. *wrote about mechanical and organic solidarity*
c. *analyzed everyday life in terms of dramaturgy*
d. *studied the concept of personal space*
e. *wrote a theorem about the nature of social reality*

MATCH EACH CONCEPT WITH ITS DEFINITION

1. Status Set
2. Ascribed Status
3. Achieved Status
4. Status Inconsistency
5. Division of Labor

a. *position one inherits at birth*
b. *positions that are earned*
c. *all the statuses one occupies*
d. *status contradiction*
e. *splitting of tasks into specialties*

ESSAY QUESTIONS

1. Choose a research topic and discuss how to approach this topic using both macrosociological and microsociological approaches.

2. The concept of a social structure is often difficult to grasp. Yet the social structure is a central organizing feature of social life. Identify the ways in which it takes shape in our society and in our lives.

3. Today we see many examples of people wanting to recreate a simpler way of life. Using Tönnies' framework, analyze this tendency.

4. Assume that you have been asked to give a presentation to your sociology class on Goffman's dramaturgy approach. Describe what information you would want to include in such a presentation.

5. Explain what sociologists mean by "the social construction of reality."

STUDENT PROJECTS

1.   Once you have finished reading this chapter, try and analyze the statuses, roles, and so on in your own life. How does when and where you were born affect your life? What are your current statuses and roles? What kinds of role conflict or role strain have you experienced in these roles? Do you think your situation would be different if you had a different ascribed status? For example, would your situation different if you had been born a member of the opposite sex?

2.   What are some things you do on a daily basis to practice impression management? Have you ever had a case where your attempts to manage impressions backfired? Explain. What types of face-saving behavior did you use afterwards? Explain.

CHAPTER 5

SOCIAL GROUPS AND FORMAL ORGANIZATIONS

CHAPTER SUMMARY

- **Groups** are the essence of life in society. An essential feature of a group is that its members have something in common and believe that what they have in common is significant. Society is the largest and most complex group that sociologists study.
- The following types of groups exist within society: **primary groups, secondary groups, in-groups** and **out-groups, reference groups,** and **social networks.** The new technology has given birth to a new type of group, the **electronic community.**
- **Robert Michels** noted that formal organizations tend to be controlled by a small group; this elite group bypasses members and limits leadership roles to its own inner circle. Michels called this tendency the **iron law of oligarchy.**
- A **bureaucracy** is a hierarchical organization with a division of labor, written rules, written communications, and the impersonality of positions. Bureaucracies endure because they are efficient and because when their original goals are met, they are replaced with other goals (goal displacement). Bureaucracies tend to become a central feature of societies, taking over more and more of everyday tasks.
- The concept of **corporate culture** refers to an organization's traditions, values, and norms. Much of this culture is invisible. It can affect its members either negatively or positively, depending upon the members' available opportunities to achieve.
- The Japanese corporate model provides a contrast to the United States corporate model in terms of hiring and promotion practices, guarantees of lifetime security, worker involvement outside the work setting, the broad training of workers, and the collective decision-making that takes place.
- **Group dynamics** refer to the ways in which individuals and groups influence one another. Size affects the dynamics of a group. Different types of leaders serve different functions in the group: **instrumental leaders** are task-oriented, while **expressive leaders** focus on maintaining harmony. **Authoritarian leaders** give orders, **democratic leaders** lead by consensus, and **laissez-faire leaders** are highly permissive.
- The **Asch** experiment illustrates the power of peer pressure, while the **Milgram** experiment demonstrates the influence of authority. Both show how easily we succumb to **groupthink,** a kind of collective tunnel vision.

LEARNING OBJECTIVES

As you read Chapter 5, use these learning objectives to organize your notes. After completing your reading, you should be able to answer each of the objectives.

1. Distinguish between groups, aggregates, and categories and explain why they are important to individuals and societies.
2. Define primary groups and explain the role they play in our lives.
3. Compare secondary groups to primary groups in terms of the characteristics of each.
4. Describe voluntary associations and explain why there is a tendency for an oligarchy to control this type of secondary group, especially in socially diverse societies.
5. Distinguish between in-groups and out-groups.
6. Explain what the purpose of reference groups is and why, within a socially diverse society, we often receive contradictory messages from reference groups.

7.   Explain the relationship between cliques and social networks. Discuss how *networking* addresses some of the social barriers within a socially diverse society.

8.   State the definition of bureaucracy, list its essential characteristics, explain why it tends to endure over time, and plays an increasingly more central role in our social lives.

9.   Discuss the dysfunctions of bureaucracies, and give examples of each type of problem.

10.   Identify the consequences of hidden values in the corporate culture, especially noting their impact on women and minority participants.

11.   Compare and contrast the Japanese and United States corporate organizational models.

12.   Explain the concept of group dynamics and indicate how group size affects interaction.

13.   Describe the two types of leaders in groups and the three basic styles of leadership.

14.   Analyze the roles of peer pressure and authority in the Asch and Milgram experiments.

15.   Discuss groupthink and explain how it can be dangerous for a society.

CHAPTER OUTLINE

I. **Social Groups**

A. **Groups** are the essence of life in society. An essential element of a social group is that its members have something in common and believe that what they have in common makes a difference.

    1. An **aggregate** is individuals who temporarily share the same physical space but do not see themselves as belonging together.

    2. A **category** is people who share similar characteristics but do not interact with one another or consider each other's interest.

B. **Primary groups** refer to those groups characterized by cooperative, intimate, long-term, face-to-face relationships.

    1. The group becomes part of the individual's identity and the lens through which to view life.

    2. They are essential to an individual's psychological well-being since humans have an intense need for associations that provide feelings of self-esteem.

C. **Secondary groups** are larger, more anonymous, formal, and impersonal than are primary groups, and are based on some shared interest or activity.

    1. Members are likely to interact based on specific roles, such as president, manager, worker, or student.

    2. Secondary groups tend to break down into smaller primary groups, such as friendship cliques at school or work. This primary group then serves as a buffer between the individual and the needs of the secondary group.

    3. **Voluntary associations** are secondary groups made up of volunteers who have organized on the basis of some mutual interest.

    4. Within voluntary associations is an inner core of individuals who stand firmly behind the group's goals and are firmly committed to maintaining the organization. **Robert Michels** used the term **iron law of oligarchy** to refer to the tendency of this inner core to dominate the organization by becoming a small, self-perpetuating elite. Within a socially diverse society, people who do not represent the appearances, values, or background of the inner circle may be excluded from leadership.

D. Groups toward which individuals feel loyalty are called **in-groups**, while those toward which they feel antagonisms are called **out-groups**.

        1.   This division is significant sociologically because in-groups provide a sense of identification or belonging, give feelings of superiority, and command loyalty, thus exercising a high degree of control over their members. The antagonisms that out-groups produce help reinforce the loyalty of members of the in-group.

        2.   According to **Robert K. Merton**, the behaviors of an in-group's members are seen as virtues, while the same behaviors by members of an out-group are viewed as vices. This double standard can pose a danger for pluralistic societies, when out-groups come to symbolize some evil, arousing hatred and motivating members of the in-group to strike out against the out-group.

E.   **Reference groups** are the groups we use as standards to evaluate ourselves, whether or not we actually belong to those groups.

        1.   **Reference groups** exert great influence over our behavior. People may change their clothing, hairstyle, speech, and other characteristics to match reference group expectations.

        2.   Having two reference groups that clearly conflict with each other can produce intense internal conflict.

F.   **Social networks** consist of people linked by various social ties. **Cliques** are a kind of social network. Our interactions within social networks connect us to the larger society.

        1.   Stanley Milgram's research on social networks established *how small* our social world is. He randomly selected a set of names from across the country—half the names were designated *senders* and the other half were designated *receivers*. Milgram asked the senders to mail the envelope (with the receiver's name on it) to someone they knew who might know the receiver. This continued until the envelope finally reached the receiver—it turned out that on the average there were only five links between the original sender and the designated receiver.

        2.   Social networks tend to perpetuate social inequality; who you know may be more important than what you know. The *old boy* network, for instance, tends to keep the best positions available to men only, rather than women.

G.   In the 1990s a new type of human group—**electronic communities**—was created through the technology of the Internet. Every day, hundreds of thousands of people meet in chat rooms to talk on almost any conceivable topic.

II.   Bureaucracies

A.   Almost 100 years ago, **Max Weber** noted the emergence of **bureaucracies**, a new type of organization whose goal was to maximize efficiency and results.

B.   The essential characteristics of bureaucracies are: (1) a hierarchy with assignments flowing downward and accountability flowing upward; (2) a division of labor; (3) written rules; (4) written communications and records; and (5) impersonality.

C.   Once bureaucracies come into existence, they tend to perpetuate themselves by replacing old goals with new ones.

D.   Weber predicted that bureaucracies would dominate social life because they are such a powerful form of social organization. He called this process the **rationalization of society.**

E.   Bureaucracies also have a dark side. As they carry out their functions, certain dysfunctions emerge.

        1.   Sometimes the rules that govern bureaucratic activity can become too detailed or too cumbersome, such that procedures are no longer carried out efficiently.

        2.   Bureaucratic **alienation**, a feeling of powerlessness and normlessness, occurs when workers are assigned to repetitive tasks in order for the corporation to

achieve efficient production, thereby cutting them off from the product of one's labor.

3.　To resist alienation in secondary organization, workers form **primary groups.**

III.　Working for the Corporation

A.　**Rosabeth Moss Kanter's** organizational research demonstrates that the corporate elite maintains hidden values—to keep itself in power and provide better access to information, networking, and "fast tracks" for workers like themselves, usually white and male.

1.　Workers who fit in are given opportunities to advance. They outperform others and are more committed. Those judged outsiders experience few opportunities, think poorly of themselves, are less committed, and work below their potential.

2.　The hidden values that create this self-fulfilling prophecy remain largely invisible. Because of this, the inner circle reproduces itself, thereby contributing to the **iron law of oligarchy**.

3.　Females and minorities do not match the hidden values of the corporate culture and may by treated differently. They may experience *showcasing*—being put in highly visible, but relatively powerless, positions so that the company can show how *progressive* it is. These are often *slow-track* positions—promotions are slow because accomplishments seldom come to the attention of top management.

B.　The Japanese have become a giant in today's global economy because they developed a different corporate model.

1.　In Japan, newly hired college graduates are viewed as a team working towards the same goal of success for the organization. In the United States, employees try to outperform one another and are loyal to themselves rather than the company.

2.　In Japan, lifetime security is taken for granted, with employees and firms maintaining mutual loyalties. In the United States, lifetime security is unusual, with companies routinely laying workers off in slow times and workers looking out for number one.

3.　In Japan, work is like a marriage; company and employee are mutually committed. In the United States, the work relationship is a highly specific and often temporary one.

4.　In Japan, workers move from one job to another within the corporation. In the United States, workers are expected to perform one job only, and if they do it well they may be promoted up the ladder to the next level.

5.　In Japan, decision making is a lengthy process, with everyone affected by the decision being given an opportunity to have input. In the United States, decisions are made without necessarily consulting those who will be affected. However, in reality, most Japanese workers do not work in corporations that reflect the model and in recent years, Japan has turned to the United States for clues on how to be more efficient.

IV.　Group Dynamics

A.　How individuals affect groups and groups affect individuals is known as **group dynamics.** Sociologists often study dynamics in **small groups,** where everyone interacts directly with all the other group members.

B.　The size of the group is significant for its dynamics.

1.　Sociologist **Georg Simmel** (1858-1918) noted the significance of group size, making distinctions between a **dyad**, the smallest and most fragile of all human groupings with only two members, and a **triad**, stronger than dyads because there are three members but still are extremely unstable. It is not uncommon for the bonds between two members to seem stronger, with the third person feeling hurt and excluded.

    2.   As more members are added to a group, intensity decreases and stability increases, for there are more linkages between more people within the group. The groups develop a more formal structure to accomplish their goals, for instance by having a president, treasurer, etc.

C.   Group size also influences our attitudes and behaviors.

    1.   As the group grows in size, its members feel a diffusion of responsibility.

    2.   As the size increases, the group loses its sense of intimacy.

    3.   As the size increases, the group tends to divide itself into smaller groups.

D.   A leader is defined as someone who influences the behavior of others.

    1.   There are two types of group leaders. **Instrumental** (task-oriented) leaders are those who try to keep the group moving toward its goals. **Expressive** (socioemotional) leaders are those who are less likely to be recognized as leaders but help with the group's morale. These leaders may have to minimize the friction that instrumental leaders necessarily create.

    2.   There are three types of leadership styles. **Authoritarian leaders** are those who give orders and frequently do not explain why they praise or condemn a person's work. **Democratic leaders** are those who try to gain a consensus by explaining proposed actions, suggesting alternative approaches, and giving *facts* as the basis for their evaluation of the members' work. **Laissez-faire leaders** are those who are very passive and give the group almost total freedom to do as it wishes.

    3.   Psychologists **Ronald Lippitt** and **Ralph White** discovered that these leadership styles produced different results when used on small groups of young boys. Under authoritarian leaders, the boys became either aggressive or apathetic; under democratic leaders, they were more personal and friendly; and under laissez-faire leaders they asked more questions, made fewer decisions, and were notable for their lack of achievement.

    4.   Different situations require different styles of leadership. People who become leaders are seen as strongly representing the group's values or as able to lead a group out of a crisis. They tend to be more talkative and to express determination and self-confidence. Taller people and those judged better looking are more likely to become leaders.

E.   A study by **Dr. Solomon Asch** indicates that people are strongly influenced by peer pressure. Asch was interested in seeing whether individuals would resist the temptation to change a correct response to an incorrect response because of peer pressure.

    1.   Asch held cards up in front of small groups of people and asked them which sets of cards matched; one at a time. People were supposed to respond aloud. All but one of the group members were confederates, having been told in advance by the researcher how to answer the question.

    2.   After two trials in which everyone answered correctly, the confederates intentionally answered incorrectly, as they had been instructed to do.

    3.   Of the fifty people tested, thirty-three percent always gave the incorrect answers at least half of the time because of peer pressure, even though they knew the answers were wrong. Only twenty-five percent always gave the right answer despite the peer pressure.

F.   Sociologist **Irving Janis** coined the word **groupthink** to refer to situations in which people in a group think alike and any suggestion or alternative becomes a sign of disloyalty. Even moral judgments are put aside for the perceived welfare of the group.

    1.   The Asch and Milgram experiments demonstrate how groupthink can develop.

2.   U.S. history provides examples of governmental groupthink: presidents and their inner circles have committed themselves to a single course of action (refusal to believe the Japanese might attack Pearl Harbor; continuing and expanding the war in Vietnam) even when objective evidence showed the course to be wrong. The leaders became cut off from information that did not coincide with their own opinions.

3.   Groupthink can be prevented only by insuring that leaders regularly are exposed to individuals who have views conflicting with those of the inner circle.

KEY TERMS

After studying the chapter, review each of the following terms.

aggregate: individuals who temporarily share the same physical space but do not see themselves as belonging together (p. 114)

alienation: Marx's term for the workers' lack of connection to the product of their labor; caused by their being assigned repetitive tasks on a small part of a product which leads to a sense of powerlessness and normlessness; also used in the general sense of not feeling a part of something (p. 126)

authoritarian leader: a leader who leads by giving orders (p. 131)

bureaucracy: a formal organization with a hierarchy of authority, a clear division of labor; emphasis on written rules, communications, and records; and impersonality of positions (p. 121)

category: people who have similar characteristics (p. 114)

clique: a cluster of people within a larger group who choose to interact with one another; an internal faction (p. 119)

coalition: the alignment of some members of a group against others (p. 129)

corporate culture: the orientations that characterize corporate work settings (p. 126)

democratic leader: a leader who leads by trying to reach a consensus (p. 131)

dyad: the smallest possible group, consisting of two persons (p. 129)

electronic community: individuals who regularly interact with one another on the Internet and who think of themselves as belonging together (p. 121)

expressive leader: an individual who increases harmony and minimizes conflict in a group; also known as a socioemotional leader (p. 131)

goal displacement: the adoption of new goals by an organization; also known as goal replacement (p. 123)

group: people who have something in common and who believe that what they have in common is significant; also called a social group (p. 114)

group dynamics: the ways in which individuals affect groups and groups influence individuals (p. 129)

groupthink: Irving Janis term for a narrowing of thought by a group of people leading to the perception that there is only one correct answer; in groupthink, to suggest alternatives becomes a sign of disloyalty (p. 135)

in-groups: groups toward which one feels loyalty (p.117)

instrumental leader: an individual who tries to keep the group moving toward its goals; also known as a *task oriented leader* (p. 131)

(the) iron law of oligarchy: Robert Michels' phrase for the tendency of formal organizations to be dominated by small, self-perpetuating elite (p. 117)

laissez-faire leader: an individual who leads by being highly permissive (p. 131)

leader: someone who influences other people (p. 131)

leadership styles: ways in which people express their leadership (p. 131)

out-groups: groups toward which one feels antagonism (p. 117)

primary group: a group characterized by intimate, long-term, face-to-face association and cooperation (p. 115)

(the) rationalization of society: a widespread acceptance of rationality and a social organization largely built around this idea (p. 124)

reference group: Herbert Hyman's term for groups we use as standards to evaluate ourselves (p. 118)

secondary group: compared with a primary group, a larger, relatively temporary, more anonymous, formal, and impersonal group based on some interest or activity, whose members are likely to interact on the basis of specific roles. (p. 115)

small group: a group small enough for everyone to interact directly with all the other members (p. 129)

social network: the social ties radiating outward from the self that link people together (p. 119)

triad: a group of three people (p. 129)

voluntary association: a group made up of people who voluntarily organize on the basis of some mutual interest, also known as voluntary memberships. (p. 115)

KEY PEOPLE

Review the major theoretical contributions or research findings of these theorists and thinkers.

George Arquitt and Elaine Fox: These sociologists studied local posts of the VFW and found three types of members and evidence of the iron law of oligarchy.

Solomon Asch: Asch is famous for his research on conformity to group pressure.

Charles H. Cooley: It was Cooley who noted the central role of primary groups in the development of one's sense of self.

John Darley and Bibb Latane: These researchers investigated what impact the size of the group has on individual members' attitudes and behaviors. They found that as the group grew in size, individuals' sense of responsibility diminished, their interactions became more formal, and the larger group tended to break down into small ones.

Lloyd Howells and Selwyn Becker: These social psychologists found that factors such as location within a group underlie people's choices of leaders.

Irving Janis: Janis coined the term *groupthink* to refer to the tunnel vision that a group of people sometimes develop.

Rosabeth Moss Kanter: Kanter studied the *invisible* corporate culture which for the most part continually reproduces itself by promoting those workers who fit the elite's stereotypical views.

Judith Kleinfeld: a psychologist who criticized Milgram's research on social networks. She did not find evidence for the "small world phenomenon."

Ronald Lippitt and Ralph White: These social psychologists carried out a classic study on leadership styles and found that the style of leadership affected the behavior of group members.

Robert K. Merton: Merton observed that the traits of in-groups become viewed as virtues, while those same traits in out-groups are seen as vices.

Robert Michels: Michels first used the term "the iron law of oligarchy" to describe the tendency for the leaders of an organization to become entrenched in a collective tunnel vision.

Stanley Milgram: Milgram's research has contributed greatly to sociological knowledge of group life. He did research on social networks and on individual conformity to group pressure.

George Ritzer: Ritzer coined the term *the McDonaldization of society* to describe the increasing standardization of modern social life.

Georg Simmel: This early sociologist was one of the first to note the significance of group size; he used the terms dyad and triad to describe the smallest groups.

Max Weber: Weber studied the rationalization of society by investigating the link between Protestantism and capitalism and identified the characteristics of bureaucracy.

SELF-TEST

After completing this self-test, check your answers in the Answer Key of this Study Guide.

MULTIPLE CHOICE QUESTIONS

1. People who have something in common and who believe that what they have in common is significant are called a(n):
    a. group.
    b. category.
    c. aggregate.
    d. reference organization

2. _____ groups are essential to an individual's psychological well-being.
    a. Primary
    b. Secondary
    c. Therapy
    d. Interpersonal

3. Secondary groups:
    a. have members who are likely to interact on the basis of specific roles.

b.   are characteristic of industrial societies.
c.   are essential to the functioning of contemporary societies.
d.   all of the above.

4.   Secondary groups tend to break down into:
a.   aggregates.
b.   categories.
c.   primary groups.
d.   none of the above.

5.   The tendency for organizations to be dominated by a small, self-perpetuating elite is called:
a.   the Peter Principle.
b.   bureaucratic engorgement.
c.   the iron law of oligarchy.
d.   the corporate power struggle.

6.   Sociologists refer to groups that provide a sense of identification or belonging as:
a.   personal groups.
b.   in-groups.
c.   my-group.
d.   homeboys' groups.

7.   The groups we use as a standard to evaluate ourselves are:
a.   primary groups.
b.   secondary groups.
c.   reference groups.
d.   evaluation groups.

8.   Clusters, or internal factions, within a large group are known as:
a.   categories.
b.   cliques.
c.   secondary groups.
d.   out-groups.

9.   To study the phenomenon of social networks, Milgram conducted an experiment called:
a.   the small town phenomenon.
b.   the primary group cluster.
c.   the small world phenomenon.
d.   the in-group phenomenon.

10.   All of the following are characteristics of bureaucracy, *except*:
a.   a division of labor.
b.   a hierarchy with assignments flowing upward and accountability flowing downward.
c.   written rules, communications, and records.
d.   impersonality.

11.   Goal displacement occurs when:
a.   a bureaucrat is unable to function as a cooperative, integrated part of the whole.
b.   goals conflict with one another.
c.   an organization has achieved its original goals and then adopts new goals.
d.   members of an organization are promoted until they reach their level of incompetence.

12. The idea that bureaucracies, with their rules, regulations, and emphasis on results, would increasingly govern our lives is:
    a. goal displacement.
    b. the rationalization of society.
    c. alienation.
    d. discrimination.

13. Which of the following is not one of the dysfunctions of bureaucracies?
    a. red tape
    b. bureaucratic alienation
    c. a and b are both dysfunctions
    d. none of the above

14. Karl Marx use the term _____ to refer to what happens in a bureaucracy when people begin to feel more like objects than people.
    a. communism
    b. proletariat
    c. alienation
    d. resistance

15. Group-wise, one of the common ways to reduce a feeling of alienation at work is to:
    a. assault someone.
    b. create more red tape.
    c. daydream.
    d. form a primary group.

16. Kanter stresses that corporate culture contains:
    a. hidden values.
    b. alienation.
    c. rules.
    d. fairness.

17. The *hidden values* of corporate culture contribute to:
    a. equal pay for equal work.
    b. secondary group formation.
    c. the iron law of oligarchy.
    d. democratization.

18. In which type of corporate model is lifetime security taken for granted?
    a. The United States model.
    b. The Japanese model.
    c. Both the United States and Japanese models.
    d. It is not taken for granted in either the United States or Japanese models.

19. In the United States, lifetime job security is limited primarily to:
    a. researchers.
    b. teachers.
    c. executives.
    d. boards of trustees.

20.   In Japan, decision making is by:
       a.   democratic process.
       b.   corporate heads.
       c.   consensus.
       d.   board of trustees.

21.   Small groups:
       a.   are primary groups.
       b.   are secondary groups.
       c.   can be either primary or secondary groups.
       d.   neither primary nor secondary groups, but fall between these two types of groups.

22.   Dyads:
       a.   are the most intense or intimate of human groups.
       b.   require continuing active participation and commitment of both members.
       c.   are the most unstable of social groups.
       d.   all of the above.

23.   When some group members align themselves against others in the group:
       a.   a coalition forms.
       b.   nationalization develops.
       c.   primary groups collapse.
       d.   secondary groups collapse.

24.   Larger groups are more_____than small groups.
       a.   intimate
       b.   intense
       c.   stable
       d.   none of the above

25.   An expressive leader:
       a.   tries to keep the group moving toward its goals.
       b.   is also known as a task-oriented leader.
       c.   increases harmony and minimizes conflict in a group.
       d.   is the director of the drama club.

26.   All of the following are styles of leadership *except*:
       a.   authoritarian.
       b.   democratic.
       c.   laisse-faire.
       d.   bureaucratic.

27.   Which of the following has been found to be the best leadership style?
       a.   authoritarian
       b.   bureaucratic
       c.   democratic
       d.   none of the above

28.   The Asch experiment demonstrates:
       a.   the power of conformity.

b.   the power of authority.
c.   the importance of individualism.
d.   the importance of groupthink.

29.   The Milgram experiment demonstrates:
a.   that people who know they are being studied will behave differently as a result.
b.   the awesome influence of peer groups over their members.
c.   how strongly people are influenced by authority.
d.   how isolated political leaders can become.

30.   Irving Janis uses the term _____ to refer to the collective tunnel vision that group members sometimes develop.
a.   groupthink
b.   bureaucratic alienation
c.   peer pressure
d.   conformity pressure

TRUE-FALSE QUESTIONS

T F   1.   An aggregate consists of people who temporarily share the same physical space but who do not see themselves as belonging together.
T F   2.   Members of primary groups are likely to interact on the basis of specific roles.
T F   3.   Voluntary associations are a special type of primary group.
T F   4.   As organizations grow larger they become more democratic.
T F   5.   Tensions between in- and out-groups disappear in socially diverse societies.
T F   6.   Reference group standards in a diverse society are often contradictory.
T F   7.   Networks tend to limit inequalities by giving more people access to opportunities.
T F   8.   Universities are examples of bureaucracies.
T F   9.   In a bureaucracy, each worker is a replaceable unit.
T F   10. In a division of labor workplace, most workers perform multiple tasks.
T F   11. The NATO organization exhibits goal displacement.
T F   12. Bureaucracies are likely to disappear as our dominant form of social organization in the near future.
T F   13. A self-employed auto mechanic is likely to feel alienation from their work.
T F   14. The *corporate culture* produces self-fulfilling prophecies.
T F   15. Being absorbed into the dominant culture is an example of cultural pluralism.
T F   16. In Japan, lifetime security in the workplace is a reality.
T F   17. Management by consensus is a myth in Japanese corporations.
T F   18. As a small group grows larger, its intensity decreases and its stability increases.
T F   19. The smallest possible group is a triad.
T F   20. Expressive leaders increase harmony and minimize conflicts.

FILL-IN QUESTIONS

1.   A large introductory sociology class is an example of _____.
2.   A _____ group is characterized by more anonymous, formal, and impersonal relationships.

3. _____ refers to the tendency of formal organizations to be dominated by a small, self-perpetuating elite.

4. _____ provide a sense of identification or belonging while producing feelings of antagonisms towards _____.

5. _____ groups are the groups we use as standards to evaluate ourselves.

6. Links between people, their cliques, their family, their friends, are called

_____.

7. A new type of human community using the internet to interact is referred to as the _____ community.

8. _____ occurs when new goals are adopted by an organization to replace previous goals that may have been fulfilled.

9. The phrase _____ refers to the increasing influence of bureaucracies in society.

10. _____ is a feeling of powerlessness and normlessness; the experience of being cut off from the product of one's labor.

11. The belief that Japanese workers have lifetime job security is mostly a _____.

12. Sociologists use the term _____ to refer to how groups influence us and how we affect groups.

13. As a _____ grows larger, it becomes more stable, but its intensity, or intimacy, decreases.

14. An individual who tries to keep the group moving toward its goals is a(n)

_____.

15. _____ is a narrowing of thought by a group of people, which results in overconfidence and tunnel vision.

MATCH THESE THEORISTS/PHILOSOPHERS WITH THEIR CONTRIBUTIONS

1. Simmel
2. Michels
3. Milgram
4. Asch
5. Cooley

a. *primary groups*
b. *obedience to authority*
c. *dyad*
d. *iron law of oligarchy*
e. *power of peer pressure*

MATCH EACH CONCEPT WITH ITS MEANING

1. primary group
2. secondary group
3. reference group
4. cliques
5. social networks

a. *friends of friends*
b. *provides intimacy*
c. *provide standards to evaluate us*
d. *more formal and impersonal*
e. *internal factions*

ESSAY QUESTIONS

1. Define the concept of primary group, and the concept of secondary group. Discuss how the two are linked in the workplace.
2. Define the iron law of oligarchy and discuss why this problem occurs in voluntary associations.
3. Explain the three different leadership styles. Include in your answer a discussion on which style is the best.
4. Discuss and compare Japanese and American corporations. What are the myths and realities?
5. Explore the factors that influence the emergence of groupthink and consider strategies for minimizing the development of this collective tunnel vision.

STUDY PROJECTS

1. Do you have a reference group that you use or have used to evaluate your life? How important is this reference group to you? Explain.

2. Do you belong to any electronic communities? If so, list them and explain the extent of your participation in each of these communities. If you do not belong to any electronic communities, explain why. Overall, do you think electronic communities serve an important social networking function in society? Why or why not?

CHAPTER 6

DEVIANCE AND SOCIAL CONTROL

CHAPTER SUMMARY

- **Deviance**, which refers to violations of social norms, is relative; what people consider deviant varies from one culture to another and from group to group within a society. It is not the act itself, but the reaction to the act, that makes something deviant. To explain deviance, biologists and psychologists look for reasons within people, such as genetic predispositions or personality disorders, while sociologists look for explanations in social relationships.

- **Symbolic interactionists** have developed several theories to explain deviance. They use differential association theory, control theory, and labeling theory to analyze deviance such as crime. Many people succeed in neutralizing the norms of society and are able to commit deviant acts while thinking of themselves as conformists. Although most people resist being labeled deviant, there are those who embrace deviance.

- **Functionalists** state that deviance is functional because it affirms norms and promotes social unity and social change. **Strain theory** suggests that while people are socialized to accept the norms of material success, many are unable to achieve this goal in socially acceptable ways so they turn to deviance as a means to the goal. Accordingly, **illegitimate opportunity structures** give some people easier access to illegal means of achieving goals than others.

- **Conflict theorists** argue that the group in power imposes its definitions of deviance on other groups—the ruling class directs the criminal justice system against members of the working class, who commit highly visible property crimes. At the same time it diverts its own criminal activities out of the criminal justice system. The use of imprisonment is motivated by the goals of retribution, deterrence, rehabilitation, and incapacitation.

- In recent years, the U.S. has taken the "get-tough" position on crime which has resulted in the imprisonment of millions of people. There is a growing tendency towards the medicalization of deviance; according to this view, deviant acts are external symptoms of internal disorders. **Thomas Szasz** argues that mental illnesses are neither mental nor illnesses, but are simply problem behaviors. With deviance inevitable, the larger issues are how to protect people from deviant behaviors that are harmful to their welfare, to tolerate those that are not, and to develop systems of fairer treatment for deviants.

LEARNING OBJECTIVES

As you read Chapter 6, use these learning objectives to organize your notes. After completing your reading, you should be able to answer each of the objectives.

1. Define "deviance" and understand why, from a sociological perspective, deviance is relative.
2. Know why human groups need norms to exist and, consequently, develop a system of social control for enforcing norms.
3. Describe some of the sanctions human groups use to enforce norms, including shaming and degradation ceremonies.
4. Differentiate between socio-biological, psychological, and sociological explanations of why people violate norms.
5. Talk about deviance from the symbolic interactionist perspective—describe and apply the various components of differential association theory, control theory, and labeling theory.
6. List and discuss the five techniques of neutralization.

7.	Know from the functionalist perspective what functions deviance fulfills for society.
8.	Understand strain theory and discuss its social implications.
9.	Describe the different ways street crime and white-collar crime are perceived by the public and treated by the criminal justice system.
10.	Talk about the role power plays in defining and punishing deviance while discussing, from the conflict perspective, how the criminal justice system legitimates and perpetuates social inequality.
11.	Discuss the reasons for, and implications of, "get tough" policies on crime in the United States.
12.	Discuss the controversy within the discipline of sociology concerning the declining crime rates.
13.	Explain what is meant by the recidivism rate.
14.	Talk about the gender, social class, and racial and ethnic biases in the application of the death penalty.
15.	Explain what is meant by the term "hate crime."
16.	Know what is meant by the medicalization of deviance and why some sociologists view mental illness as more of a social, rather than biological, condition.
17.	Explain why the United States needs to develop a more fair and humane approach to dealing with deviance.

CHAPTER OUTLINE

## I.	What Is Deviance?

A.	Sociologists use the term deviance to refer to a violation of norms.
1.	According to sociologist **Howard S. Becker**, it is not the act itself that makes an action deviant, but rather how society reacts to it.
2.	Deviance is a relative concept; since different groups have different norms, what is deviant to some is not deviant to others.
3.	Crime is the violation of rules that have been written into law.
4.	Sociologists use the term *deviance* nonjudgementally to refer to any act to which people respond negatively. To sociologists, all people are deviants because everyone violates rules from time to time.
5.	**Erving Goffman** used *stigma* to refer to attributes that discredit one's claim to a "normal" identity; a stigma (e.g. physical deformities, skin color) defines a person's master status, superseding all other statuses the person occupies.
B.	Norms allow social order—a group's customary social arrangements—because they lay out the basic guidelines for how we play our roles and how we interact with others.
1.	Deviance is often seen as threatening because it violates a group's customary social arrangements and undermines the predictability that is the foundation of social life.
2.	Human groups develop a system of social control; formal and informal means of enforcing the norms.
C.	Society's disapproval of deviance takes the form of negative sanctions and ranges from frowns and gossip to imprisonment and capital punishment, although most negative sanctions are informal. Positive sanctions are used to reward people for conforming to norms.
D.	The sociological explanations of deviance differ from biological and psychological ones.
1.	Psychologists and sociobiologists explain deviance by looking within individuals; sociologists look outside the individual.

2. Biological explanations focus on genetic predisposition—factors such as intelligence, "XYY" theory (that an extra Y chromosome in men leads to crime), or body type (squarish, muscular persons more likely to commit street crimes).

3 Psychological explanations focus on personality disorders (e.g., "bad toilet training," "suffocating mothers," etc.). Yet these do not necessarily result in the presence or absence of specific forms of deviance in a person.

4 Sociological explanations search outside the individual; social influences–such as socialization, subcultural group memberships, or social class (people's relative standing in terms of education, occupation, income and wealth)–account for why some people break norms.

II. The Symbolic Interactionist Perspective

A. **Edwin Sutherland** used the term *differential association* to suggest that we learn to deviate from or conform to society's norms mostly from the people with whom we associate.

1. The key to differential association is the learning of ideas and attitudes favorable to following the law. Because we learn both from the various people we associate with, the end result is an imbalance; we conform or deviate depending on which set of messages is stronger.

2. Studies have demonstrated that families do teach their members to violate the norms of society; families involved in crime tend to set their children on a lawbreaking path.

3. The neighborhood is also likely to be influential; sociologists have found that delinquents tend to come from neighborhoods in which their peers are involved in crime.

4. Symbolic interactionists stress that we are not mere pawns, but help produce our orientation to life; our choice of associates helps to shape our sense of self.

B. According to **Walter Reckless**, who developed control theory, everyone is propelled towards deviance, but two control systems work against these motivations to deviate.

1. Inner controls are one's capacity to withstand temptations toward deviance, and include internalized morality, integrity, fear of punishment, and desire to be good. Outer controls involve groups (e.g., family, friends, the police) that influence a person to stay away from crime.

2. Sociologist **Travis Hirschi** noted that strong bonds to society lead to more effective inner controls; bonds are based on attachments, commitments, involvements, and beliefs.

3. The likelihood that we will deviate from social norms is related to the strength of our control systems–if the systems are strong we are less likely to deviate than if they are weak.

C. **Labeling theory** is the view that the labels people are given affect their own and others' perceptions of them, and thus channel their behavior either into deviance or into conformity.

1. Most people resist being labeled as deviant, even when engaging in deviant behavior. There are five different techniques of neutralizations: (1) denial of responsibility ("I didn't do it"); (2) denial of injury ("Who really got hurt?"); (3) denial of a victim ("She deserved it"); (4) condemnation of the condemners ("Who are you to talk?"); and (5) appeal to higher loyalty ("I had to help my friends").

2. Some people invite a deviant label (e.g. motorcycle gangs may pride themselves on getting into trouble, laughing at death, etc.).

3. **William J. Chambliss's** study of law-breaking activities among two groups—the Saints (boys from respectable middle class families) and the Toughnecks (boys from working class families who hang out on the streets)—provides an excellent illustration of labeling theory. There were social class differences not only in terms of the visibility of the law-breaking behavior, but also in the styles of interaction with those in authority. These influenced the way in which teachers and the police saw them and treated them. The study showed how labels open and close the door of opportunity for the individuals involved.

III.   The Functionalist Perspective

A.   **Emile Durkheim** stated that deviance is functional, for it contributes to social order.
1.   Deviance clarifies moral boundaries (a group's ideas about how people should act and think) and affirms norms.
2.   Deviance promotes social unity.
3.   Deviance promotes social change (if boundary violations gain enough support, they become new, acceptable behaviors).

B.   **Robert Merton** developed strain theory to analyze what happens when people are socialized to desire a cultural goal but denied the institutionalized (i.e., legitimate) means to reach it.
1.   Merton used "anomie" (Durkheim's term) to refer to the strain people experience when they are blocked in their attempts to achieve those goals. He identified five reactions to cultural goals and institutionalized means.
2.   The first reaction is conformity (using acceptable means to seek the goals society sets), which is the most common. The other four responses are deviant innovation (using illegitimate means to achieve them); ritualism (giving up on achieving cultural goals, but clinging to conventional rules of conduct); retreatism (rejecting cultural goals, dropping out); and rebellion (seeking to replace society's goals).
3.   According to strain theory, deviants are products of their society. Some people experience greater frustration in achieving cultural goals because of their location in society, making them more likely to deviate.

C.   According to illegitimate opportunity theory social classes have distinct styles of crime due to unequal access to institutionalized means of achieving socially acceptable goals.
1.   Many poor children in industrialized societies, who are socialized into wanting to own things, end up dropping out of school because of educational failure, thereby closing the door on many legitimate avenues to financial success.
2.   **Richard Cloward** and **Lloyd Ohlin** suggest that opportunities for remunerative crime are woven into the texture of life and may result when legitimate structures fail. In this way the poor may be drawn into certain crimes in unequal numbers.
3.   Illegal income-producing activities, such as robbery, drug dealing, prostitution, pimping, gambling, and other "hustles," are functional for those who want to make money, but whose access to legitimate activities is blocked.
4.   Gangs offer disadvantaged youth an illegitimate opportunity structure. Research by **Martin Sanchez Jankowski** demonstrated that young men joined gangs because they provided them with access to steady money, recreation, anonymity in criminal activities, protection, and a way to help the neighborhood.
5.   White-collar crime refers to crimes that people of respectable and high social status commit in the course of their occupations. Such crimes exist in greater numbers than commonly perceived, and can be very costly—totaling about $400 billion a year. They can involve physical harm and sometimes death (concealing information that silicone breast implants might leak, for example).

IV.   The Conflict Perspective

A.   Conflict theorists address the issue of why the legal system is inconsistent in terms of providing "justice for all". This inequality is central to their analysis of crime and the criminal justice system—the police, courts, and prisons.

B.   The criminal justice system is controlled by the wealthy and powerful—a power elite; this group determines the basic laws whose enforcement is essential to the preservation of its power.

C.   According to conflict theory, the law is an instrument of repression, a tool designed to maintain the powerful in privileged positions and keep the powerless from rebelling and overthrowing the social order. When members of the working class get out of line, they are arrested, tried and imprisoned in the criminal justice system.

    1.   While the criminal justice system tends to overlook the harm done by the corporations, flagrant violations are prosecuted. The publicity given to white collar criminals helps to stabilize the system by providing evidence of fairness.

    2.   Usually the powerful bypass the courts altogether, appearing instead before some agency, whose members are people from the same wealthy background. Given this, it is not surprising that the usual sanction is a token fine.

    3.   Property crimes of the masses are handled by the courts; these crimes not only threaten the sanctity of private property, but ultimately, the positions of the powerful.

V.   Reactions to Deviance

A.   Imprisonment—a reflection of a "get-tough" orientation—is an increasingly popular reaction to crime.

    1.   There has been a tremendous growth in the U.S. prison population; it is estimated that more than 1.8 million people are currently incarcerated. About 95 percent are men, and about half are African American.

    2.   The recidivism rate (the proportion of persons who are rearrested) in the United States runs as high as 85-90 percent, and those given probation do no better.

    3.   Research on the death penalty reveals that the death penalty is not administered evenly. Biases including differential treatment based on geographic location, gender, social class, as well as racial and ethnic biases.

    4.   As opinions change, or different groups gain access to power, definitions of deviance and laws will also change. Some examples of new types of crime are identity theft and hate crimes.

B.   Medicalization of deviance is the view that deviance is a symptom of some underlying illness that needs to be treated by physicians.

    Thomas Szasz argues that mental illness is simply problem behaviors: some forms of "mental" illnesses have organic causes (e.g., depression caused by a chemical imbalance in the brain); while others are responses to trouble with various coping devices.

    Some sociologists find Szasz's analysis refreshing because it indicates that social experiences, and not some illness of the mind, underlie bizarre behaviors.

C.   In considering the homeless, just the experience of being homeless can cause mental illness. Because you are on the streets and often have no place to wash yourself or your clothes, you are stared at or ignored, resulting in withdrawal. Homelessness and mental illness can be reciprocal: just as "mental illness" can cause homelessness, so can the trials of being homeless and of living on the streets can lead to unusual and unacceptable thinking and behaviors.

D. With deviance inevitable, one measure of a society is how it treats its deviants. The larger issues are how to protect people from deviant behaviors that are harmful to their welfare, to tolerate those that are not, and to develop systems of fairer treatment for deviants.

KEY TERMS

After studying the chapter, review each of the following terms.

Capital punishment: the death penalty (p. 157)

capitalist class: the wealthy who own the means of production and buy the labor of the working class (p. 153)

control theory: the idea that two control systems—inner controls and outer controls—work against our tendencies to deviate (p. 145)

crime: the violation of norms written into law (p. 140)

criminal justice system: the system of police, courts, and prisons set up to deal with people who are accused of having committed a crime (p. 152)

cultural goals: the legitimate objectives held out to the members of a society (p. 148)

deviance: the violation of rules or norms (p. 140)

differential association: Edwin Sutherland's term to indicate that associating with some groups results in learning an "excess of definitions" of deviance, and, by extension, in a greater likelihood that one will become deviant (p. 144)

genetic predisposition: inborn tendencies, in this context, to commit deviant acts (p. 143)

hate crime: crimes to which more severe penalties are attached because they are motivated by hatred (dislike, animosity) of someone's race-ethnicity, religion, sexual orientation, disability, or national origin (p. 161)

illegitimate opportunity structure: opportunities for crimes that are woven into the texture of life (p. 150)

institutionalized means: approved ways of reaching cultural goals (p. 148)

labeling theory: the view, developed by symbolic interactionists, that the labels people are given affect their own and others' perceptions of them, thus channeling their behavior either into deviance or into conformity (p. 146)

marginal working class: the most desperate members of the working class, who have few skills, little job security, and are often unemployed (p. 153)

medicalization of deviance: to make some deviance a medical matter, a symptom of some underlying illness that needs to be treated by physicians (p. 161)

negative sanction: an expression of disapproval for breaking a norm; ranging from a mild, informal reaction such as a frown to a more formal reaction such as a prison sentence or an execution (p. 142)

personality disorders: the view that a personality disturbance of some sort causes an individual to violate social norms (p. 143)

positive sanction: a reward given for following norms, ranging from a smile to a prize (p. 142)

recidivism rate: the proportion of people who are rearrested (p. 156)

social control: a group's formal and informal means of enforcing its norms (p. 142)

social order: a group's usual and customary social arrangements, on which its members depend and on which they base their lives (p. 142)

stigma: 'blemishes" that discredit a person's claim to a "normal" identity (p. 140)

strain theory: Robert Merton's term for the strain engendered when a society socializes large numbers of people to desire a cultural goal (such as success) but withholds from many the approved means to reach that goal; one adaptation is crime, the choice of an innovative but illegitimate means (one outside the approved system) to attain the cultural goal (p. 148)

street crime: crimes such as mugging, rape, and burglary (p. 143)

techniques of neutralization: ways of thinking or rationalizing that help people deflect society's norms (p. 146)

white-collar crime (corporate crime): Edwin Sutherland's term for crimes committed by people of respectable and high social status in the course of their occupations; examples include bribery of public officials, securities violations, embezzlement, false advertising, and price fixing (p. 150)

working class: people who sell their labor to the capitalist class (p. 153)

KEY PEOPLE

Review the major theoretical contributions or research findings of these theorists and thinkers.

Howard Becker: Becker observed that an act is not deviant in and of itself, but only when there is a reaction to it.

William Chambliss: Chambliss demonstrated the power of the label in his study of two youth gangs—the Saints and the Roughnecks.

Richard Cloward and Lloyd Ohlin: These sociologists identified the illegitimate opportunity structures that are woven into the texture of life in urban slums and provide an alternative set of opportunities for slum residents when legitimate ones are blocked.

Emile Durkheim: Durkheim noted the functions that deviance has for social life.

Robert Edgerton: An anthropologist who reported how differently human groups react to similar behaviors.

Erving Goffman: Goffman wrote about the role of stigma in the definition of whom and what is deviant.

Travis Hirschi: In order to understand the effectiveness of inner controls, Hirschi studied the strength of the bonds an individual has to society.

Ruth Horowitz: Horowitz did participant observation in a lower-class Chicano neighborhood in Chicago and discovered how associating with people who have a certain concept of "honor" can propel young men to deviance.

Robert Merton: Merton developed strain theory to explain patterns of deviance within a society.

Walter Reckless: Reckless developed control theory, suggesting that our behavior is controlled by two different systems, one external (*outer controls* like the police, family, and friends) and the other internal (*inner controls* like our conscience, religious principles, and ideas of right and wrong).

Edwin Sutherland: Sutherland not only developed differential association theory, but was the first to study and give a name (white collar crime) to crimes that occur among the middle class in the course of their work.

Gresham Sykes and David Matza: These sociologists studied the different strategies delinquent boys use to deflect society's norms—techniques of neutralization.

Thomas Szasz: Szasz argued that mental illness represents the medicalization of deviance.

Mike Watson: Watson studied motorcycle gangs and found that they actively embraced the deviant label.

SELF-TEST
After completing this self-test, check your answers in the Answer Key of this Study Guide.

MULTIPLE CHOICE QUESTIONS

1. In sociology, to what does the term deviance refer?
    a. behavior that sociologists believe is bad enough to warrant being punished by society
    b. all violations of social rules
    c. the violation of serious rules
    d. crime

2. Why is deviance often seen as threatening?
    a. because it is always harmful to society
    b. because it undermines the predictability of social life
    c. because it costs society a great deal of money
    d. because it is bad

3. Of what are frowns, gossip, and crossing people off guest lists all examples?
    a. retribution
    b. degradation ceremonies
    c. negative sanctions
    d. institutionalized means to achieve goals

4. Most negative sanctions are:
    a. very punitive.
    b. universally the same.
    c. generally informal.
    d. all of the above.

5. According to Erving Goffman, what is the function of stigma?
    a. to punish the person because she or he violates the norms
    b. to reward society for conforming to the norms
    c. to identify the person who violates the norm as deviant
    d. to regulate behavior

6. A smile or an award are examples of:
    a. positive sanctions.
    b. social reaffirmation ceremonies.
    c. stigmatization.
    d. deinstitutionalization.

7. Differential association theory is based on the:
    a. functionalist perspective.
    b. conflict perspective.
    c. symbolic interactionist perspective.
    d. psychological perspective.

8. According to differential association theory, why does someone become a deviant?
    a. because of genetic predispositions
    b. because of personality disorders
    c. because of a lack of opportunities to engage in conventional activities
    d. because he learns to deviate from or conform to society's norms

9. The idea that two control systems, inner and outer controls, work against our tendencies toward deviance is called:
    a. conflict theory.
    b. differential association theory.
    c. control theory.
    d. strain theory.

10. According to Travis Hirschi, what affects the effectiveness of our inner controls?
    a. our social class background
    b. our gender
    c. our bonds to society
    d. our age

11. Which of the following is *not* one of the ways of neutralizing deviance?
    a. appeal to higher loyalties
    b. denial of responsibility
    c. denial of deviant labels
    d. denial of injury and of a victim

12. What does William Chambliss's study of the Saints and the Roughnecks suggest?
    a. Labels are easy to cast off once a person gets away from the group doing the labeling.
    b. People often live up to the labels that a community gives them.
    c. People often rebel against the labels given them and lead a completely different life.
    d. Sociological research on labeling has produced few conclusions.

13. For Chambliss, what factors influence whether people are seen as deviant?
    a. social class
    b. the visibility of offenders
    c. styles of interaction
    d. all of the above

14. Which perspective stresses that deviance promotes social unity and social change?
    a. functionalist
    b. conflict
    c. symbolic interactionist
    d. differential association

15. Which of the following is/are example(s) of *institutionalized means*?
    a. getting an education
    b. getting a good job
    c. working hard
    d. all of the above

16. All of the following are responses to anomie as identified by Robert Merton, *except*:
    a. ritualism.
    b. rebellion.
    c. retreatism.
    d. recidivism.

17. According to strain theory, who gives up pursuit of success by abusing alcohol or drugs?
    a. rebels
    b. retreatists
    c. neurotics
    d. ritualists

18. Steve lives in a neighborhood with high crime rates and poor schools. He believes he will never make it to college. He decides to quit school and sell drugs for a local drug dealer. He is quickly making a lot of money. He buys new clothes and a new car. Steve's behavior reflects which of Merton's deviant paths?
    a. innovation
    b. ritualism
    c. retreatism
    d. rebellion

19. The illegitimate opportunity structures theory is based on:
    a. the conflict perspective.
    b. the symbolic interactionist perspective.
    c. the exchange perspective.
    d. the functionalist perspective.

20. What are crimes committed by high-status people in the course of their occupations called?
    a. upper-class crime
    b. crimes of respectability
    c. white-collar crime
    d. tuxedo crime

21. Sears defrauded the poor of more than $100 million. This is an example of:
    a.   good business practices.
    b.   innovation.
    c.   corporate crime.
    d.   negative sanctions.

22. Who falls into the marginal working class?
    a.   people with few skills
    b.   people with low-paying, part-time, seasonal jobs
    c.   the most desperate members of the working class
    d.   all of the above

23. Which country today has the largest percentage of its population in prison?
    a.   Cuba
    b.   United States
    c.   Russia
    d.   China

24. Which racial/ethnic group is disproportionately represented among the prison population of the United States?
    a.   whites
    b.   Latinos
    c.   African Americans
    d.   Native Americans

25. Which of the following statements about the recidivism rate in the United States is *correct*?
    a.   As a result of the U.S. government's "get-tough" policy in recent years, there has been a sharp drop in the recidivism rate.
    b.   About one-half of all recidivists have been convicted of violent crimes.
    c.   Approximately two-thirds of all released prisoners will be rearrested within a year.
    d.   It is estimated that slightly more than one-half of all prisoners have served time in the past.

26. Who is disproportionately at risk of being put to death under the death penalty?
    a.   whites
    b.   African Americans
    c.   Latinos
    d.   Asian Americans

27. According to statistics on hate crimes, which group is most likely to be victimized?
    a.   African Americans
    b.   whites
    c.   Latinos
    d.   Asian Americans

28. A _____ crime is a crime that is motivated by bias against someone's race, religion, ethnicity, sexual orientation, disability, or national origin.
    a.   vicious
    b.   hate
    c.   prejudicial
    d.   none of the above

29. The medicalization of deviance refers to:
    a. the castration of sex offenders.
    b. use of lethal injections for the death penalty.
    c. viewing deviance as a medical matter.
    d. all of the above.

30. With deviance inevitable, the author of your textbook suggests that one measure of a society is:
    a. how low the overall rates of deviance are.
    b. what types of deviance there is.
    c. what gets defined as deviance and what doesn't.
    d. how deviants are treated.

TRUE-FALSE QUESTIONS

T F 1. Across all cultures, certain acts are considered to be deviant by everyone.
T F 2. According to your text, a college student cheating on an exam and a mugger lurking on a dark street have nothing at all in common.
T F 3. To be considered deviant, a person does not even have to do anything.
T F 4. Social control includes both formal and informal means of enforcing norms.
T F 5. All sanctions are negative.
T F 6. Sociologists search for explanations of deviance among factors outside the individual.
T F 7. According to differential association theory, the source of deviant behavior may be found in a person's socialization, or social learning.
T F 8. Symbolic interactionists stress that we are mere pawns in the hands of others.
T F 9. No one embraces deviance or wants to be labeled with a deviant identity.
T F 10. Outlaw bikers hold the conventional world in contempt and are proud of getting into trouble.
T F 11. In the study by Chambliss, the Saints and the Roughnecks both turned out largely as their labels would have predicted.
T F 12. The functionalist perspective states that deviance contributes to the social order.
T F 13. According to strain theory, everyone has a chance to get ahead in society, but some people prefer to use illegal means to achieve their goals.
T F 14. According to strain theory, some people experience greater pressures to deviate from society's norms because of their social location.
T F 15. Illegitimate opportunity structures are readily available in urban slums.
T F 16. White-collar crime is not as costly as street crime.
T F 17. Both functionalists and conflict theorists agree that the criminal justice system functions for the well-being of all citizens.
T F 18. Researchers have found that the U.S. recidivism rate is as high as 75 percent.
T F 19. The death penalty is not administered evenly in the United States.
T F 20. The classification of hate crime fits all crimes involving murder.

FILL-IN QUESTIONS

1. Sociologists use the term _____ to refer to any violation of a norm.
2. Expressions of disapproval of deviance are called _____ sanctions.
3. Psychologists focus on abnormalities within the _____.

4. Sociologists stress that people _____ deviance.
5. Researchers have found that delinquents are more likely to come from _____ that get in to trouble with the law.
6. Travis Hirschi noted that the stronger our bonds are with society, the more effective our _____ controls are.
7. According to Robert Merton, people who experience strain, are likely to feel _____, a sense of normlessness.
8. _____ crime refers to crimes that people of respectable and high social status commit in the course of their occupations.
9. A major change in the nature of crime is the growing number of _____ offenders.
10. _____ are the most desperate members of the working class.
11. In the United States, the _____ rate-the percentage of former prisoners who are rearrested-is extremely high.
12. Thomas Szasz argued that mental illnesses are simply _____ behaviors.

MATCH THESE THEORISTS/PHILOSOPHERS WITH THEIR CONTRIBUTIONS

1. Edwin Sutherland
2. Robert Merton
3. Erving Goffman
4. Thomas Szasz
5. Emile Durkheim
6. William Chambliss
7. Gresham Sykes and David Matza
8. Walter Reckless
9. Howard Becker
10. Richard Cloward and Lloyd Ohlin

a. *strain theory*
b. *control theory*
c. *differential association*
d. *functions of deviance*
e. *effects of labeling*
f. *importance of stigma*
g. *techniques of neutralization*
h. *myth of mental illness*
i. *illegitimate opportunity structure*
j. *societal reaction to deviance*

ESSAY QUESTIONS

1. Discuss how the different sociological perspectives could be combined to provide a more complete picture of deviance.
2. Explain how forms of deviance such as street gangs can be both functional and dysfunctional at the same time.
3. Using any one of the different sociological perspectives, develop an explanation for why white-collar crime is generally treated as less serious than other crimes in our society.
4. Answer the question, "Is the criminal justice system biased?"
5. Obesity could be viewed as deviance because it is a condition that violates our cultural norms regarding appearance. Develop an explanation for how this type of deviance is increasingly subject to medicalization.

STUDENT PROJECTS

1.   In thinking about contemporary U.S. society, what broader social changes have contributed to the passage of hate crime legislation? What are some problems associated with enforcement of these laws? Do you agree that we need such legislation? Why or why not?

2.   Do you agree with the author that there is a need for a more humane approach to those who are labeled deviant? Why or why not?

CHAPTER 7

GLOBAL STRATIFICATION

CHAPTER SUMMARY

- **Social stratification** is a hierarchy of relative privilege based on power, property, and prestige. Every society stratifies its members. The major systems of social stratification include: (1) **slavery**—owning other people; (2) **caste**—life-long status determined by birth; and (3) **class**—based on possession of money or material possessions. Class systems are characteristic of industrialized societies. Gender discrimination cuts across all systems of social stratification.

- Early sociologists disagreed about the meaning of social class in industrialized nations. **Karl Marx** argued that a person's relationship to the means of production was the only factor determining social class. **Max Weber** argued that three elements—*property, prestige*, and *power*—dictate an individual's standing in society.

- Various arguments have been developed to explain the universal presence of stratification. Functionalist sociologists **Kingsley Davis** and **Wilbert Moore** argued that society must offer rewards in order to assure that important social positions are filled by the most competent people. **Melvin Tumin** made the point that society would be a meritocracy if this were case. Conflict theorists see stratification as the consequence of group struggles for scarce resources. **Gaetano Mosca** believed that leadership perpetuates inequality. **Gerhard Lenski** combined several different views to explain the historical evolution of stratification systems.

- To maintain stratification within a nation, the ruling class relies on an ideology that justifies existing social arrangements, the control of information, and the use of brute force. Social networks of the rich and powerful also perpetuate social inequality.

- In Britain, the most striking features of the class system are differences in speech and accent, and in education. In the former Soviet Union, the 1917 Revolution was supposed to eliminate class differences, but instead one set of social classes were replaced by another.

- The most common model of global stratification divides nations into three groups: the **Most Industrialized**, the **Industrializing**, and the **Least Industrialized**.

- Four theories explaining the origins of global stratification are (1) **colonialism**, (2) **world system theory**, (3) **dependency theory**, and (4) a **culture of poverty**. International stratification is maintained through both **neocolonialism**—the ongoing dominance of the Least Industrialized Nations by the Most Industrialized Nations—and **multinational corporations**, which operate across national boundaries.

LEARNING OBJECTIVES

As you read Chapter 7, use these learning objectives to organize your notes. After completing your reading, you should be able to answer each of the objectives.

1. Define social stratification and explain why it is sociologically significant.
2. Describe and provide examples of the three major systems of social stratification.
3. Discuss the relationship between gender and social stratification.
4. Describe the major points of disagreement between Karl Marx and Max Weber regarding the meaning of social class in industrialized societies.

5. List the functions that social stratification provides for society as articulated by Kingsley Davis and Wilbert Moore.
6. List and discuss Melvin Tumin's counter-arguments to the functionalist view of social stratification.
7. Talk about the conflict perspective of social stratification as it relates to class conflict and scarce resources.
8. Discuss and evaluate Gerhard Lenski's attempt to synthesize the functionalist and conflict perspectives on social stratification.
9. Define ideology and understand how elite classes use it to maintain social stratification.
10. Compare the social stratification systems in Great Britain and the former Soviet Union to that in the United States.
11. Identify the major characteristics associated with the Most Industrialized Nations, Industrializing Nations, and Least Industrialized Nations.
12. Describe and evaluate the major theories pertaining to the origins and maintenance of global stratification.

CHAPTER OUTLINE

I. Systems of Social Stratification

A. Social stratification is a system in which people are divided into layers according to their relative power, property, and prestige.
  1. Social stratification refers to the ranking of large groups of people rather than individual people.
  2. Every society stratifies its members, although the degree of inequality varies.
  3. No matter what system a society may use to divide people into different layers, gender is always an essential part of the distinctions within each layer. On the basis of gender, people are sorted into categories and given differential access to rewards. Social distinctions have usually favored males.

B. Slavery is a form of social stratification in which some people own other people.
  1. Initially slavery was based on debt, punishment for violation of the law, or defeat in battle. Given this last practice, many of the first slaves were women, captured after the defeat of their village.
  2. Slavery could be temporary or permanent and was not necessarily passed on to one's children. Typically, slaves owned no property and had no power; this was not universally true, however.
  3. American colonists first tried to enslave Indians and then turned to Africans, who were being brought to North and South America by the British, Dutch, English, Portuguese, and Spanish. When American slave owners found it was profitable to own slaves for life, they developed an ideology to it and to make slavery inheritable.
  4. Although illegal, slavery still exists in places like the Sudan and Mauritania; apparently villages are raided, the men killed, and the women and children captured and sold.

C. In a caste system, status is determined by birth and is lifelong.
  1. Ascribed status is the basis of a caste system. Caste societies try to make certain that boundaries between castes remain firm by practicing endogamy (marriage within their own group) and developing rules about ritual pollution, teaching that contact with inferior castes contaminates the superior caste.

2.   Although abolished by the Indian government in 1949, the caste system remains part of everyday life in India, as it has for almost 3,000 years. This system is based on religion and is made up of four main castes, or *varnas*, which are subdivided into thousands of specialized subcastes or *jati*. The lowest caste is considered to be "untouchable," and *ablution* (washing rituals) is required to restore purity for those contaminated by individuals from this group.

3.   An American racial caste system developed in the United States when slavery ended. Even in the earlier parts of this century, all whites were considered higher than all African Americans and in the South, separate accommodations were maintained for each race.

D.   A class system is a form of social stratification based primarily on the possession of money or material possessions.

1.   An individual's initial social class position is based on that of her or his parents (ascribed status).

2.   A class system allows for social mobility—movement up or down the social class ladder—based on achieved status.

E.   Gender cuts across slavery, caste, and class. In all societies, gender becomes the basis for the distribution of the good things available in the society.

II.   What Determines Social Class?

A.   According to **Karl Marx**, social class is determined by one's relationship to the means of production—the tools, factories, land, and investment capital used to produce wealth.

1.   Modern society is composed of just two classes of people—the **bourgeoisie** (capitalists) own the means of production and the **proletariat** (workers) work for those who own the means of production.

2.   As capital becomes more concentrated, the two classes will become increasingly more hostile to one another.

3.   Class consciousness—awareness of a common identity based on one's position in the means of production—will develop. According to Marx this is the essential basis for the unity of workers.

4.   Marx believed that the workers would revolt against the capitalists, take control of the means of production, and usher in a classless society. However, the workers' unity and revolution are held back by false class consciousness—the mistaken identification of workers with the interests of capitalists.

B.   Unlike Marx, **Max Weber** did not believe that property was the sole basis of a person's position in the stratification system, but rather that property, prestige, and power determined social class.

1.   Property is an essential element; but some powerful people, like managers of corporations, *control* the means of production even though they do not own them.

2.   Prestige may be derived from ownership of property; but it also may be based on other factors, such as athletic skills.

3.   Power is the ability to control others, even over their objections.

III.   Why Is Social Stratification Universal?

A.   According to the functionalist view expressed by **Kingsley Davis** and **Wilbert Moore**, stratification is inevitable.

1.   Society must make certain that its important positions are filled with qualified people, and to guarantee this the society offers them greater rewards.

2.   Davis and Moore argued that because society offers greater rewards for its more responsible, demanding, and accountable positions, qualified people compete for them.

B.   **Melvin Tumin** offered a critique of the functionalist position.
1.   He argued that the importance of a position can not be measured by the rewards; that such an argument is circular. There must be independent indicators of importance.
2.   He noted that if stratification worked as Davis and Moore describe it, society would be a meritocracy; a form of social stratification in which all positions are awarded on the basis of merit. But it does not work this way (e.g., the best predictor of college entrance is family income, not ability). He also argued that money and fringe benefits are not the only reasons people take jobs.
3.   Finally, he noted that stratification is dysfunctional to many people, not functional.

C.   Conflict theorists stress that conflict, not function, is the basis of social stratification.
1.   Every society has limited resources to go around and in each, groups struggle with one another for those resources.
2.   Whenever a group gains power, it uses that power to extract what it can from the groups beneath it. The dominant group takes control of the social institutions, using them to keep other groups weak and preserve the best resources for itself.

D.   **Gaetano Mosca** argued that it is inevitable that every society will be stratified by power, because the ruling class is well organized and enjoys easy communication among its relatively few members; it is extremely difficult for the majority they govern to resist.
1.   Society cannot exist unless it is organized, thus, there must be politics to get the work of society done.
2.   Politics results in inequalities of power because some people take leadership positions and others follow.
3.   It is human nature to be self-centered, thus, people in positions of power use their positions to bring greater rewards to themselves.

E.   Marx argued that the bourgeoisie are in power because they control society's resources, using those resources to benefit themselves and to oppress those beneath them.

F.   Modern conflict theorists, such as **Randall Collins,** stress that conflict between capitalists and workers is not the only important conflict in contemporary society. The competition for scarce resources results in conflict not only between groups from different classes, but also between groups within the same social class (e.g., young vs. old; women vs. men).

G.   **Gehard Lenski** offered a synthesis between functionalist and conflict theories.
1.   Functionalists are right when it comes to societies that have only basic resources and do not accumulate wealth, such as hunting and gathering societies.
2.   Conflict theorists are right when it comes to societies with a surplus. In such societies humans pursue self-interests and struggle to control those surpluses. This leads to the emergence of a small elite who then builds inequality into the society, resulting in a full-blown system of social stratification.

IV.   How Do Elites Maintain Stratification?

A.   Social stratification is maintained within a nation because elites control ideas and information, maintain social networks, and use force.

B.   Ideology can be more effective than the use of brute force in maintaining inequality.
1.   The control of ideas is used by elites everywhere to maintain their positions of power—whether in dictatorships or in democracies. To the degree that their ideologies are accepted by the masses, political arrangements are stable.

2. In a dictatorship, elites use the threat of force to try to control information; in a democracy, they manipulate the media by the selective release of information.
3. Technology aids the elite in its desire to preserve its position. Technology enables elites to monitor citizens' activities without their even being aware that they are being observed.
4. Social networks provide valuable information and tend to perpetuate inequality.

V. Comparative Social Stratification

A. Great Britain's class system can be divided into upper, middle, and lower classes.
1. A little over half of the population is in the lower or working class, half is in the middle class, and about 1 percent is in the upper class.
2. The British are extremely class conscious. Language and speech patterns are important class indicators and education is the primary way the class system is perpetuated from one generation to the next.
B. The ideal of communism—a classless society—was never realized in the Soviet Union.
1. The major basis for stratification was membership in the Communist Party, which consisted of top party officials, a relatively small middle class, and a massive lower class of peasants and unskilled workers.
2. Soviet leaders, frustrated over time with the system's inability to be economically successful, initiated capitalistic reforms in the hopes of turning things around.
3. The transition to capitalism has taken bizarre twists, with some Russians organizing into criminal groups, stealing vast amounts of state property, amassing great wealth, and intimidating business people.

VI. Global Stratification: Three Worlds

A. Until recently global stratification was depicted using a simple model consisting of **First** (industrialized capitalist nations), **Second** (communist nations), and **Third** (all the rest of the nations) **Worlds**. With the collapse of communism, these terms became outdated, while other models implied moral judgments about levels of development. A more neutral framework describes degrees of industrialization and depicts, on a global level, the three primary dimensions of social stratification: property, power, and prestige.
B. The **Most Industrialized Nations** are the U.S., Canada, Great Britain, France, Germany, Switzerland and other industrialized nations of western Europe, as well as Japan, Australia, and New Zealand; they are capitalistic, although variations exist in their economic systems. Their wealth is enormous and the poor in these countries live better/longer than the average citizens in the Least Industrialized Nations.
C. The **Industrializing Nations** include the former Soviet Union and its satellite countries in Eastern Europe. People living in these countries have considerably lower income and a poorer standard of living than people in the Most Industrialized Nations, but better than those living in the Least Industrialized Nations.
D. The **Least Industrialized Nations** are those where most people live on farms or in villages with low standards of living; 68 percent of the world's population lives in these nations.

VII. How Did the World's Nations Become Stratified?

A. **Colonialism** occurred when industrialized nations made colonies of weaker nations and exploited their labor/natural resources. European nations tended to focus on Africa, while the U.S. concentrated on Central and South America.

1. The more powerful European nations planted their national flags in a colony and sent representatives to run the government. The U.S. planted corporate flags in the particular colony, letting corporations dominate the territory's government.

2. Western imperialism and colonialism shaped the Least Industrialized Nations, drawing lines across a map to divide up their spoils, thereby creating states without regard for tribal or cultural considerations. The legacy of European conquests still erupts in tribal violence because tribes with no history of national identity were arbitrarily incorporated into the same political boundaries.

B. According to world system theory (as espoused by **Immanuel Wallerstein**) countries are politically and economically tied together.

1. There are four groups of interconnected nations: (1) core nations, where capitalism first developed; (2) semi-periphery (Mediterranean area), which are highly dependent on trade with core nations; (3) periphery (eastern Europe), those mainly limited to selling cash crops to core nations, with limited economic development; and (4) external area (most of Africa/Asia), which have been left out of the growth of capitalism and have few economic ties to core nations.

2. A capitalist world economy (capitalist dominance) results from relentless expansion; even external area nations are drawn into this commercial web.

3. **Globalization** (the extensive interconnections among nations resulting from the expansion of capitalism) has speeded up because of new forms of communication and transportation. The consequence is that no nation lives in isolation.

C. Dependency theory attributes lack of economic development in the Least Industrialized Nations to dominance of the world economy by the Most Industrialized Nations.

1. It asserts that those nations that industrialized first turned other nations into their plantations and mines, taking whatever they needed; as a result, many of the Least Industrialized Nations began to specialize in a single cash crop.

2. By becoming dependent on the Most Industrialized Nations, these other countries did not develop independent economies of their own.

D. **John Kenneth Galbraith** argued that some nations remain poor because they are crippled by a culture of poverty, a way of life based on traditional values and religious beliefs that perpetuate poverty from one generation to the next and keep some of the Least Industrialized Nations from developing.

E. Most sociologists find colonialism/world system/dependency theory explanations preferable to the culture of poverty theory because the later places the blame on the victim. But each theory only partially explains global stratification.

VIII. Maintaining Global Stratification

A. **Neocolonialism** is the economic and political dominance of the Least Industrialized Nations by the Most Industrialized Nations. Michael Harrington asserts that this occurs because the Most Industrialized Nations control markets, set prices, etc. They move hazardous industries into the Least Industrialized Nations and sell weapons and manufactured goods to the Least Industrialized Nations, preventing them from developing their own industrial capacity.

B. **Multinational corporations** contribute to the exploitation of the Least Industrialized Nations.

1. Some exploit these nations directly by controlling national and local politics, running them as a fiefdom. Multinational corporations work closely with elites of the Least Industrialized Nations, funneling investments to this small circle of power in exchange for its cooperation.

2. The Most Industrialized Nations are primary beneficiaries of profits made in the Least Industrialized Nations.

3.   In some situations, multinational corporations may bring prosperity to the Least Industrialized Nations as new factories provide salaries and opportunities which otherwise would not exist for workers in those countries.

4.   In the quest to maintain global domination, new technologies create even more advantages for the Most Industrialized Nations by allowing them to use the profits generated to invest huge sums in the latest technologies.

C.   The new technology favors the Most Industrialized Nations, enabling them to maintain their global domination.

1.   The profits of multinational corporations can be invested in developing   and acquiring the latest technology, thereby generating even greater profits.

2.   Many of the Least Industrialized Nations do not have the resources to invest in new technology, creating an even greater gap between the levels of industrialization globally.

KEY TERMS

After studying the chapter, review each of the following terms.

bourgeoisie: Karl Marx's term for capitalists, those who own the means of production (p. 173)

caste system: a form of social stratification in which one's status is determined by birth and is lifelong (p. 171)

class consciousness: Karl Marx's term for awareness of a shared identity based on one's position in the means of production (p. 173)

class system: a form of social stratification based primarily on the possession of money or material possessions (p. 172)

colonialism: the process by which one nation takes over another nation, usually for the purpose of exploiting its labor and natural resources (p. 186)

culture of poverty: the assumption that the values and behaviors of the poor make them fundamentally different from other people, that these factors are largely responsible for their poverty, and that parents perpetuate poverty across generations by passing these characteristics to their children (p. 188)

divine right of kings: the idea that the king's authority comes directly from God (p. 177)

endogamy: the practice of marrying within one's own group (p. 171)

false class consciousness: Karl Marx's term to refer to workers identifying with the interests of capitalists (p. 173)

globalization of capitalism: capitalism (investing to make profits within a rational system) becoming the globe's dominant economic system (p. 186)

ideology: beliefs about the way things ought to be that justify social arrangements (p. 169)

means of production: the tools, factories, land, and investment capital used to produce wealth (p. 173)

meritocracy: a form of social stratification in which all positions are awarded on the basis of merit (p. 176)

multinational corporations: companies that operate across many national boundaries, also called transnational corporations (p. 188)

neocolonialism: the economic and political dominance of the Least Industrialized Nations by the Most Industrialized Nations (p. 188)

proletariat: Marx's term for the exploited class, the mass of workers who do not own the means of production (p. 173)

slavery: a form of social stratification in which some people own other people (p. 168)

social class: according to Weber, a large number of people who rank close to one another in power, property, and prestige; according to Marx, one of two groups: capitalists who own the means of production or workers who sell their labor (p. 174)

social mobility: movement up or down the social class ladder (p. 172)

social stratification: the division of large numbers of people into layers according to their relative power, property, and prestige; applies to both nations and to people within a nation, society, or other group (p. 168)

world system theory: economic and political connections that tie the world's countries together (p. 186)

KEY PEOPLE
Review the major theoretical contributions or research findings of these theorists and thinkers.

Randall Collins: Collins is a contemporary conflict theorist who has broadened conflict theory to include analysis of competition between groups within the same class for scarce resources.

Kingsley Davis and Wilbert Moore: These functionalists developed the theory of stratification that suggests inequality is universal because it helps societies survive by motivating the most qualified members of society to strive to fill the most important social positions.

John Kenneth Galbraith: This economist argued that the Least Industrialized Nations remain poor because their own culture holds them back.

Michael Harrington: Harrington saw that colonialism had been replaced by neocolonialism.

Martha Huggins: Huggins has studied poverty in the Least Industrialized Nations.

Gehard Lenski: Lenski offered a synthesis of the functionalist and conflict views of stratification.

Gerda Lerner: This historian has noted that women were the first people who were enslaved as a result of war and conquest.

Oscar Lewis: Lewis is the anthropologist who first suggested the reason some people are poor is because they live in a culture of poverty.

Karl Marx: Marx concluded that social class depended exclusively on the means of production; an individual's social class depended on whether or not he owned the means of production.

Gaetano Mosca: Mosca argued that every society is inevitably stratified by power.

James Schellenberg: Schellenberg is a contemporary conflict theorist.

Melvin Tumin: Tumin was the first to offer a criticism of the functionalist view on stratification.
Immanuel Wallerstein: Wallerstein proposed a world system theory to explain global stratification.
Max Weber: Weber argued that social class was based on three components—class, status, and power.

SELF-TEST
After completing this self-test, check your answers in the Answer Key of this Study Guide.

MULTIPLE CHOICE QUESTIONS

1. A system in which groups of people are divided into layers according to their relative power, property, and prestige is:
   a. a social stratification system.
   b. neocolonialism.
   c. industrialization.
   d. globalization.

2. Gender stratification is a:
   a. cultural and social universal.
   b. system characteristic of no contemporary societies.
   c. form of post-modern industrialism.
   d. none of the above are correct.

3. Lerner notes that the first people who were enslaved through warfare were:
   a. criminals.
   b. debtors.
   c. minority groups.
   d. women.

4. Which of the following is not true concerning slavery?
   a. Slavery in some cases was temporary
   b. Slavery was not necessarily inheritable
   c. Slaves were not necessarily powerless and poor
   d. All of the above are true

5. Beliefs that justify social arrangements constitute:
   a. a theory.
   b. an ideology.
   c. power.
   d. prestige.

6. The practice of endogamy is most likely found in:
   a. a class system.
   b. a caste system.
   c. a meritocracy.
   d. a socialist system.

7. The basis of a caste system is:
   a. achieved status.

b.   ascribed status.
c.   slavery.
d.   social class.

8.   Class systems are characterized by:
a.   social mobility.
b.   geographic mobility.
c.   distribution of social standings belonging to an extended network of relatives.
d.   all of the above.

9.   Marx concluded that social class depends on:
a.   wealth, power, and prestige.
b.   the means of production.
c.   where one is born in the social stratification system.
d.   what a person achieves during his or her lifetime.

10.   Those people who work for the owners, according to Marx, are:
a.   the proletariat.
b.   the bourgeoisie.
c.   the socially mobile.
d.   the lumpenproletariat.

11.   Marx said that farmers, beggars, and vagrants lacked:
a.   false class consciousness.
b.   ascribed statuses.
c.   class consciousness.
d.   technological skills.

12.   According to Max Weber, social class is determined by:
a.   one's property, prestige, and power.
b.   one's relationship to the means of production.
c.   one's tasks and how important they are to society.
d.   one's political power.

13.   The ability to control others, even over their objections, is:
a.   social stratification.
b.   power.
c.   socialism.
d.   authority.

14.   Which of the following is *not* one of the criticisms of the functionalist view
provided by Melvin Tumin?
a.   The functionalists do not provide an adequate method for measuring the social
importance of the position.
b.   The functionalists assume that social stratification is beneficial to everyone, which it is
not.
c.   The functionalists consider that stratification is the same everywhere and at all points in
history.
d.   The functionalists view society as a meritocracy in which positions are awarded on the
basis of merit, when in reality other factors such as income and gender influence one's
placement in the system of stratification.

15. Gaetano Mosca argued that every society will be stratified by:
    a. wealth.
    b. class.
    c. individuals' relation to the means of production.
    d. power.

16. Lenski suggested that conflict theory and functionalism should look at:
    a. surpluses.
    b. false class consciousness.
    c. democracy.
    d. the proletariat.

17. The idea that a king's authority comes directly from God is:
    a. Marxism.
    b. functionalism.
    c. the Divine Right of Kings.
    d. conflict theory.

18. The British perpetuate their class system between generations by:
    a. emphasizing material possessions such as clothes.
    b. religion.
    c. education.
    d. encouraging persons in all class to marry others within their own class.

19. Historically, the intermediate step between capitalism and communism (in the former Soviet Union) was:
    a. conflict theory.
    b. functionalism.
    c. socialism.
    d. slavery.

20. In the former Soviet Union, the system of stratification was based on:
    a. occupation.
    b. trade union membership.
    c. Communist Party membership.
    d. education.

21. The United States, Canada, Great Britain, and France are examples of:
    a. the Most Industrialized Nations.
    b. Industrialized Nations.
    c. the Least Industrialized Nations.
    d. none of the above.

22. In Brazil, the "poorest of the poor" children are part of:
    a. the proletariat.
    b. the working class.
    c. the dangerous class.
    d. the marginal class.

23.   Most people in the Least Industrialized Nations live on less than _____ a year.
    a. $1,000
    b. $5,000
    c. $8,000
    d. $10,000

24.   _____is the control of weak nations' labor and natural resources by powerful nations.
    a.   Communism
    b.   Colonialism
    c.   Globalism
    d.   A banana republic

25.   What theorist is associated with world system theory?
    a.   Immanuel Wallerstein
    b.   Karl Marx
    c.   C. Wright Mills
    d.   Max Weber

26.   According to world system theory, all of the following are groups of interconnected nations, *except*:
    a.   core nations.
    b.   nations on the semiperiphery.
    c.   nations on the periphery.
    d.   nations on the internal area which have extensive connections with the core nations.

27.   Assembly for export plants in Mexico are know as:
    a.   NAFTA.
    b.   Maquiladoras.
    c.   outsourcing plants.
    d.   none of the above.

28.   Who claimed that the culture of the least industrialized countries held them back?
    a.   Oscar Lewis
    b.   John Kenneth Galbraith
    c.   Immanuel Wallerstein
    d.   Max Weber

29.   Michael Harrington argues that colonialism fell out of style and was replaced by:
    a.   communism.
    b.   socialism.
    c.   capitalism.
    d.   neocolonialism.

30.   _____ that operate across many national boundaries also help to maintain the global dominance of the Most Industrialized Nations.
    a.   Military operations
    b.   United Nation organizations
    c.   Multinational corporations
    d.   Technological systems

TRUE-FALSE QUESTIONS

T F   1.   According to sociologists, your location in the system of social stratification has a profound effect on your chances in life.

T F   2.   Gender discrimination cuts across all systems of stratification.

T F   3.   Slavery has been common in world history.

T F   4.   States have always had two separate school systems.

T F   5.   The oldest example of a caste system is Saudi Arabia.

T F   6.   A class system is primarily based on ascribed statuses.

T F   7.   According to Karl Marx, the means of production is the only factor in determining social class.

T F   8.   Marx believed that the tendency for workers to mistakenly identify with the interests of capitalists hindered their unity and impeded revolution.

T F   9.   Max Weber agreed with Karl Marx that property was the basis for social class.

T F   10.   For Weber, property and prestige were "two-way streets."

T F   11.   Social inequality is universal.

T F   12.   The functional theorists Moore and Davis tried to justify social inequality, not promote it.

T F   13.   If ability is the sole predictor of who goes to college, we have a meritocracy.

T F   14.   Contemporary conflict theorists argue that competition over scarce resources occurs not only between classes, but also between groups within the same social class.

T F   15.   In maintaining stratification, elites find that brute force is more effective than the control of information or ideas.

T F   16.   From under the leadership of Lenin and Trotsky, the former Soviet Union was able to create a classless society.

T F   17.   The Communist Party was highly stratified.

T F   18.   The "First World" referred to the Least Industrialized Nations.

T F   19.   One of the ways to control the number of poor children in Brazil is to shoot them.

T F   20.   The culture of poverty thesis is generally preferred by sociologists as an explanation of global stratification.

FILL-IN QUESTIONS

1.   _____ is a way of ranking large groups of people in a hierarchy that shows their relative privileges.

2.   The gray area between a contract and slavery is _____ service.

3.   In a _____ system, status is determined by birth.

4.   _____ provides the best example of a caste system.

5.   In every society in the world, _____ is a basis for social stratification.

6.   Karl Marx argued that workers suffer from _____, workers mistakenly thinking of themselves as capitalists.

7.   _____ is a form of social stratification in which all positions are awarded on the basis of merit.

8. The divine right of kings was an _____ that made the king God's direct representative on earth.

9. _____ is the primary way by which the British perpetuate their class system.

10. The _____ theory focuses on how the countries that industrialized first got the jump on the rest of the world.

11. Immanuel Wallerstein calls those countries that industrialized first the _____ nations.

12. Assembly-for-export plants on the Mexican-United States border are known as _____.

13. John Kenneth Galbraith claimed that the _____ of the Least Industrialized Nations held them back.

14. Neocolonialism theory argues that keeping least industrialized countries in _____ makes them submit to trading terms dictated by the neocolonialists.

15. Multinational corporations try to work closely with the _____ of Least Industrialized Nations.

MATCH THESE THEORISTS/PHILOSOPHERS WITH THEIR CONTRIBUTIONS

1. Max Weber
2. Karl Marx
3. Melvin Tumin
4. Gaetana Mosca
5. Davis and Moore

a. *false consciousness*
b. *functionalist view of stratification*
c. *class based on property, prestige, and power*
d. *forerunner of conflict view of stratification*
e. *criticized functionalist view of stratification*

MATCH EACH CONCEPT WITH ITS DEFINITION

1. Proletariat
2. Slavery
3. Bourgeoisie
4. Caste system
5. Social class system

a. *Those who own the means of production*
b. *Ownership of some people by others*
c. *Based on money and material possessions*
d. *Those who work for the owners*
e. *Status determined by birth and is lifelong*

ESSAY QUESTIONS

1. Compare Marx's theory of stratification with Weber's. Discuss why Weber's is more widely accepted by sociologists.

2. Using the different theories presented in this chapter, answer the question, "Why is stratification universal?"

3. Consider why ideology is a more effective way of maintaining stratification than brute force.

4. In the 1960s, most former colonies around the globe won their political independence. Since that time, the position of these countries has remained largely unchanged within the global system of stratification. Provide some explanation as to why political independence alone was not enough to alter their status.

5. Within a society, the elite rely on ideology, control of information, and use of force to maintain stratification. Develop an explanation for how the Most Industrialized Nations maintain their status at the top of the global system of stratification.

STUDENT PROJECTS

1. Why do you think social stratification is universal? What role do you think technology plays in continuing social stratification in the United States? What technological gadgets do you currently own? What ones would you like to own? Do you think having access to a computer gives a college student an advantage over college students who do not have access to a computer? Explain.

2. What role do you play in perpetuating global stratification? Go home and look at the tags on the back of five shirts hanging in your closet. List the countries where your shirts were assembled. How many of them are Least Industrialized Nations? What do you pay for your shirts? What do you think workers in those countries get paid? What does this example have to do with world systems theory? Explain.

CHAPTER 8

SOCIAL CLASS IN THE UNITED STATES

CHAPTER SUMMARY

- Most sociologists have adopted Weber's definition of social class as a large group of people who rank closely to one another in terms of wealth, power, and prestige. **Wealth**, consisting of property and income, is concentrated in the upper class. **Power** is the ability to carry out one's will despite the resistance of others. **Prestige** is the regard or respect accorded an individual or social position.

- **Status** is social ranking. Most people are status consistent, meaning that they rank high or low on all three dimensions of social class. People who rank high on some dimensions and low on others are status inconsistent. The frustration of status inconsistency tends to produce political radicalism.

- Sociologists use two main models to portray the social class structure. **Erik Wright** developed a four class model based on the ideas of Karl Marx. **Dennis Gilbert** and **Joseph Kahl** developed a six class model based on the ideas of Max Weber.

- Social class leaves no aspect of life untouched. Class membership affects life changes, physical and mental health, family life, politics, religion, education, and whether or not we benefit from new technology.

- In studying the mobility of individuals within society, sociologists look at **intergenerational mobility** (the individual changes in social class from one generation to the next), **exchange mobility** (the movement of large numbers of people from one class to another), and **structural mobility** (the social and economic changes that affect the social class position of large numbers of people).

- Poverty is unequally distributed in the United States. Latinos, African Americans, Native Americans, children, female-headed households, and the rural poor are more likely to be poor. Sociologists generally focus on structural factors such as employment opportunities, in explaining poverty. The **Horatio Alger myth** encourages people to strive to get ahead, and blames failures on individual shortcomings.

LEARNING OBJECTIVES
As you read Chapter 8, use these learning objectives to organize your notes. After completing your reading, you should be able to answer each of the objectives.

1. Define social class, describe its various components, and discuss the debate between different theorists over those components.
2. Differentiate between wealth, power, and prestige and talk about how each is distributed in the United States.
3. Discuss the relationship between occupations and prestige.
4. Define status inconsistency and discuss its implications.
5. Compare Erik Wright's model of social class with Dennis Gilbert and Joseph Kahl's model of social class.
6. Describe each of the six classes in Gilbert and Kahl's model of social class.
7. Know the consequences of social class on family life, education, religion, politics, physical health, and mental health.
8. Describe — and distinguish between — the three types of social mobility.

9. Understand the issues with women and social mobility.
10. Know the fears surrounding the development of new technology.
11. Know how the United States government defines poverty and the implications of that definition.
12. Identify the major characteristics of the poor in the United States.
13. Compare structural vs. individual explanations of poverty in the United States.
14. Talk about recent changes in welfare policy in the United States and the controversies associated with those changes.
15. Identify the social functions of the Horatio Alger myth and discuss the myth's sociological implications.

CHAPTER OUTLINE

I. What Is Social Class?

    A.   **Social class** can be defined as a large group of people who rank close to each other in wealth, power, and prestige.

    B.   **Wealth** consists of property (what we own) and income (money we receive). Wealth and income are not always the same—a person may own much property yet have little income, or vice versa. Usually, however, wealth and income go together.

        1.   Ownership of property (real estate, stocks and bonds, etc.) is not distributed evenly: 10 percent of the U.S. population owns 68 percent of the wealth, and the richest 1 percent of U.S. families are worth more than the entire bottom 90 percent of Americans.

        2.   Income is also distributed disproportionately: the top 20 percent of U.S. residents earn 47 percent of the income; the bottom 20 percent receive less than 5 percent. Each fifth of the U.S. population received approximately the same proportion of national income today as it did in 1945. The changes that have occurred indicate growing inequality; the richest 20 percent of U.S. families have grown richer while the poorest 20 percent have grown poorer.

        3.   Apart from the very rich, the most affluent group in U.S. society is the executive officers of the largest corporations. Their median compensation is $2.8 million a year. A CEO's income is 100 times higher than the average pay of U.S. workers.

    C.   **Power** is the ability to carry out your will in spite of resistance. Power is concentrated in the hands of a few—the "power elite"—who share the same ideologies and values, belong to the same clubs, and reinforce each other's world view. No major decision in U.S. government is made without their approval.

    D.   **Prestige** is the respect or regard people give to various occupations and accomplishments.

        1.   Occupations are the primary source of prestige. Occupations with the highest prestige pay more, require more education, entail more abstract thought, and offer greater autonomy. Occupational prestige rankings tend to be consistent across countries and over time.

        2.   For prestige to be valuable, people must acknowledge it. The elite traditionally create rules to emphasize their higher status.

        3.   Status symbols, which vary according to social class, are ways of displaying prestige. In the United States, they include designer label clothing, expensive cars, prestigious addresses, and attendance at particular schools.

E.   **Status inconsistency** is the term used to describe the situation of people who have a mixture of high and low rankings in the three components of social class (wealth, power, and prestige).

1.   Most people are status consistent—they rank at the same level in all three components. People who are status inconsistent want others to treat them on the basis of their highest status, but others tend to judge them on the basis of their lowest status.

2.   Sociologist **Gerhard Lenski** determined that people suffering the frustrations of status inconsistency are more likely to be radical and approve political action aimed against higher status groups.

II.   Sociological Models of Social Class

A.   The number of classes that exist in an industrial society is a matter of debate, but there are two main models: one that builds on Marx and the other on Weber.

B.   Sociologist **Erik Wright** realized that not everyone falls into Marx's two broad classes (capitalists and workers, based upon a person's relationship to the means of productions). For instance, although executives, managers, and supervisors would fall into Marx's category of workers, they act more like capitalists.

1.   Wright resolved this problem by regarding some people as simultaneously members of more than one class, occupying what he called *contradictory class locations*.

2.   Wright identified four classes: (1) capitalists, the owners of large enterprises; (2) petty bourgeoisie, the owners of small businesses; (3) managers, the employees with authority over others; and (4) workers, who sell their labor to others.

C.   Using the framework originally developed by Weber, sociologists **Dennis Gilbert** and **Joseph Kahl** also created a model to describe class structure in the U.S. and other capitalist countries.

1.   The capitalist class (1 percent of the population) is composed of investors, heirs, and a few executives; it is divided into "old" money and "new" money. The children of "new" money move into the old money class by attending the right schools and marrying "old" money.

2.   The upper-middle class (15 percent of the population) is composed of professionals and upper managers, most of whom have attended college or university and frequently have postgraduate degrees. Of all the classes, this class is the one most shaped by education.

3.   The lower-middle class (34 percent of the population) is composed of lower managers, craftspeople and foremen. They have at least a high school education.

4.   The working class (30 percent of the population) is composed of factory workers and low-paid white collar workers. Most have a high school education.

5.   The working poor (16 percent of the population) is composed of relatively unskilled blue-collar and white-collar workers, and those with temporary and seasonal jobs. If they graduated from high school, they probably did not do well.

6.   The underclass (4 percent of the population) is concentrated in the inner cities and has little connection with the job market. Welfare is their main support.

D.   The automobile industry provides an example of the social class ladder. At the top of the capitalist class, one finds the Ford family, who own and control Ford Motor Co.; directly below them are the executives of the company, classified at the lower end of the capitalist class. The owners of a Ford agency would be considered part of the upper middle class, while a salesman would belong to the lower middle class. Mechanics are in the working class; those who "detail" used cars for the agency are working poor. Usually the underclass exists entirely outside the industry.

III. Consequences of Social Class

A. **Social class** plays a role in family life.

    1. Children of the capitalist class are under great pressure to select the right mate in order to assure the continuity of the family line. Parents in this social class play a large role in mate selection.

    2. Marriages are more likely to fail in the lower social classes; the children of the poor thus are more likely to live in single-parent households.

B. The amount of education increases and type of education changes as one goes up the social class ladder, with children of the upper classes bypassing public schools in favor of private education.

C. Religious orientation also follows class lines. Classes tend to cluster in different denominations; and patterns of worship also follow class lines.

D. Political views and involvement are influenced by social class as well.

    1. People in lower classes are more likely to vote Democrat, and those in higher classes to vote Republican; the parties are seen as promoting different class interests.

    2. People in the working class are more likely to be liberal on economic issues and more conservative on social issues.

    3. Political participation is not equal; people at the bottom of the class structure are less likely to vote or get involved in politics.

E. Social class affects our health; the lower classes have more sickness and higher death rates. This pattern is influenced by unequal access to medical care.

F. Mental health is also affected by social class. Studies show that the mental health of the lower classes is worse than that of the higher classes due to the stresses of poverty. Social class is also a deciding factor in how the mentally ill are treated, with poorer individuals having less access to mental health facilities.

G. New technologies benefit some classes and hurt others. It opens and closes opportunities for people largely by virtue of where they are located on the social class ladder.

    1. For those at the top of the social class ladder, new technology enables them to globalize production and maximize profits.

    2. The educational background of the upper middle class prepares them to take a leading role in managing this new global production system.

    3. For those below these two classes, new technology is transforming the workplace, eliminating jobs and causing workers' skills to become outdated. They are hit hardest by technological changes.

IV. Social Mobility

A. There are three basic types of social mobility: intergenerational, structural, and exchange.

    1. Intergenerational mobility is the change that family members make in their social class from one generation to the next. As a result of individual effort, a person can rise from one level to another; in the event of individual failure, the reverse can be true.

    2. Sociologists are more interested in structural mobility—social changes that affect large numbers of people. By way of example, as the economy shifted from factory machines to computers vast numbers of new jobs were created and shifts from blue-collar jobs to white-collar positions occurred.

    3. Exchange mobility is the movement of people up and down the social class system, while, on balance, the proportions remain the same. The term refers to a general, overall movement of large numbers of people exchanging place on the social ladder that leaves the class system basically untouched.

B. Studies of social mobility in the United States have focused on men. Compared with their fathers, one-half of all men have moved up in social class; one-third have stayed in the same place; and one-sixth have moved down.

    1. In the past it was assumed that women had no class position of their own; they were simply assigned to the class of their husbands.

    2. Structural changes in the U.S. economy have created opportunities for women to move up the social class ladder. One study indicated that women who did move up were encouraged by their parents to postpone marriage and get an education.

C. If the U.S. does not keep pace with global changes, its economic position will decline. The U.S. is rushing to integrate advanced technology into all spheres of social life. As this happens, the technologically illiterate are left behind and their future looks grim.

V. Poverty

A. The U.S. government classifies the **poverty line** as including families whose incomes are less than three times a low-cost food budget. Any modification of this measure instantly adds or subtracts millions of people, and thus has significant consequences.

B. Certain social groups are disproportionately represented among the poor population.

    1. Poverty is not evenly distributed among the states; the poor are clustered in the South more than in other region, and in California more than in other states. The poverty rate for the rural poor is slightly higher than the national average. While they show the same racial/ethnic characteristics as the nation as a whole, the rural poor are less likely to be single parents, are less skilled and less educated, and the jobs available to them pay less.

    2. Race-ethnicity is a major factor in determining poverty. Although 2 out of 3 poor people are white, only 10 percent of whites, 22 percent of Latinos, 24 percent of African Americans, and 26 percent of Native Americans live in poverty.

    3. Only two percent of people who finish college end up in poverty, compared to one in four of those who drop out of high school.

    4. The sex of the person who heads a family is one of the best predictors of whether or not a family is poor. The major causes of this phenomenon, called the feminization of poverty, are divorce, births to unwed mothers, and the lower wages paid to women.

    5. The percentage of poor people over age 65 who are poor is lower than the national average, although elderly Latino and African Americans are almost three times more likely to be poor than elderly white Americans.

C. Children are more likely to live in poverty than are adults or the elderly. This holds true regardless of race-ethnicity, but poverty is much greater among minority children: two out of every five Latino children and almost one out of every two African-American children are poor.

D. In the 1960s **Michael Harrington** and **Oscar Lewis** suggested that the poor get trapped in a "culture of poverty" as a result of having values and behaviors that make them "fundamentally different" from other U.S. residents.

    1. Research indicates that most poverty is of short duration, lasting only a year or less, and that most often it is due to a dramatic life change. Only 12 percent of poverty lasts five years or more.

    2. Since the number of people who live in poverty remains fairly constant, this means that as many people move into poverty as move out of it.

    3. About one-fourth of the U.S. population is or has been poor for at least a year.

E. New federal laws require that states place a lifetime cap on welfare assistance to require welfare recipients to look for work and take available jobs.

    1.   Defenders of the new rules say that they will rescue people from poverty. In some states the welfare rolls dropped sharply, and nationally the recipients of welfare decreased by 44 percent.

    2.   Conflict theorists note that welfare rolls declined during a period of economic prosperity—the poor moved into the workforce as part of the army of reserve workers. They predict that welfare rolls will swell once our economy moves into a recession.

F.   In trying to explain poverty, two choices compete: individual explanations or social structural explanations.

    1.   Sociologists look to such factors as inequalities in education, access to learning job skills, racial, ethnic, age, and gender discrimination, and large-scale economic change to explain the patterns of poverty in society.

    2.   Another explanation focuses on how characteristics of individuals are assumed to contribute to their poverty. Sociologists reject explanations that focus on qualities of laziness or lack of intelligence to explain poverty.

    3.   Real-life examples of people from humble origins who climbed far up the social ladder reinforces the widely-held belief of most U.S. residents (including minorities and the working poor) that they have a chance of getting ahead (the **Horatio Alger myth**), even though this is obviously a statistical impossibility. Functionalists would stress that this belief is functional for society because it encourages people to compete for higher positions, while placing the blame for failure squarely on the individual.

KEY TERMS

After studying the chapter, review each of the following terms.

anomie: a condition resulting from status inconsistency (p. 201)

contradictory class locations: Erik Wright's term for a position in the class structure that generates contradictory interests (p. 202)

culture of poverty: the assumption that values and behaviors of the poor make them fundamentally different from other people, that these factors are largely responsible for their poverty, and that parents perpetuate poverty across generations by passing these characteristics on to their children (p. 215)

downward social mobility: movement down the social class ladder (p. 208)

exchange mobility: the same number of people move both up and down the social class ladder, such that, on balance, the social class system shows little change (p. 210)

(the) feminization of poverty: a trend in U.S. poverty where most poor families are headed by women (p. 214)

Horatio Alger myth: the belief that due to limitless possibilities anyone can get ahead if he or she tries hard enough (p. 217)

income: a flow of money (p. 194)

intergenerational mobility: the change that family members make in social class from one generation to the next (p. 208)

poverty line: the official measure of poverty; calculated to include those whose incomes are less than three times a low-cost food budget (p. 211)

power: the ability to carry out your will, even over the resistance of others (p. 197)

power elite: C. Wright Mills' term for the top people in U.S. corporations, military, and politics who make the nation's major decisions (p. 197)

prestige: respect or regard (p. 198)

social class: according to Weber, a large number of people who rank close to one another in wealth, power, and prestige; according to Marx, one of two groups: capitalists, who own the means of production or workers, who sell their labor (p. 194)

status: social ranking; the position that someone occupies in society or in a social group (p. 200)

status consistency: people ranking high or low on all three dimensions of social class (p. 200)

status inconsistency: ranking high on some dimensions of social class and low on others (p. 200)

structural mobility: movement up or down the social class ladder that is due to changes in the structure of society, not to individual efforts (p. 208)

underclass: a group of people for whom poverty persists year after year across generations (p. 205)

upward social mobility: movement up the social class ladder (p. 208)

wealth: property and income (p. 194)

KEY PEOPLE

Review the major theoretical contributions or research findings of these theorists and thinkers.

William Domhoff: Drawing upon the work of C. Wright Mills, Domhoff analyzed the workings of the ruling class.

Dennis Gilbert and Joseph Kahl: These sociologists developed a more contemporary stratification model based on Max Weber's work.

Ray Gold: In research on status inconsistency, Gold studied tenant reactions to janitors who earned more than they did. He found that the tenants acted "snooty" to the janitors, and at the same time the janitors took pleasure in knowing the intimate details of the tenants' lives.

Daniel Hellinger and Dennis Judd: In analyzing the exercise of power in the U.S., these two men suggest that there is a "democratic façade" that conceals the real sources of power within this society.

Elizabeth Higginbotham and Lynn Weber: These sociologists studied the mobility patterns for women. They found that those women who experienced upward mobility were most likely to have strong parental support to defer marriage and get an education.

Gerhard Lenski: Lenski noted that everyone wants to maximize their status, but are often judged on the basis of their lowest status despite the individual's efforts to be judged on the basis of their highest status.

C. Wright Mills: Mills used the term *power elite* to describe the top decision makers in the nation.

Daniel P. Moynihan: Moynihan was a sociologist as well as a U.S. senator; he attributed the high rate of child poverty to the breakdown of the U.S. family.

Max Weber: Weber expanded the concept of social class beyond economics—one's relationship to the means of production—to include power and prestige as well.

Erik Wright: Wright proposed an up-dated version of Marx's theory of stratification.

SELF-TEST

After completing this self-test, check your answers in the Answer Key of this Study Guide.

MULTIPLE CHOICE QUESTIONS

1. According to your text, on what do most sociologists agree concerning social class?
   a. It has a clear-cut, accepted definition in sociology.
   b. It is best defined by the two classes set out by Marx.
   c. It is best defined by Weber's dimensions of social class.
   d. It has no clear-cut, accepted definition and thus is used differently by all sociologists.

2. What percent of the nation's families own 68 percent of the wealth in the United States?
   a. 1
   b. 5
   c. 10
   d. 20

3. According to Paul Samuelson, if an income pyramid were made out of a child's blocks, where would most U.S. residents be?
   a. near the top of the pyramid
   b. near the middle of the pyramid
   c. near the bottom of the pyramid
   d. none of the above

4. Which of the following statements best describes changes in the distribution of U.S. income?
   a. The income distribution has remained virtually unchanged across time.
   b. The percentage of income going to the richest 20 percent of U.S. families has declined while the percentage going to the poorest 20 percent has increased.
   c. The percentage of income going to the middle income groups has increased at the expense of groups at both the top and bottom of the income scale.
   d. The percentage of income going to the richest 20 percent of U.S. families has increased while the percentage going to the poorest 20 percent has decreased.

5. What term do Hellinger and Judd use to describe the myth that the average citizen exercises power when he or she votes for representatives to Congress or the U.S. president?
   a. democratic charade
   b. popular façade
   c. democratic façade

    c.   democratic façade
    d.   political power myth

6.   What term did Mills use to refer to decision makers at the top of society?
    a.   the decision elite
    b.   the power elite
    c.   the power corps
    d.   the power brokers

7.   Which of these statements regarding the jobs that have the most prestige is *not* true?
    a.   They pay more.
    b.   They require more education.
    c.   They require special talent or skills.
    d.   They offer greater autonomy.

8.   Based on his research, what did Ray Gold discover about status inconsistency?
    a.   College professors tend to be politically radical.
    b.   Most people ignore their own inconsistent status while focusing on others.
    c.   Tenants related to the inconsistent status of the apartment building janitors by acting "snooty" toward them.
    d.   Status inconsistency is a very uncommon situation because most people try to be placed in approximately the same place in all three dimensions of stratification.

9.   How did Erik Wright update Marx's class categories in response to criticisms that they were too broad?
    a.   He divided each of the two classes into three sub-classes, making six classes in all.
    b.   He created an open scale in which people place themselves into classes.
    c.   He recommended listing people's different associations and then classifying them on the basis of their most important one.
    d.   He recognized that people can be members of more than one class at the same time.

10.   According to Gilbert and Kahl, the members of which social class can attribute their location in the class system to having a college or postgraduate education?
    a.   the capitalist class
    b.   the upper middle class
    c.   the lower middle class
    d.   the working class

11.   According to Gilbert and Kahl, all of the following describe the working class *except*:
    a.   most are employed in relatively unskilled blue-collar and white-collar jobs.
    b.   most have attended college for one or two years.
    c.   most hope to get ahead by achieving seniority on the job.
    d.   about 30 percent of the population belong to this class.

12.   Which of the following statements best describes the place of the homeless in our system today?
    a.   They are on the lowest rung with little or no chance of climbing anywhere.
    b.   They are the "fallout" of our developing postindustrial economy.
    c.   In another era, they would have had plenty of work as unskilled laborers.
    d.   All of the above.

13. One area of life which is affected by social class:
    a. is choice of mate.
    b. is politics.
    c. is sickness and health.
    d. is actually any/all of the above.

14. The poor are more likely than other classes to die:
    a. in infancy.
    b. in old age.
    c. at every age of the life cycle.
    d. ` as young adults.

15. Which social class experiences the most stress in daily life?
    a. Upper class
    b. Middle class
    c. Lower class
    d. All of the above classes experience about the same amount of stress, although the kind of stress and the source of stress may be different.

16. Full-time workers who must still rely on food stamps are part of:
    a. the working poor.
    b. the lower working class.
    c. the lower-lower class.
    d. the poverty class.

17. What type of mobility refers to the upward or downward movement in social class by family members from one generation to another?
    a. intergenerational
    b. intragenerational
    c. structural
    d. exchange

18. A homeless person whose father is/was a physician has experienced:
    a. exchange mobility.
    b. structural mobility.
    c. upward mobility.
    d. downward mobility.

19. What type of mobility refers to changes in society that cause large numbers of people to move up or down the class ladder?
    a. exchange
    b. automatic
    c. structural
    d. intragenerational

20. What type of mobility occurs when large numbers of people move up or down the social class ladder, but, on balance, the proportions of the social classes remain the same?
    a. exchange mobility
    b. structural mobility
    c. upward mobility
    d. job mobility

21. As compared with their fathers, about one-half of men in the United States have:
    a. a status higher than that of their fathers.
    b. the same status their fathers did.
    c. a status lower than that of their fathers.
    d. It is impossible to compare the statuses of fathers and sons because of structural mobility.

22. In addition to structural changes in the economic system, Higgenbotham and Weber found that women in Memphis from working-class backgrounds who subsequently occupied professional, managerial, and administrative positions had all been:
    a. encouraged by their parents to get an education.
    b. in the top 5 percent of their graduating class.
    c. the eldest child in the family.
    d. encouraged by their husbands to return to school.

23. The official measure of poverty calculated to include those whose incomes equal less than three times a low-cost food budget is the:
    a. adjusted income level.
    b. welfare distribution scale.
    c. poverty line.
    d. welfare line.

24. In what area of the United States is poverty clustered?
    a. inner cities
    b. South
    c. North
    d. West

25. Only _____ of white Americans are poor compared to 24 percent of African Americans and 22 percent of Latinos.
    a. 11 percent
    b. 10 percent
    c. 9 percent
    d. 8 percent

26. The most likely segment of the population in the United States to experience poverty today is:
    a. children.
    b. the elderly.
    c. middle-age adults.
    d. young single males.

27. Which of the following is a major cause of the feminization of poverty?
    a. divorce
    b. births to unmarried mothers
    c. lower wages paid to female workers
    d. all of the above are correct

28. Who are the least likely segment of the population to be poor?
    a. the elderly
    b. children
    c. women-headed families
    d. all of the above are not likely to experience poverty

29. What explanation for poverty is based on the assumption that the poor are fundamentally different from other people in the society?
    a.   social structure
    b.   social interaction
    c.   liberal
    d.   culture of poverty

30. The Horatio Alger myth:
    a.   is beneficial for society, according to the functionalists.
    b.   reduces pressures on the social system.
    c.   motivates people to try harder to succeed because anything is possible.
    d.   all of the above are correct.

TRUE-FALSE QUESTIONS

T F   1.   Wealth includes property and liquid assets.
T F   2.   Wealth and income are the same.
T F   3.   The richest one percent of United States families are also the people who have, since the 1904's, become richer than any other group.
T F   4.   The most affluent group in the United States is the Fortune 500 company CEOs.
T F   5.   The "democratic façade" refers to the political machinery in large cities.
T F   6.   Occupational prestige rankings are quite uniform across different countries.
T F   7.   Intergenerational mobility refers to mobility experienced between, not within, generations.
T F   8.   At or very near the top of most occupational prestige rankings is the occupation of physician.
T F   9.   Income is more unequally distributed in the United States than wealth.
T F   10.   College professors are, typically, an example of status inconsistency.
T F   11.   In the United States the social class that is most shaped by education is the working class.
T F   12.   The capitalist class helps to shape the consciousness of the United States.
T F   13.   The nouveau riche are the group with "old money."
T F   14.   People who "detail" cars at an automobile dealership are in the lower-middle social class.
T F   15.   It is exchange mobility when large numbers of people move up and down the social class ladder but the proportions of the social classes remains about the same.
T F   16.   Divorce is more common among the middle class than the poor.
T F   17.   Health care in the United States is a citizen's right.
T F   18.   Most poverty in the United States is of short duration, lasting only a year or less.
T F   19.   The greatest predictor of whether Americans are poor is geography.
T F   20.   Children in the United States are less likely than the general population to be poor.

FILL-IN QUESTIONS

1.   According to Weber, the three dimensions of social class are: (1) _____; (2) _____; and (3) _____.
2.   Since 1940, the income and wealth gap between the rich and poor have become _____. 188)
3.   According to Mills, the _____ makes the big decisions in United States society. (189)

4. Wages, rents, interest, royalties, and proceeds from a business are _____.
5. Almost 68 percent of all the wealth in the United States is owned by _____ of the nation's families.
6. The ability to carry out your will, despite resistance, is _____.
7. According to Wright, a position in the class structure that generates conflicting interests is _____.
8. Our social ranking is our _____.
9. The _____ is the powerful elite that consists of just 1 percent of the United States population.
10. The _____ consists of a small group of people for whom poverty persists year after year and across generations.
11. _____ is movement up the social class ladder.
12. For the upper middle class, the new technology is _____.
13. The "blue-bloods" of society fit into the concept of _____ money.
14. The official measure of poverty is referred to as _____.
15. Most poor families in the United States are headed by _____.

MATCH THESE THEORISTS/PHILOSOPHERS WITH THEIR CONTRIBUTIONS

1. Mills
2. Moynihan
3. Weber
4. Wright
5. Lewis

a. *the power elite*
b. *poverty and family breakdown*
c. *culture of poverty*
d. *three dimensions of social class*
e. *status inconsistency*

MATCH EACH SOCIAL CLASS WITH ITS DESCRIPTION

1. The working class
2. The working poor
3. The underclass
4. The capitalists
5. The upper-middle class

a. *have unskilled, temporary jobs.*
b. *fear recession.*
c. *many are philanthropists.*
d. *often manage corporations.*
e. *welfare is the main support.*

ESSAY QUESTIONS

1. Identify the three dimensions of social class and discuss their consequences.
2. Discuss why you think women have been largely ignored in studies of mobility.
3. Describe which groups are at the greatest risk of poverty and then suggest ways in which poverty can be reduced by targeting these populations.
4. Explore why individual explanations of poverty are easier for the average American to accept than structural explanations.
5. Given what you have learned in this chapter about stratification, what do you think are the chances that welfare reform will ultimately be successful in moving people out of poverty?

STUDENT PROJECTS

1. In what social class are your parents? What social class are you in now? How did your social class impact your choice of a college or university? Explain. Do you think your college educational experiences will lead to a change in your social class? Why?

2. Develop a budget for a single mother and her child based on the fact that the mother earns $6.00 per hour and works 35 hours a week (She can not find a 40 hour week job who will pay her health benefits). She does not receive any child support and her child is in daycare when she is working. Calculate food, clothing, transportation, shelter, and daycare. How difficult is it to make it in American society? What assistance would this family need to live a decent life?

CHAPTER 9

INEQUALITIES OF RACE AND ETHNICITY

CHAPTER SUMMARY

- **Race** is a complex and often misunderstood concept. Race is a reality in the sense that inherited physical characteristics distinguish one group from another. However, race is a myth in the sense of one race being superior to or more pure than another. The *idea* of race is powerful, shaping basic relationships between people.
- An **ethnic group** is a group of people who identify with one another on the basis of common ancestry and cultural heritage.
- A **minority group** is composed of people who are singled out for unequal treatment by members of the dominant group, the group with more power, privilege, and social status. Minorities originate with migration and the expansion of political boundaries.
- The extent of **ethnic identification** depends upon the relative size of the group, its power, broad physical characteristics, and the amount of discrimination it faces. Ethnic work, ranging from efforts to enhance and maintain the group's distinctions to attempts to recover one's heritage, is the process of constructing an ethnic identity.
- **Prejudice** is an attitude and **discrimination** is unfair treatment.
- **Individual discrimination** is the negative treatment of one person by another, while **institutional discrimination** is discrimination built into society's social institutions.
- Psychological theories explain the origin of prejudice in terms of stress, frustration that gets directed towards scapegoats, and in terms of the development of authoritarian personalities. Sociologists emphasize how different social environments affect levels of prejudice. They look at the benefits and costs of discrimination, the exploitation of racial-ethnic divisions by those in power, and the self-fulfilling prophecies that are the outcome of labeling.
- Dominant groups typically practice one of these five patterns toward minority groups: genocide, population transfer, internal colonialism, segregation, assimilation, and multiculturalism.
- From largest to smallest, the major ethnic groups are (1) European Americans, (2) Latinos, (3) African Americans, (4) Asian Americans, and (5) Native Americans.
- While each minority group in the United States has had different experiences, they are all familiar with discrimination. African Americans are increasingly divided into middle and lower classes; Latinos are divided by country of origin; Asian Americans are better off than whites, but their well-being varies by country origin; Native Americans are concerned with poverty, nationhood, and the settlement of treaty obligations. For all minorities, the overarching issue is overcoming discrimination.
- Today the main issues related to racial/ethnic relations are immigration, affirmative action, and how to develop a true multicultural society.

LEARNING OBJECTIVES
As you read Chapter 9, use these learning objectives to organize your notes. After completing your reading, you should be able to answer each of the objectives.

1. Explain how the concept of race is both a reality and a myth.
2. Distinguish between race and ethnicity.
3. Describe the characteristics of minority groups and dominant groups.

4. Know what is meant by ethnic identity and the four factors that heighten or reduce it.
5. Differentiate between prejudice and discrimination.
6. Distinguish between individual discrimination and institutional discrimination.
7. Understand the psychological and sociological theories of prejudice.
8. List the six patterns of intergroup relations that develop between minority and dominant groups and provide examples for each.
9. Compare and contrast the experiences of White Europeans, Latinos, African Americans, Asian Americans, and Native Americans in the United States.
10. Talk about the major issues—and debates— currently dominating race and ethnic relations in the United States.

CHAPTER OUTLINE

I. Laying the Sociological Foundation

A. **Race** is a reality in the sense that humans do come in different colors and shapes; however, two of the myths regarding race are that one race is superior to another, and that a pure race exists. These myths make a difference in social life because people believe they are real and they act on their beliefs.

B. **Race** and **ethnicity** are often confused due to the cultural differences people see and the way they define race. *Ethnicity* refers to cultural characteristics that distinguish a people.

C. Minority groups are people singled out for unequal treatment and regard themselves as objects of collective discrimination.

1. Shared characteristics of minorities worldwide: (1) the physical or cultural traits that distinguish them are held in low esteem by the dominant group, which treats them unequally; (2) they tend to marry within their own group; and (3) they tend to feel strong group solidarity.

2. They are not necessarily in the numerical minority. Sociologists refer to those who do the discriminating as the dominant group—they have greater power, more privileges, and higher social status. The dominant group attributes its privileged position to its superiority, not to discrimination.

3. A group becomes a minority through the expansion of political boundaries by another group. Another way for group to become a minority, either *voluntarily* or *involuntarily*, is by migration into a territory.

D. Individuals vary considerably in terms of how they construct their racial-ethnic identity; some people feel an intense sense of ethnic identity, while others feel very little.

1. Ethnic identity is influenced by the relative size and power of the ethnic group, its appearance, and the level of discrimination aimed at the group. If a group is relatively small, has little power, has a distinctive appearance, and is an object of discrimination, its members will have a heightened sense of ethnic identity.

2. *Ethnic work* refers to how people construct their ethnic identity and includes enhancing and maintaining a group's distinctiveness or attempting to recover their ethnic heritage. The idea of the U.S. as a melting pot, with different groups quietly blending together into an ethnic stew is undermined by the fact that many people today are engaged in ethnic work; a better metaphor would be "tossed salad" or "ethnic mosaic."

E. Prejudice and discrimination are common throughout the world.

1. **Discrimination** is unfair treatment directed toward someone. When based on race, it is known as **racism**. It can also be based on features such as age, sex, sexual preference, religion, or politics.
2. **Prejudice** is prejudging of some sort, usually in a negative way.
3. **Ethnocentrism** is so common that each racial/ethnic group views other groups as inferior in some way. Studies confirm that there is less prejudice among the more educated and among younger people.

F. Sociologists distinguish between *individual* and *institutional* discrimination.
1. **Individual discrimination** (negative treatment of one person by another) is too limited a perspective because it focuses only on individual treatment.
2. **Institutional discrimination** (negative treatment of a minority group that is built into a society's institutions) focuses on human behavior at the group level. Examples include certain mortgage lending practices and health care availability.

II. Theories of Prejudice

A. Psychological Perspectives:
1. According to **John Dollard**, prejudice results from frustration: people unable to strike out at the real source of their frustration find scapegoats to unfairly blame.
2. According to **Theodor Adorno,** highly prejudiced people are characterized by excess conformity, intolerance, insecurity, heightened respect for authority, and submission to superiors. He called this complex of personality traits the authoritarian personality. Subsequent studies have generally concluded that people who are older, less educated, less intelligent, and from a lower social class are more likely to be authoritarian.

B. Sociological Perspectives:
1. To functionalists, the social environment can be deliberately arranged to generate either positive or negative feelings about people. Prejudice can be a product of pitting groups against each other in an "I win/you lose" situation. Prejudice is functional in that it creates in-group solidarity and out-group antagonism. It is dysfunctional in that it destroys social relationships and intensifies conflict.
2. To conflict theorists, the ruling class benefits when it systematically pits group against group by: (1) creating a split labor market which divides workers along racial-ethnic lines and weakens solidarity among the workers; and by (2) maintaining higher unemployment rates for minorities, creating a reserve labor force from which owners can draw when they need to temporarily expand production. Workers from different racial-ethnic groups learn to fear and distrust one another instead of recognizing common interests and working for their mutual benefit.
3. To symbolic interactionists, the labels people learn color their perception, leading them to see certain things and be blind to others. Racial and ethnic labels are especially powerful because they are shorthand for emotionally laden stereotypes. The stereotypes that we learn not only justify prejudice and discrimination, but they also lead to a self-fulfilling prophecy.

III. Global Patterns of Intergroup Relations

A. **Genocide** is the actual or attempted systematic annihilation of a race or ethnic group who has been labeled as less than fully human by the dominant group. Dehumanizing labels are powerful forces that help people to compartmentalize—separate their acts from any feelings that would threaten their self-concept—thereby making it difficult for them to participate in the act. The Holocaust and the treatment of Native Americans are examples.

B. **Population transfer** is the involuntary movement of a minority group. Indirect transfer involves making life so unbearable that the minority group members leave; direct transfer involves forced expulsion. A combination of genocide and population transfer occurred in Bosnia (a part of the former Yugoslavia) as Serbs engaged in ethnic cleansing—the wholesale slaughter of Muslims and Croats, which forced survivors to flee the area.

C. **Internal colonialism** is a society's policy of exploiting a minority by using social institutions to deny it access to full benefits. Slavery is an extreme example.

D. **Segregation**, the formal separation of groups, often accompanies internal colonialism. The dominant group exploits the labor of the minority while maintaining social distance.

E. **Assimilation** is the process by which a minority is absorbed into the mainstream. Forced assimilation occurs when the dominant group prohibits the minority from using its own religion, language, and customs. *Permissive assimilation* is when the minority adopts the dominant group's patterns in its own way, and at its own speed.

F. **Multiculturalism (pluralism)** permits or encourages racial and ethnic variation. Switzerland provides an outstanding example of this.

IV. Race and Ethnic Relations in the United States

A. The major racial-ethnic groups in the U.S. are White European Americans, African Americans, Latinos, Asian Americans, and Native Americans.

B. In the United States, the dominant group is made up of whites whose ancestors emigrated here from European countries.

1. White Anglo-Saxon Protestants (WASPs) were highly ethnocentric and viewed white ethnics—the Irish, Germans, Poles, Jews, and Italians—as inferior.

2. Immigrants were expected to blend into the mainstream, speak English and adopt the dominant group's way of life. It was the grandchildren of the immigrants, the third generation, who most easily adjusted. As these white ethnics assimilated into Anglo culture, the definition of WASP was expanded to include them.

3. Because the English first settled the colonies, they established the institutions and culture to which later immigrants had to conform.

C. **Latinos** are the largest ethnic group in the United States, and include Chicanos, Puerto Ricans, Cuban Americans, and people from Central or South America. Concentrated primarily in four states (California, Texas, New York, and Florida), they are causing major demographic shifts.

1. The Spanish language distinguishes them from other minorities: perhaps half are unable to speak English without difficulty. This is a major obstacle to getting well-paid jobs.

2. Divisions based on social class and country of origin prevent political unity among these Latino groups.

3. Compared with non-Hispanic whites and Asian American, Latinos are worse off on all indicators of well-being. The country of origin is significant, with Cuban Americans scoring the highest on indicators of well-being and Puerto-Rican Americans scoring the lowest.

D. **African Americans** face a legacy of racism. Following the end of the Civil War, southern states passed *Jim Crow* laws that separated blacks and whites.

1. In 1955, African Americans in Montgomery, Alabama, using the nonviolent tactics advocated by Martin Luther King, Jr., protested laws they believed to be unjust. This led to the civil rights movement that challenged existing patterns of racial segregation throughout the south.

2.	The 1964 Civil Rights Acts (banning discrimination in public facilities) and the 1965 Voting Rights Act (banning literacy tests used to prevent African Americans from voting) heightened expectations. Frustration over the slow pace of change led to urban riots and passage of the 1968 Civil Rights Act.

3.	Since then, African Americans have made political and economic progress. For example, African Americans have quadrupled their membership in the U.S. House of Representatives in the past 25 years. As college enrollment continues to increase, the middle class has expanded so that now one of every four African American families makes more than $50,000 annually. African Americans such as Jesse Jackson, Douglas Wilder, and Clarence Thomas are politically prominent.

4.	Despite these gains, however, African Americans continue to lag behind in politics, economics, and education. African Americans average 61 percent of whites' incomes; only 17 percent of African Americans graduate from college, and about one of every five African American families makes less than $15,000 annually.

5.	According to William J. Wilson, social class (not race) is the major determinant of quality of life. The African American community today is divided into two groups. Middle-class African Americans seized opportunities created by civil rights legislation and advanced economically, moving out of the inner city; they have moved up the class ladder, live in good housing, have well-paid jobs, and send their children to good schools. However, as opportunities for unskilled labor declined, a large group of poorly educated and unskilled African Americans were left behind; they still live in poverty, face violent crime and dead-end jobs, attend terrible schools, and live in hopelessness and despair.

6.	Charles Willie challenges Wilson, arguing that discrimination on the basis of race persists, despite gains made by some African Americans.

7.	It is likely that both discrimination and social class contribute to the African American experience.

E.	**Asian Americans** have long faced discrimination in the United States.

1.	The history of Asian Americans is one of discrimination and prejudice. Chinese Americans were frequently the victims of vigilante groups and anti-Chinese legislation. After the attack on Pearl Harbor in World War II, hostilities increased, with many Japanese Americans being imprisoned in "relocation camps".

2.	When immigrants from Japan began to arrive they experienced "spillover bigotry," a stereotype that lumped all Asians together, depicting them as sneaky, lazy, and untrustworthy.

3.	Today Asian Americans are the fastest growing minority in the U.S. and they are a diverse group divided by separate cultures. Although there are variations in income among Asian American groups, on the average Asian Americans have been extremely successful. This success can be traced to three factors: (1) a close family life; (2) educational achievement; and (3) assimilation into the mainstream.

4.	Asian Americans are becoming more prominent in politics, serving as governors of Hawaii and Washington.

F.	Due to the influence of old movie westerns, many Americans tend to hold stereotypes of **Native Americans** as uncivilized savages and a single group of people subdivided into separate bands.

1.	In reality, Native Americans represent a diverse group of people with a variety of cultures and languages. Although originally numbering between 5 and 10 million, their numbers were reduced to a low of 500,000 at the beginning of the twentieth century due to a lack of immunity to European diseases and warfare. Today there are about 2 million Native Americans.

2.   At first, relations between European settlers and the Native Americans were peaceful. However, as the number of settlers increased, tensions grew. Because they stood in the way of expansion, many were slaughtered. Government policy shifted to population transfer, with Native Americans confined to reservations.

3.   Today they are an invisible minority. Almost half live in rural areas, with one-third concentrated in Oklahoma, California, and Arizona; most other Americans are hardly aware of them. They have the highest rates of poverty, unemployment, suicide, and alcoholism of any U.S. minority. These negative conditions are the result of Anglo domination.

4.   In the 1960's Native Americans won a series of legal victories that restored their control over the land and their right to determine economic policy. Many Native American tribes have opened businesses, ranging from industrial parks to casinos.

5.   Many tribes maintain the right to remain separate from the U.S. government and U.S. society; this separatism is a highly controversial issue.

6.   Today, many Native Americans are interested in recovering their own traditions. Pan-Indianism emphasizes common elements that run through Native American cultures in order to develop self-identification that goes beyond any one tribe.

V.   Looking toward the Future

A.   As U.S. society moves toward the twenty-first century, two issues that will have to be resolved are immigration and affirmative action.

B.   **Immigration** and the fear of its consequences are central to U.S. history.

1.   The first great wave of immigrants arrived from Europe at the end of the nineteenth and beginning of the twentieth centuries. The second wave, since 1980, has brought immigrants from around the world and is contributing to the changing U.S. racial/ethnic mix.

2.   In some states, such as California, all minorities combined represent the majority of the population.

3.   Many are concerned that this influx of immigrants will change the character of U.S. society, including the primacy of the English language.

C.   **Affirmative action** is at the core of the national debate about how to steer a course in race and ethnic relations.

1.   Some see affirmative action as the more direct way to level the playing field of economic opportunity, while others say that it results in reverse discrimination.

2.   Several controversial rulings suggest that there is still no consensus about the proper role of affirmative action in a multicultural society.

3.   In order to achieve a multicultural society in which different racial-ethnic groups not only co-exist but actually respect one another will require that groups with different histories and cultures learn to accept one another. We must begin to examine our history and question many of its' assumptions and symbols.

KEY TERMS

After studying the chapter, review each of the following terms.

assimilation: the process of being absorbed into the mainstream culture (p. 234)

authoritarian personality: Adorno's term for people who are prejudiced and rank high on scales of conformity, intolerance, insecurity, respect for authority, and submissiveness to superiors (p. 230)

compartmentalize: to separate acts from feelings or attitudes (p. 233)

discrimination: an act of unfair treatment directed against an individual or a group (p. 227)

dominant group: the group with the most power, greatest privileges, and highest social status (p. 226)

ethnic work; activities designed to discover, enhance, or maintain ethnic and racial identification (p. 227)

ethnicity (and **ethnic**): having distinctive cultural characteristics (p. 223)

genocide: the systematic annihilation or attempted annihilation of a people based on their presumed race or ethnic group (p. 223)

individual discrimination: the negative treatment of one person by another on the basis of that person's perceived characteristics (p. 229)

institutional discrimination: the negative treatment of a minority group that is built into a society's institutions, also called systematic discrimination (p. 229)

internal colonialism: the policy of economically exploiting a minority group (p. 233)

melting pot: the view that Americans of various backgrounds would blend into a sort of ethnic stew, leaving behind their distinctive ethnic identities and forming a new ethnic group (p. 227)

minority group: people who are singled out for unequal treatment on the basis of their physical and cultural characteristics, and who regard themselves as objects of collective discrimination (p. 226)

multiculturalism: (also called **pluralism**) a philosophy or political policy that permits or encourages groups to express their individual, unique racial and ethnic identities (p. 234)

pan-Indianism: a movement that focuses on common elements in the culture of Native Americans in order to develop a cross-tribal self identity and to work toward the welfare of all Native Americans (p. 249)

pluralism: the diffusion of power among many interest groups which prevents any single group from gaining control of the government (p. 234)

population transfer: forcing a minority group to relocate (p. 233)

prejudice: an attitude of prejudging, usually in a negative way (p. 228)

race: a group whose inherited physical characteristics distinguish it from other groups (p. 222)

racism: prejudice and discrimination on the basis of race (p. 227)

reserve labor force: the term used by conflict theorists for the unemployed who can be put to work during times of high production and then discarded when no longer needed (p. 231)

rising expectations: the sense that better conditions are soon to follow, which, if unfulfilled, creates mounting frustration (p. 242)

scapegoat: an individual or group unfairly blamed for someone else's troubles (p. 230)

segregation; the policy of keeping racial or ethnic groups separated (p. 234)

selective perception: seeing certain features of an object or situation, but remaining blind to others (p. 232)

split labor market: a term used by conflict theorists for the practice of weakening the bargaining power of workers by splitting them along racial, ethnic, gender, age, or any other lines (p. 232)

WASP: white Anglo-Saxon Protestant; narrowly, an American of English descent; broadly, an American of western European ancestry (p. 235)

white ethnics: white immigrants to the U.S. whose culture differs from that of WASPs (p. 235)

KEY PEOPLE

Review the major theoretical contributions or research findings of these theorists and thinkers.

Theodor Adorno: Adorno identified the authoritarian personality type.

Emery Cowen, Judah Landes and Donald Schaet: In an experiment, these psychologists found that students directed frustrations onto people who had nothing to do with their problem.

Ashley Doane: Doane identified four factors that affect an individual's sense of ethnic identity.

John Dollard: This psychologist first suggested that prejudice is the result of frustration and scapegoats become the targets for people's frustrations.

Eugene Hartley: Known for his work on prejudice, Hartley found that people who are prejudiced against one racial or ethnic group tend to be prejudiced against others and that prejudice is not necessarily based on personal negative experiences.

Douglas Massey: Massey and his students designed a research project to test discrimination in the housing market. Students from different racial and social class backgrounds made calls about apartment units available for rent. When compared with white students, the African Americans were less likely to actually speak to a rental agent, less likely to be told a unit was available, more likely to have to pay an application fee, and more likely to have their credit mentioned.

Ashley Montagu: This physical anthropologist pointed out that some scientists have classified humans into two races while others have identified as many as two thousand.

Alejandro Portes and Rueben Rumbaut: These sociologists looked at the impact that immigration has had on our country, noting that there has always been an anti-immigrant sentiment present.

Barbara Reskin: Reskin examined the results of affirmative action, concluding that it has had only a modest impact on hiring, promotion, and college admission.

Muzafer & Carolyn Sherif: The Sherifs researched the functions of prejudice and found that it builds in-group solidarity.

Charles Willie: Willie has criticized William Wilson's work, arguing that race is still an important criterion for discrimination.

William Wilson: Known for his work on racial discrimination, Wilson argues that class is a more important factor than race in explaining patterns of inequality.

Louis Wirth: Wirth offered a sociological definition of a minority group.

SELF-TEST

After completing this self-test, check your answers in the Answer Key of this Study Guide.

MULTIPLE CHOICE QUESTIONS

1. Race:
   a. means having distinctive cultural characteristics.
   b. means having inherited physical characteristics that distinguish one group from another.
   c. means people who are singled out for unequal treatment.
   d. is relatively easy to determine.

2. People often confuse race and ethnicity because:
   a. they dislike people who are different from themselves.
   b. of the cultural differences people see and the way they define race.
   c. they are unaware of the fact that race is cultural and ethnicity is biological.
   d. all of the above.

3. A minority group:
   a. is discriminated against because of physical or cultural differences.
   b. is discriminated against because of personality factors.
   c. does not always experience discrimination.
   d. all of the above.

4. The dominant group in a society almost always considers its position is due to:
   a. its own innate superiority.
   b. its ability to oppress minority group members.
   c. its ability to control political power.
   d. all of the above.

5. The factors affecting a group's sense of ethnic identity are:
   a. The amount of power the group has.
   b. the size of the group.
   c. the degree to which the group's physical appearance differs from the mainstream.
   d. all of the above.

6. Many people today are tracing their family lines. This is an example of:
   a. ethnic identity.
   b. ethnic enclaves.
   c. ethnic work.
   d. ethnic pride.

7. The best description of a melting pot is:
   a. a society in which groups quietly blend into a sort of ethnic stew.
   b. a society in which each ethnicity maintains its distinctiveness.
   c. a society where everyone adapts to the dominant group's ways.
   d. none of the above.

8. Prejudice and discrimination:
   a. are less prevalent in the United States than in other societies.
   b. are more prevalent in the United States than in other societies.

    c.   appear to characterize every society, regardless of size.

    d.   appear to characterize only large societies.

9.   Prejudice:
    a.   is an attitude.
    b.   may be positive or negative.
    c.   is often the basis for discrimination.
    d.   all of the above.

10.   Sociologist Kathleen Blee, in interviews with women who were members of the KKK or Aryan nation, found:
    a.   most women were recruited by someone who already belonged to the group.
    b.   some women learned to be racists after they joined the group.
    c.   Intense racism was not the cause of their joining but the result of their membership.
    d.   all of the above

11.   When a group of people learn to be prejudiced against their own group this is referred to as:
    a.   group racism.
    b.   reverse discrimination.
    c.   internalization of the norms of the dominant group.
    d.   none of the above.

12.   Negative treatment on the basis of personal characteristics is:
    a.   individual discrimination.
    b.   individual prejudice.
    c.   institutional discrimination.
    d.   institutional prejudice.

13.   What do the findings of research on patterns of mortgage lending confirm?
    a.   Discrimination is the result of individual bankers' decisions.
    b.   Decisions to reject loans reflect sound banking practices.
    c.   While African Americans and Latinos were rejected more often than whites, the rate was not significant.
    d.   Discrimination is built into the country's financial institutions.

14.   According to John Dollard, the source of prejudice is:
    a.   the authoritarian personality.
    b.   frustration.
    c.   a split-labor market.
    d.   selective perception.

15.   Why do functionalists consider prejudice functional for some groups?
    a.   It is a useful weapon in maintaining social divisions.
    b.   It contributes to the creation of scapegoats.
    c.   It helps to create solidarity within the group by fostering antagonisms directed against other groups.
    d.   It affects how members of one group perceive members of other groups.

16.   According to conflict theorists, prejudice:
    a.   benefits capitalists by splitting workers along racial or ethnic lines.
    b.   contributes to the exploitation of workers, thus producing a split-labor market.

c.   keeps workers from demanding higher wages and better working conditions.
d.   all of the above.

17.   Symbolic interactionists stress that prejudiced people:
    a.   are born that way.
    b.   have certain types of personalities.
    c.   learn their prejudices in interaction with others.
    d.   none of the above.

18.   Genocide:
    a.   occurred when Hitler attempted to destroy all Jews.
    b.   is the systematic annihilation of a race or ethnic group.
    c.   often requires the cooperation of ordinary citizens.
    d.   all of the above.

19.   The process of expelling a minority from a country or a particular area is called:
    a.   population redistribution.
    b.   direct population transfer.
    c.   indirect population transfer.
    d.   expelled population transfer.

20.   A society's policy of exploiting a minority group, using social institutions to deny the minority access to the society's full benefits, is referred to as:
    a.   segregation.
    b.   pluralism.
    c.   internal colonialism.
    d.   genocide.

21.   What frequently accompanies internal colonialism?
    a.   genocide
    b.   population transfer
    c.   ethnic cleansing
    d.   segregation

22.   The process of being absorbed into the mainstream culture is:
    a.   pluralism.
    b.   assimilation.
    c.   cultural submersion.
    d.   internal colonialism.

23.   Prior to the fall of the Soviet Union, the government required all Armenian children to attend schools where they were taught only in Russian, even when Armenian was their first language. This would be an example of:
    a.   ethnic cleansing.
    b.   forced assimilation.
    c.   internal colonialism.
    d.   pluralism.

24.   Which of the following statements about WASPs is *incorrect*?
    a.   They embraced whites from other European nations, helping them assimilate.
    b.   They took power and determined the national agenda, controlling the destiny of the nation.

c. The term refers to White Anglo-Saxon Protestants whose ancestors came from England.

d. They were highly ethnocentric and viewed other immigrants as inferior.

25. According to your text, Latinos are distinguished from other ethnic minorities in the United States by:
a. the Spanish language.
b. the fact that virtually all Latinos entered the United States illegally.
c. the short length of time Latinos have been in the United States.
d. all of the above.

26. According to William Wilson, new opportunities enabling middle-class African Americans to move up the social class ladder were created by:
a. economic prosperity.
b. organized religion.
c. civil rights legislation.
d. technological advances.

27. Which of the following statements about reparations is *incorrect*?
a. It is widely accepted that blacks deserve compensation for slavery, the only disagreement is what form that compensation should take.
b. It has been argued that the greater wealth of today's white Americans is built on centuries of unpaid labor of black slaves.
c. Reparations are a form of back wages.
d. Most of today's white population descended from people who immigrated to the U.S. after slavery ended and therefore had nothing to do with slavery.

28. Which of the following statements about the experiences of Asian Americans is *incorrect*?
a. Much of the hostility directed toward Japanese Americans was due to Pearl Harbor.
b. Asian Americans are becoming more prominent in politics.
c. The view that Asian Americans have been successful in this country is basically correct.
d. Most Asian Americans grow up in tight-knit families.

29. Which of the following groups is often referred to as an "invisible minority?"
a. African Americans
b. Asian Americans
c. Latinos
d. Native Americans

30. What is a difference between the earlier wave of immigration at the turn of the last century and the current wave?
a. The current wave is much smaller.
b. The current wave is more global in content.
c. The current wave is experiencing a more welcoming environment.
d. All of the above.

TRUE-FALSE QUESTIONS

T F   1.   Scientists generally agree on just how many races there are in the world.

T F   2.   Sociologists often use the terms race and ethnicity interchangeably.

T F 3. Either physical or cultural differences can be a basis of unequal treatment in societies.

T F 4. A group must represent a numerical minority to be a minority group.

T F 5. Certain characteristics are shared by minorities worldwide.

T F 6. Minorities often have a shared sense of identity and common destiny.

T F 7. Ethnic work depends on the degree to which an individual has an ethnic identity.

T F 8. Discrimination is unfair treatment based solely on racial characteristics.

T F 9. Although prejudice can be either positive or negative, most prejudice is negative and involves prejudging other groups as inferior.

T F 10. People can learn to be prejudiced against their own group.

T F 11. Sociologists believe that individual discrimination is an adequate explanation for discrimination in the United States.

T F 12. Research shows that African Americans and Latinos are 60 percent more likely than whites to be rejected for mortgages, all other factors being similar.

T F 13. According to research, even mild levels of frustration can lead to higher levels of prejudice.

T F 14. Adorno's research suggests that people of lower social class are more likely to be authoritarian.

T F 15. Functionalists focus on the role of the capitalist class in exploiting racism and ethnic inequalities.

T F 16. Symbolic interactionists stress that the labels we use encourage us to see things selectively.

T F 17. Genocide often relies on labeling and compartmentalization.

T F 18. Segregation allows the dominant group to exploit the labor of the minority while maintaining social distance.

T F 19. Today, more immigrants live in the United States than any time in history.

T F 20. Sociologist Barbara Reskin found that affirmative action had huge impacts for minorities.

FILL-IN QUESTIONS

1. The mapping of the human genome systems shows that humans are strikingly _____.

2. The _____ of race is far from a myth.

3. A _____ is a group singled out for unequal treatment and who regard themselves as objects of collective discrimination.

4. We can use the term _____ to refer to the way people construct their ethnicity.

5. Many analysts are using the term _____ rather than melting pot when referring to the American ethnic experience.

6. In her research on women who joined organizations like the KKK and the Aryan Nation, Blee found that their intense racism was not the cause of their joining, but the _____ of their membership.

7. Discrimination does not have to be _____.

8. Gender and _____ also provide common bases for scapegoating.

9. According to the text, last century's two most notorious examples of genocide occurred in Germany and _____.

10. _____ are the largest minority group in the United States.

11. African-Americans have _____ their membership in the U.S. House of Representatives in the past 30 years.

12. The majority of Asians in the United States live in the _____.

13. Native Americans can truly be called the _____.
14. A highly controversial issue among Native Americans is _____.
15. In the state of _____, racial-ethnic minorities already constitute the majority of people in that state.

MATCH EACH CONCEPT WITH ITS DESCRIPTION

1. Melting pot
2. Ethnicity
3. Genocide
4. Race
5. Dominant group

a. *inherited physical traits*
b. *an attempt to destroy a people*
c. *cultural characteristics*
d. *have the greatest power and status*
e. *many groups blending*

MATCH THESE THEORISTS/PHILOSOPHERS WITH THEIR CONTRIBUTIONS

1. Adorno
2. Doane
3. Reskin
4. Wirth
5. Willie

a. *Defined minority group*
b. *Ethnic identity*
c. *Authoritarian personality*
d. *Research on affirmative action*
e. *Racial discrimination and pay*

ESSAY QUESTIONS

1. Explain what the author means when he says that race is both a myth and a reality.
2. Using the experiences of different racial and ethnic groups in the United States, identify and discuss the six patterns of intergroup relations.
3. Explore how both psychological and sociological theories can be used together to gain a deeper understanding of prejudice and discrimination.
4. Summarize the arguments on both sides of the reparations debate and then analyze what factors influence your own views on this subject.
5. What would have to change in our society in order for us to truly be a multicultural society?

STUDENT PROJECTS

1. Does your family have a great sense of ethnicity? Why or why not? Do you engage in any activities (food, clothing, music, celebrations) that are related to your ethnic heritage? If so, explain.

2. Should race be a factor in college admissions? Why or why not? What do you think should be done to insure that everyone has equal educational opportunity in the United States? Upon what should colleges base admissions? Are grades and SAT or ACT test scores good measures? What factors do you think should be important? Why?

CHAPTER 10

INEQUALITIES OF GENDER AND AGE

CHAPTER SUMMARY

- Each society establishes a structure that, on the basis of sex and gender, permits or limits access to power, property, and prestige; this structure is referred to as *gender stratification*. **Sex** refers to biological distinctions between males and females; **gender** refers to the behaviors and attitudes a society considers proper for its males and females. In the "nature versus nurture" debate, most sociologists take the side of nurture.

- Male dominance, or **patriarchy**, appears to be universal. The primary theory about how women became a minority group focuses on the physical limitations imposed by childbirth.

- Although feminist movements in the United States have battled to eliminate some of the most blatant forms of gender discrimination, there are still many areas of inequality. More females than males now attend college, but both generally end up in gender-biased academic fields. There are signs of change, as indicated by the growing number of women in such fields as law and medicine.

- Women continue to face discrimination in health care — when complaining of chest pain, they are referred for heart surgery later than men with similar complaints and are given other unnecessary surgeries more often.

- Over the course of this century women have made up an increasing proportion of the workforce, although they continue to be paid less than men. Women continue to face sexual harassment in the workplace.

- Women are more likely to be the victims of battering, rape, incest, and murder. Female circumcision is a uniquely special case of violence against women. According to conflict theory, men use violence against women to maintain their position of power.

- In the past, the traditional expectations associated with women's roles kept them out of politics. Although still underrepresented, there is a trend toward greater political equality between men and women.

- As women's decision-making roles continue to expand, a reasonable goal is greater appreciation of differences combined with greater equality of opportunity.

- Attitudes, beliefs, and policies regarding the aged vary from one society to another ranging from exclusion and killing to integration and honor.

- The symbolic interaction perspective stresses the social construction of aging, emphasizing that age has no meaning in and of itself, but is given a meaning by each society. Ageism stereotypes are influenced by the mass media.

- The functional perspective analyzes the withdrawal of the elderly from positions of responsibility. Disengagement and activity theories are two functional theories arising from research in this area.

- Conflict theorists believe that the competition for scarce resources by rival interest groups (e.g., how age cohorts may be on a collision course regarding Social Security, Medicare, and Medicaid), is a guiding principle of social life.

- In the future, our society will be challenged to find ways to support an aging population of retired people whose lives are extended through new technologies.

LEARNING OBJECTIVES

As you read Chapter 10, use these learning objectives to organize your notes. After completing your reading, you should be able to answer each of the objectives.

1. Define gender stratification and differentiate between sex and gender.
2. Discuss the continuing controversy regarding the biological and cultural factors which come into play in creating gender differences in societies.
3. Explain why women are considered to be a minority group and summarize the theory of how male dominance occurred.
4. Describe the major factors which led to the rise of feminism in the United States and note how successful this movement has been up to this point in time.
5. Discuss ways in which educational systems may perpetuate gender inequality.
6. Identify some of the ways in which the field of health care reflects gender inequality.
7. Explain gender relations in the workplace, including changes in the labor force participation rate that have produced the quiet revolution, the pay gap, the "glass ceiling" the "glass escalator," and sexual harassment.
8. Discuss the patterns of violence against women, explain why female circumcision is a uniquely special case of violence leveled against women, and summarize the feminist explanation.
9. Explain why women were underrepresented in politics in the past and how that is changing today.
10. Describe what the future looks like in terms of gender relations in the United States.
11. Explain the process known as the social construction of aging, use the Tiwi and the Abkhasians as examples of how our notions of aging are socially constructed.
12. Discuss what effects industrialization has had on the aging process and identify factors involved in the "graying" of industrialized nations.
13. Discuss the major conclusions drawn by symbolic interactionists regarding aging.
14. Summarize the functional perspective on aging and explain both disengagement and activity theories.
15. Explain why conflict theorists see social life as a struggle between groups for scarce resources and note how this impacts different age cohorts.

CHAPTER OUTLINE

INEQUALITIES OF GENDER
I. Issues of Sex and Gender
A. Gender stratification refers to the unequal access to power, prestige, and property possessed by men and by women.
B. Sex and gender reflect different bases.
1. **Sex** is the biological characteristics distinguishing males and females — primary sex organs (organs related to reproduction) and secondary sex organs (physical distinctions not related to reproduction).
2. **Gender** is a social characteristic, and varies from one society to another; it refers to the behaviors and attitudes the group considers proper for its males and females.
3. The sociological significance of gender is that it serves as a sorting device by which society controls its members and thus is a structural feature of society.
C. There is disagreement as to what produces gender differences in behavior.
1. Some researchers argue that **biological factors** (two X chromosomes in females, one X and one Y in males) result in differences in the behavior of males (more aggressive and domineering) and females (more comforting and nurturing).

2.   The dominant sociological position is that gender differences result from sex being used to mark people for special treatment; males and females then take on the relative positions that society assigns to them.

D.   **Alice Rossi** suggested that women are better prepared biologically for "mothering" than are men; nature provides biological predispositions which are overlaid with culture. Medical accidents and studies such as the one involving Vietnam veterans suggest that the relationship between biology and social learning is a complex one.

II.   How Females Became a Minority Group

A.   Around the world, gender is *the* primary division between people. Every society sets up barriers to deny women equal access, and they are therefore referred to as a minority even though they outnumber men.

B.   Although the origin of **patriarchy** (male dominance) is unknown, one theory points to the social consequences of human reproduction.

     1.   As a result of pregnancy and breast-feeding, women were limited for much of their lives; they assumed tasks associated with the home and child care.

     2.   Men took over those tasks requiring greater speed and longer absences such as hunting animals. This enabled men to make contact with other tribes and to wage war; male prestige results from their accumulation of possessions through trade and war with other groups. Little prestige was given to women's routine tasks, in part because they were not perceived as risking their lives for the group.

     3.   Eventually men took over society, using their weapons, possessions, and knowledge to guarantee that they held more social power than did women.

C.   There is no way to test this theory because the answers lie buried in history. There may be many different causes other than the biology of human reproduction.

     1.   **Marvin Harris** argued that in prehistoric times, each group was threatened with annihilation by other groups, and each had to recruit members to fight enemies in dangerous, hand-to-hand combat. Men (bigger and stronger) were coaxed into this bravery by promises of rewards—sexual access to females.

     2.   **Frederick Engels** suggested that male dominance developed in society with the emergence of private property.

     3.   Today, male dominance is a continuation of millennia-old patterns.

III.   Gender Inequality in the United States

A.   Woman's rights resulted from a prolonged and bitter struggle.

     1.   U.S. women could not vote, hold property, or serve on a jury until this century. Males did not willingly surrender their privileges, but used social institutions to maintain their position.

     2.   **Feminism**, the view that biology is not destiny and that gender stratification is wrong and should be resisted, met with strong opposition.

     3.   The first wave of the women's movement had a radical branch, which wanted to reform all social institutions, and a conservative branch, which concentrated on winning the vote for women. The conservative branch dominated and both branches of the movement more or less disappeared after suffrage was achieved.

     4.   The second wave began in the 1960s; its goals range from changing women's work roles to changing policies on violence against women.

     5.   While women enjoy more rights today, gender inequality still exists.

B.   Despite evidence of the educational gains made by women—more females than males are enrolled in U.S. colleges and universities and females earn 57 percent of all bachelor's degrees—some traditional male-female distinctions persist.

1. At college, males and females are channeled into different fields; 87 percent of library science degrees are awarded to females; 82 percent of engineering degrees are awarded to males.
2. The proportion of females decreases in post-graduate work.
3. There is also gender stratification in both the rank and pay within higher educational institutions. Women are less likely to be in the higher ranks of academia, and at all levels are paid less than their male counterparts.
4. Changes are taking place; the proportion of professional degrees earned by women has increased in recent years.

C. Researchers have found another kind of sex discrimination in the area of medicine and health care.
1. Physicians sometimes dismiss the complaints of female patients as not serious. This neglect could be a matter of life and death; one example is in the area of diagnosing and treating heart disease.
2. Physicians regard women's reproductive organs as "potentially disease producing" and largely unnecessary after childbearing years; they frequently recommend removal. Surgeons make a lot of money from the unnecessary removal of these organs.

D. There have been significant changes in the workforce as the number of working women has increased. However, discrimination against women is still very visible.
1. In 1900, one in five workers was female; today it is almost one in two.
2. Sociologists refer ever increasing proportion of women in the workforce as a "quiet revolution." It has had profound effects on consumer matters, relationships with significant others, at work, and in women's self-concepts.
3. Women who work full-time average only 70 percent of what men are paid. Despite their level of educational achievement, women earn less than men; this is true even when they have more qualifications than their male counterparts. Half of this pay gap results from women entering lower-paying jobs.
4. One study found that in their first jobs, women business majors at one university averaged an annual starting salary that is 11 percent less than their male counterparts, even though they had higher grades and more internship experiences. Five years later, the pay gap was even wider.
5. The "**glass ceiling**" describes an invisible barrier that women face in the work force. Men, who dominate the executive suites, stereotype potential leaders as people who look like themselves. In addition, women lack mentors; male executives are reluctant to get close to female subordinates because they fear gossip and sexual harassment charges, or they believe that women are weak. In recent years women who are highly motivated, fiercely competitive, and play by "men's rules," have begun to crack the glass ceiling.
6. For men, employment in traditionally female occupations (nursing, elementary school teaching, and social work) means increased job opportunities, more desirable work assignments, higher-level positions, and larger salaries. **Christine Williams** refers to this as the "**glass escalator**."

E. Until the 1970s, women did not draw a connection between unwanted sexual advances on the job and their subordinate positions at work.
1. But as women began to discuss the problem, they named it and came to see unwanted sexual advances by men in powerful positions as a structural problem. The change resulted from reinterpreting women's experiences—giving them a name.
2. As more women move into positions of authority over men, the problem of sexual harassment is no longer exclusively a female problem.

3.   Court cases constantly result in changes as to what is and is not included within the legal definition of sexual harassment. The Court has ruled that sexual harassment laws also apply to homosexuals who are harassed by heterosexuals on the job.

F.   Women are more likely to be victims of violence than men.

1.   Every year in the U.S. 7 of every 10,000 females aged 12 and older is raped; the typical rapist is under the age of 30.

2.   Of increased concern today is the widespread incidence of date rape. Studies show that this occurs most commonly between couples who have known each other about one year; most go unreported.

3.   Males are more likely to commit murder than females, and males commit 89 percent of the murders involving women victims.

4.   Women are also disproportionate victims of family violence—spouse battering, marital rape, and incest—and of genital circumcision.

5.   Feminists use symbolic interactionism to understand violence against women. They stress that U.S. culture promotes violence by males as it teaches men to associate power, dominance, strength, virility and superiority with masculinity. Men use violence in an attempt to maintain a higher status.

6.   To solve violence we must first break the link between violence and masculinity, possibly through educational programs in schools, churches, homes and the media.

IV. The Changing Face of Politics

A.   Despite the gains U.S. women have made in recent elections, they continue to be underrepresented in political office, especially in higher office. There are different factors that contribute to this pattern.

1.   Women are still underrepresented in law and business, the careers from which most politicians are drawn.

2.   Women do not see themselves as a voting block that needs political action to overcome discrimination.

3.   Most women find the roles of mother and politician incompatible.

4.   Males seldom incorporate women into the centers of decision making or present them as viable candidates.

B.   Trends in the 1990s indicate that women do participate in political life in greater numbers than in the past. Indicators that things will change include more women going into careers in law and business, traveling and establishing wider networks of support, and the fact that child care is increasingly seen as the mutual responsibility of both parents.

C.   As women play a fuller role in society, the structural obstacles to women's participation will give way. Relationships between men and women will change and certain distinctions between the sexes will disappear. The goal is greater appreciation of sexual differences coupled with increased equality of opportunity.

INEQUALITIES OF AGING
V. Aging in a Global Perspective

A.   Every society must deal with the process of people aging.

1.   The Tiwi have a custom of "covering up" aged women who have become too feeble to look after themselves. They dig a hole, place the elderly woman in the hole, cover her body with dirt, and then leave her to die. In their culture, when the women eventually dies it is from natural causes—she has died because she is too old and frail to dig herself out of the hole and survive.

2.   In Abkhasia (a remote agricultural region in the former Soviet Union), the people commonly live to be 100, or even older. Possible reasons for their longevity include diet and eating customs (overeating is considered dangerous); lifelong physical activity (they don't begin to slow down until age 98); and social integration (the elderly are active, valued, contributing members of the society, never isolated from family and community).

3.   This reveals an important sociological principle, that aging is socially constructed. Attitudes towards aging are rooted in society and therefore differ from one social group to the next.

B.   In industrialized nations, life expectancy increases because of a more plentiful food supply, a safer water supply and the control of certain diseases.

1.   As the elderly population increases, so does the cost of meeting their particular needs; this has become a major social issue in the Most Industrialized Nations as the young face a growing tax burden to pay for benefits to the elderly.

2.   In the Least Industrialized Nations, there are no social security taxes and families are expected to take care of their own elderly.

C.   The graying of America refers to the proportion of older persons in the U.S. population. Almost 13 percent of the population has achieved age 65.

1.   The maximum length of life, the life span, has not increased.

VI.   The Symbolic Interactionist Perspective

A.   **Robert Butler** coined the term **ageism** to refer to prejudice, discrimination, and hostility directed at people because of their age.

B.   In U.S. society today, the general image of old age is negative, but researchers have found that at one time, old age had some positive meanings.

1.   Few made it to old age, so those who did were respected.

2.   In the days before Social Security provided for retirement, the elderly worked and were seen as wise and knowledgeable about work skills.

3.   Industrialization eroded traditional bases of respect. With improved sanitation and health care, living to an old age was no longer unique. The mystique that the elderly possess superior knowledge was stripped away by mass education.

4.   The aging baby boom generation, because of their size and their better financial standing, will very likely contribute to more positive symbols of aging.

VII.   The Functionalist Perspective

A.   Functionalists examine age from the standpoint of how those persons who are retiring and those who will replace them in the work force make mutual adjustments.

B.   **Elaine Cumming** and **William Henry** developed disengagement theory to explain how society prevents disruption to society when the elderly retire.

1.   The elderly are rewarded (pensions) for giving up positions rather than waiting until they become incompetent or die; this allows for a smooth transition of positions.

2.   This is criticized because it assumes that the elderly disengage and then sink into oblivion. There is evidence that the elderly actually exchange one set of social roles for another; the new role is centered on friendship.

C.   Activity theory examines people's reactions to this exchange of one set of roles for another. Older people who maintain a high level of activity tend to be more satisfied with life than those who do not. Level of activity is connected to key factors such as social class, health, and individual orientation.

VIII. The Conflict Perspective

A. Conflict theorists examine social life as a struggle between groups for scarce resources. Social Security legislation is an example of that struggle.

    1. In the 1920s-30s, two-thirds of all citizens over 65 had no savings and could not support themselves. Francis Townsend enrolled one-third of all Americans over 65 in clubs that sought a national sales tax to finance a monthly pension for all Americans over age 65. To avoid the plan without appearing to be opposed to old-age pensions, Social Security was enacted by Congress.

    2. Conflict theorists state that Social Security was not a result of generosity, but rather of competition among interest groups.

B. Since equilibrium is only a temporary balancing of social forces, some form of continuing conflict between the young and the old appears inevitable.

    1. The huge costs of Social Security have become a national concern. The dependency ratio (number of workers compared with number of recipients) is currently four working-age Americans paying to support each person over 65.

    2. Some argue that the needs of the elderly and of children are on a collision course. Data indicate that as the number of elderly poor decreased, the number of children in poverty increased. It has been argued that the comparison is misleading because the money that went to the elderly did not come from money intended for the children. Framing the issue in this way is an attempt to divide the working class, and to force a choice between the needs of children and those of the elderly.

KEY TERMS

After studying the chapter, review each of the following terms.

activity theory: the view that satisfaction during old age is related to a person's level and quality of activity (p. 283)

age cohort: people born at roughly the same time who pass through the life course together (p. 282)

continuity theory: How people adjust to retirement by continuing aspects of their lives, such as roles or coping techniques (p. 284)

dependency ratio: the ratio of the number of workers required to support dependent persons, those 65 and over and those 15 and under and others who may be on Social Security, Medicaid, or other government supported programs (p. 285)

disengagement theory: the view that society prevents disruption by having the elderly vacate (or disengage from) their positions of responsibility so the younger generation can step into their shoes (p. 282)

feminism: the philosophy that men and women should be politically, economically, and socially equal; organized activity on behalf of this principle (p. 264)

gender: the behavior and attitudes that a society considers proper for its males and females; masculinity or femininity (p. 256)

gender stratification: males' and females' unequal access to power, prestige, and property on the basis of their sex (p. 256)

glass ceiling: the invisible barrier that prevents women from reaching the executive suite (p. 271)

glass escalator: allows men to be given higher level positions and more desirable work assignments (p. 272)

graying of America: refers to the growing proportion of older people in the U.S. population (p. 278)

life expectancy: the number of years that an average newborn can expect to live to (p. 278)

life span: the maximum possible length of the life of a species (p. 280)

patriarchy: a society or group in which men dominate women; authority is invested in males (p. 262)

sex: biological characteristics that distinguish females and males, consisting of primary and secondary sex characteristics (p. 256)

sexual harassment: the abuse of one's position of authority to force unwanted sexual demands on someone (p. 272)

KEY PEOPLE

Review the major theoretical contributions or research findings of these theorists and thinkers.

Robert Butler: Butler coined the term "ageism" to refer to prejudice, discrimination and hostility directed against people because of their age.

Janet Chafetz: Chafetz studied the second wave of feminism in the 1960s, noting that as large numbers of women began to work in the economy, they began to compare their working conditions with those of men.

Elaine Cumming and William Henry: These two developed disengagement theory to explain how society prevents disruption when the elderly vacate their positions of responsibility.

Frederick Engels: Engels was a colleague of Karl Marx and wrote a book about the origins of the family in which he argued that male dominance developed with the origin of private property.

Sue Fisher: Fisher's participatory observation in a hospital uncovered evidence of doctors' recommending unnecessary surgery for female patients.

Rex Fuller and Richard Schoenberger: These economists examined the starting salaries of business majors and found that women averaged 11 percent lower pay than men right out of college, and that the gap grew to 14 percent after five years in the workforce.

Marvin Harris: This anthropologist suggested that male dominance grew out of the greater physical strength that men had which made them better suited for the hand-to-hand combat of tribal societies; women became the reward to entice men into battle.

Charles Hart: An anthropologist who did his field work during the 1920s among the Tiwi of Tunisia.

Dorothy Jerrome: This anthropologist is critical of disengagement theory, pointing out that it contains implicit bias against old people.

Gerda Lerner: Lerner suggested that patriarchy may have had different origins in different places around the world.

Meredith Minkler and Ann Robertson: These conflict sociologists investigated whether or not the government expenditures allocated for the elderly were at the expense of children and found there was no evidence of that.

Alice Rossi: This feminist sociologist has suggested that women are better prepared biologically for "mothering" than are men.

Diana Scully: Scully did research on physicians' attitudes towards female patients.

Christine Williams: Williams found that men in nontraditional careers and occupations often experience a glass escalator—moving more quickly than women into desirable work assignments, higher-level positions, and larger salaries.

SELF-TEST
After completing this self-test, check your answers in the Answer Key of this Study Guide.

MULTIPLE CHOICE QUESTIONS

1.   Males' and females' unequal access to power, prestige, and property is:
   a.   age stratification.
   b.   gender stratification.
   c.   class stratification.
   d.   economic stratification.

2.   The sociological significance of gender is that:
   a.   it is a biological given that socialization cannot change.
   b.   it is one way society controls its members.
   c.   it provides new members for society.
   d.   it provides the most important social roles.

3.   The physical distinctions between males and females that are not directly connected with reproduction are:
   a.   primary sex characteristics.
   b.   secondary sex characteristics.
   c.   sex.
   d.   gender.

4.   The term "sex" refers to:
   a.   the social characteristics that a society considers proper for its males and females.
   b.   the biological characteristics that distinguish females and males.
   c.   masculinity and femininity.
   d.   all of the above.

5.   Following a 1963 medical accident in which a male twin's penis was burned off and he was then raised as a girl:
   a.   she (he) adjusted well to the feminine role and eventually married a man.
   b.   she (he) lived her life comfortably and happily as a female with minor setbacks.

c.   she (he) rejected the feminine role, reverted back to a man, and eventually married a woman.

d.   she (he) began rejecting the feminine role by age three.

6.   Sociologists refer to women as a minority group because:
a.   they make up less than half of the United States population.
b.   the women's movement has made their problems obvious.
c.   they earn less than men.
d.   minorities are discriminated against on the basis of physical or cultural characteristics.

7.   A study of Vietnam veterans, begun in 1985, involved the measurement of testosterone and showed that the men with higher testosterone levels:
a.   tended to be less aggressive.
b.   tended to not have trouble with their parents.
c.   tended not to become delinquents.
d.   tended to have more sexual partners.

8.   Patriarchy means that:
a.   women dominate society.
b.   men dominate society.
c.   children dominate society.
d.   the elderly dominate society.

9.   *Which* of the following is not true regarding the status of women in early United States society?
a.   Women could not serve on juries or hold public office.
b.   A husband and wife were legally one person—HIM.
c.   Women could not hold property in their own name.
d.   Women could not be called to testify in court.

10.   The view that biology is not destiny and that stratification by gender is wrong and should be resisted is:
a.   testosterone world.
b.   lesbianism.
c.   feminism.
d.   none of the above.

11.   The "second wave" of the women's movement began in:
a.   the 1960's.
b.   the early 20th century.
c.   last year.
d.   none of the above

12.   The "wave" of the women's movement that is apparently switching focus from emphasizing equal opportunity for women to values that underlie work and social institutions is:
a.   destined to fail.
b.   minimizing the factor of power.
c.   the "second wave."
d.   the "third wave."

13. Which of the following is not a true statements regarding women and men in higher education (in the United States)?
    a. Women earn over half of all bachelor's degrees.
    b. Males outnumber females at the undergraduate level.
    c. Women are less likely than men to complete a doctorate degree.
    d. Women are less likely to be full professors than men.

14. The figure in the text that examines "professional degrees" shows that the greatest change for women has been the significant increase in:
    a. agronomy degrees.
    b. biology degrees.
    c. sociology degrees.
    d. dentistry degrees.

15. Regarding gender inequality and health care, surgical sexism is reinforced by the powerful motive of:
    a. greed.
    b. distribution of placebos.
    c. equality of opportunity.
    d. none of the above.

16. Sociologists use the term "quiet revolution" to refer to the increasing number of women:
    a. in graduate programs.
    b. in major professions.
    c. holding public office.
    d. in the paid work force.

17. Besides gender discrimination, the largest factor in the gender pay gap seems to be:
    a. the proportions of each gender finishing college.
    b. the fact that women are the primary caretakers of their children.
    c. differences in the career choices made by each gender.
    d. the kinds of entry level positions for which each gender applies.

18. The mostly invisible barrier that keeps women from reaching the executive suites is:
    a. the glass elevator.
    b. the glass ceiling.
    c. higher grades and fewer internships.
    d. lower grades and more internships.

19. The "motor" that drives the glass escalator is:
    a. "acting like men."
    b. the glass ceiling.
    c. pay.
    d. gender.

20. Mark took a job in a home decorating company, a traditionally female occupation. He rose rapidly to a leadership position, bypassing several females with more experience. His promotion illustrates:
    a. sexual harassment.
    b. the glass ceiling.

c.   the glass escalator.
d.   the daddy track.

21.   All *except one* of the following are reasons why people live longer in industrial societies. Which one should not be included?
    a.   Fighting disease effectively.
    b.   Having a plentiful food supply.
    c.   Purifying the water supply.
    d.   Performing regular physical fitness.

22.   The increasing proportion of older people in the United States has been referred to as the:
    a.   aging revolution.
    b.   graying of America.
    c.   new old.
    d.   geriatric generation.

23.   Although more people are living to an old age, the maximum length of life possible, the _____ has not increased.
    a.   life span
    b.   geriatric age limit
    c.   life expectancy
    d.   none of the above

24.   Robert Butler coined the term _____ to refer to prejudice, discrimination, and hostility directed against people because of their age.
    a.   prejudice
    b.   discrimination
    c.   ageism
    d.   oldism

25.   People who were born at roughly the same time and who pass through the life course together are known as:
    a.   peer groups.
    b.   age cohorts.
    c.   peer cohorts.
    d.   age groups.

26.   Disengagement theory is based on what theoretical perspective?
    a.   Functionalism.
    b.   Exchange.
    c.   Conflict.
    d.   Symbolic interactionism.

27.   Activity theory assumes that the _____ activities elderly people engage in, the more they find life satisfying.
    a.   more
    b.   less
    c.   the higher the quality of
    d.   none of the above

28. The basic criticism of continuity theory is that it is too:
    a. simplistic.
    b. broad.
    c. general.
    d. complex.

29. Conflict theorists argue that some form of conflict seems inevitable between the elderly and the young because:
    a. people protect their own interests.
    b. medicine keeps people alive longer.
    c. the number of people who collect Social Security is growing.
    d. the elderly are wealthier than young workers.

30. The _____ ratio is the number of people who collect social security compared with the number of workers who contribute to it.
    a. social security
    b. dependency
    c. inequality
    d. retirement

TRUE-FALSE QUESTIONS

T F 1. The terms "sex" and "gender" basically mean the same thing to sociologists.
T F 2. Primary sex characteristics are the physical distinctions between males and females that are not directly connected with reproduction.
T F 3. Secondary sex characteristics become clearly evident at puberty.
T F 4. Sociologist Alice Rossi has argued that women are better prepared for mothering than men.
T F 5. Women are considered to be a minority group because there are fewer women than men in the United States.
T F 6. The major theory of patriarchy points to the social consequences of human reproduction.
T F 7. Frederick Engels argued that patriarchy developed with the origin of private property.
T F 8. Feminists known as "radical" founded the National Women's Party in 1916.
T F 9. In the United States, women's rights were gained by a prolonged and bitter struggle.
T F 10. There is no gender inequality in the area of education.
T F 11. Much of the gender inequality in healthcare seems to be unintentional.
T F 12. The quiet revolution is another word for women achieving full equality with men in the workforce.
T F 13. Women current earn 70 percent of what men are paid.
T F 14. Out of the top 500 corporations, more than half are headed by women.
T F 15. One reason the glass ceiling is so powerful is that women lack mentors.
T F 16. Men in traditionally female oriented jobs experience the glass escalator.
T F 17. Females are more likely to be victims of violence than males.
T F 18. Life expectancy and life span describe the same thing.

T F 19. Disengagement theory is used to explain how society prevents disruption by having the elderly vacate their positions of responsibility.

T F 20. According to conflict theorists, the issue of social security is a good example of the struggle between the young and old in the United States.

FILL-IN QUESTIONS

1. _____ refers to biological characteristics that distinguish females and males and consists of primary and secondary sex characteristics.
2. Around the world, _____ is the primary division between people.
3. Some sociologists argue that _____ factors are involved in some human behavior.
4. Social factors in life include _____, _____, and _____.
5. Patriarchy was/is attributed to warfare and physical strength by anthropologist _____.
6. Women won the right to vote, in the United States, in _____.
7. Men in non-traditional jobs often ride the _____ to more desirable work assignments, higher-level positions, and larger salaries.
8. United States women who work full time average only _____% of what men are paid.
9. The maximum length of life is referred to as the _____.
10. The term _____ of America refers to the increasing proportion of older people.
11. _____ is the discrimination against people because of their age.
12. People who are born at roughly the same time and who pass through the life course together are considered a(n) _____.
13. The original social security legislation required people to retire at age _____.
14. The number of people it now takes to support one person on social security is _____.
15. Social Security and _____ have become national concerns.

MATCH EACH CONCEPT WITH ITS DEFINITION

1. Dependency ratio
2. Ageism
3. Life span
4. Life expectancy
5. Sexual harassment
6. Glass escalator
7. Glass ceiling
8. Feminism
9. Patriarchy
10. Gender

a. *Social traits for males and females*
b. *Biology is not destiny*
c. *Men dominate women*
d. *Women don't get to the executive suite*
e. *Unwelcome sexual attention*
f. *Number of years people can expect to live*
g. *Prejudice against older people*
h. *Maximum length of life possible*
i. *stereotype that someone is male and, therefore, more capable*
j. *number of workers needed to support one social security recipient*

ESSAY QUESTIONS

1. Summarize the sociobiology argument concerning behavioral differences between men and women. Explain which position most closely reflects your own: biological, sociological, or sociobiological.
2. Compare and contrast the two waves of the feminist movement in this country by identifying the forces that contributed to both waves.
3. Discuss why women are so often the victims of violence.
4. Explain why sociologists say that aging is socially constructed.
5. Choose one of the three different sociological perspectives and discuss how that perspective approaches the subject of aging. Consider both the strengths and weaknesses of the perspective you chose.

STUDENT PROJECTS

1. Your text discusses a variety of potential circumstances surrounding the issue of gender inequality. Look around you. Do you see everyday instances of gender inequality? Explain one example that you have observed or heard about.

2. After reading about the Social Security system, list some of the problems with the current system. What do you think of the proposed recommendations for solving the crisis? Would you support them? Why or why not?

3. In this chapter you read about how the media shapes our image(s) of older people. Think about people you know who are over 60 years of age. How does the reality of their lives fit with the images of older people that are presented in movies, advertisements, and television? Explain and compare.

CHAPTER 11

POLITICS AND THE ECONOMY

CHAPTER SUMMARY

- **Authority** refers to the legitimate use of power, while **coercion** is viewed as the unjust, illegitimate use of power. The state is a political entity that claims a monopoly on the use of violence over a particular territory. **Max Weber** identified three types of authority—traditional, rational-legal, and charismatic. The orderly transfer of authority at the death, resignation, or incapacitation of a leader is critical for social stability.

- Three forms of government are **monarchies** (power is based on hereditary rule), **democracies** (power is given by the citizens), and **dictatorships** (power is seized by an individual or a small group).

- In the United States, with its winner-takes-all electoral system, the two main political parties must appeal to the center, and minority parties make little headway. The more people feel they have a stake in the political system, the more likely they are to vote. Special interest groups, with their lobbyists and PACs, play a significant role in U.S. politics.

- Functionalists and conflict theorists have very different views on who rules the United States. According to the functionalists, no one group holds power; instead competing interest groups balance one another (pluralism). According to conflict theorists, the United States is governed by a ruling class composed of members drawn from the elite (power elite).

- The earliest hunting and gathering societies were characterized by subsistence economies; economic systems became more complex as people discovered how to cultivate (horticultural and pastoral societies), farm (agricultural societies) and manufacture (industrial societies). Trade resulted from the emergence of a surplus; one outcome of trade was the creation of social inequality, as some people began to accumulate more than others.

- The two major economic systems are **capitalism**, in which the means of production are privately owned, and **socialism**, in which the means of production are state owned. In recent years, each of these systems has adopted features of the other.

- The term **corporate capitalism** is used to describe the economic dominance by giant corporations. Those in the inner circle are intent on making sure that corporate capitalism is protected; the interests of this inner circle exist beyond national boundaries.

- There are indications that a new world order is developing as communications, transportation, and trade expands globally. For human welfare, the consequences of this transformation is still unclear; predictions range from excellent to calamitous.

LEARNING OBJECTIVES
As you read Chapter 11, use these learning objectives to organize your notes. After completing your reading, you should be able to answer each of the objectives.

1. Distinguish between power, authority, and coercion, and discuss the role of the state in the exercise of legitimate violence.
2. Describe the sources of authority identified by Weber, and explain how the orderly transfer of authority is achieved under each type or authority.
3. Differentiate between monarchies, democracies, and dictatorships and oligarchies.
4. Explain the nature of the two-party system in the United States and consider why third parties do poorly within this system.

5. Describe American voting patterns, identify the groups most and least likely to vote in elections, and explain the social factors behind these patterns.
6. Analyze the ways in which special-interest groups influence the political process.
7. Distinguish between the functionalist and conflict perspectives on how the U.S. political process operates, and compare the power elite perspective of C. Wright Mills with William Domhoff's ruling class theory.
8. Know Timasheff's seven fuels for war and understand the nature of terrorism.
9. Trace the transformation of economic systems through each historical stage and state the degree to which social inequality existed in each economy.
10. Discuss some of the "ominous" economic trends in the United States.
11. State the essential features of capitalism and of socialism and explain why neither exists in its "pure" form.
12. Identify the ideologies behind capitalism and socialism.
13. State the criticisms of capitalism and of socialism, describe the recent changes in socialist economies, and explain why some theorists believe the two systems are converging.
14. Define corporate capitalism, corporations, interlocking directorates, and multinational corporations, and discuss the role each plays in the global economy.
15. Explain why some theorists believe that there is a possibility that global political and economic unity could come about.

CHAPTER OUTLINE

POLITICS: ESTABLISHING LEADERSHIP
I.   Power, Authority, and Violence

A. **Max Weber** noted that power—the ability to get your way, even over the resistance of others—can be either legitimate or illegitimate. **Authority** is legitimate power that people accept as right, while **coercion** is power that people do not accept as just.

B. The **state** is the source of legitimate force or violence in society; violence is the ultimate foundation of political order. The ultimate proof of the state's authority is that the state can kill someone because he or she has done something which is considered absolutely horrible; an individual can't do the same without facing consequences.

C. The first source of authority, as identified by Weber, is **traditional authority**. Based on custom, this type of authority is prevalent in preliterate groups where custom sets relationships. When society changes, traditional authority is undermined, but does not die, even in postindustrial societies. For example, parental authority is a traditional authority.

D. **Rational-legal authority**, based on written rules (also called bureaucratic authority), is the second source of authority that Weber identified. It derives from the position an individual holds, not from the person. Everyone (no matter how high the office) is subject to the rules.

E. **Charismatic authority** is the third source of authority that Weber identified. It is based on an individual's ability to attract followers and may pose a threat to because charismatic leaders work outside the established political system and may threaten it. Authorities are often quick to oppose this type of leader.

F. Orderly transfer of authority upon the death, resignation, or incapacity of a leader is critical for stability. Succession is more of a problem with charismatic authority than with traditional or rational-legal authority. *Routinization of charisma* refers to the transfer of authority from a charismatic leader to either traditional or rational-legal authority.

II. Types of Government

A. As cities developed, each city-state (an independent city whose power radiated outward, bringing adjacent areas under its rule) had its own **monarchy**, a type of government headed by a king or queen.

    1. As city-states warred with one another, the victors would extend their rule, and eventually cover an entire region.

    2. As the size of these regions grew, people developed identification with the region; over time, this gave rise to the state.

B. A **democracy** is a government whose authority is derived from the people.

    1. Direct democracy (voters meet to discuss issues and make decisions) existed 2,000 years ago in Athens. This type of democracy was appropriate in small communities.

    2. Representative democracy (voters elect representatives to govern and make decisions on their behalf) emerged as the United State became more populated, making direct democracy impossible. This concept was revolutionary; its implementation meant the reversal of traditional ideas because the government was to be responsive to the people's wishes, not the people to the wishes of the government.

    3. Today, citizenship (the idea that citizens have basic rights) is taken for granted in the U.S. Universal citizenship (everyone having the same basic rights) came into practice very slowly and only through fierce struggle.

C. **Dictatorship** is government where power is seized and held by an individual; oligarchy results when a small group of individuals seizes power. Dictators and oligarchies can be totalitarian; when the government exercises almost total control of a people

III. The U.S. Political System

A. The **Democratic** and **Republican** parties had emerged by the time of the Civil War.

    1. The Democrats are often associated with the poor and working class and the Republicans with people who are financially better off.

    2. Since each party appeals to a broad membership it is difficult to distinguish conservative Democrats from liberal Republicans; however, it is easy to discern the extremes. Those elected to Congress may cross party lines because, although office-holders support their party's philosophy, they do not necessarily support all of its specific proposals.

    3. Despite their differences, both parties support the fundamentals of U.S. society such as freedom of religion, free public education, and capitalism.

    4. Third parties do play a role in U.S. politics, although generally they receive little public support. Ross Perot's "United We Stand" party was one exception.

B. Year after year Americans show consistent voting patterns.

    1. U.S. voting patterns are consistent: the percentage of people who vote increases as they age. In addition, whites are more likely to vote than African Americans or Asian Americans, while Latinos are considerably less likely to vote than either. Those with higher levels of education are more likely to vote, as are people with higher levels of income, and females are slightly more likely to vote in presidential elections than are males.

    2. The more that people feel they have a stake in the system, the more likely they are to vote. Those who have been rewarded by the system are more socially

integrated and perceive that elections directly affect their lives and the society in which they live.

3.   People who gain less from the system in terms of education, income, and jobs are more likely to be alienated.

4.   Voter apathy is indifference/inaction to the political process. As a result of apathy, half of all eligible American voters do not vote for president; two-thirds of eligible voters do not vote for members of Congress.

C.   **Special-interest groups** are people who think alike on a particular issue and can be mobilized for political action.

1.   *Lobbyists* are people who try to influence legislation on behalf of their clients; they have become a major force in politics. In an effort to curb the influence of lobbyists, Congress passed legislation in the 1970s that set limits on the amount of money special-interest groups can donate to political candidates.

2.   *Political action committees (PACs)* solicit and spend funds to influence legislation and bypass laws intended to limit the amount any individual, corporation, or group can give a candidate. PACs have become a powerful influence, bankrolling lobbyists and legislators, and those PACs with the most clout gain the ear of Congress.

D.   The major criticism against lobbyists and PACs is that their money buys votes. Rather than representing the people who elected them, legislators support the special interests of groups able to help them stay in power.

IV.   Who Rules the United States?

A.   The functionalists say that **pluralism**—the diffusion of power among interest groups—prevents any one group from gaining control of the government. Functionalists believe this helps keep the government from turning against its citizens.

1.   To balance the interests of competing groups, the founders of the U.S. system of government created a system of checks and balances. Separation of powers among the three branches of government ensures that each is able to nullify the actions of the other two, thus preventing the domination of any single branch.

2.   According to this perspective, each group within society pursues its own interests and is balanced by other groups pursuing theirs. As groups negotiate with one another and reach compromises, conflict is minimized.

B.   According to the conflict perspective, lobbyists, and even Congress, are not at the center of decision making. Rather, members of the power elite make the decisions that direct the country and shake the world.

1.   As stated by **C. Wright Mills**, the power elite (heads of leading corporations, powerful generals and admirals in the armed forces, and certain elite politicians) rule the United States. The power elite views capitalism as essential to the welfare of the country; thus, business interests come first.

2.   According to **William Domhoff**, the ruling class (the wealthiest and most powerful individuals in the country) runs the United States. Its members control the U.S.'s top corporations and foundations; presidential cabinet members and top ambassadors to the most powerful countries are chosen from this group. They promote the view that these positions come through merit and that everyone has a chance of becoming rich.

3.   The ruling class does not act in complete unity; the interests of one segment may conflict with those of another. But at the same time, the members generally see eye to eye for they have a mutual interest in solving the problems of business.

C.   While the functionalist and conflict views of power in U.S. society cannot be reconciled, it is possible to employ both. The middle level of C. Wright Mills' model best reflects the functionalist view of competing interests holding each other at bay. At the top is an elite that follows its special interests, as conflict theorists suggest.

V. War and Terrorism: Ways of Implementing Political Objectives

A.   The state uses violence to protect citizens from individuals and groups, sometimes turning violence against other nations. War (armed conflict between nations or politically distinct groups) often is a part of national policy.

B.   Nicholas Timasheff identified three essential conditions of war.

    1.   There is a cultural tradition of war; because they have fought wars in the past, leaders see war as an option.

    2.   An antagonistic situation exists, with two or more states confronting incompatible objectives.

    3.   A "fuel" heats the antagonistic situation to the boiling point so that people move from thinking about war to engaging in it; Timasheff identified seven fuels including revenge, power, prestige, unity, position, ethnicity, and beliefs.

C.   War has an effect on morality.

    1.   Exposure to brutality and killing often causes dehumanization (reducing people to objects that do not deserve to be treated as humans).

    2.   Characteristics of dehumanization include (1) increased emotional distance from others; (2) an emphasis on following procedures; (3) inability to resist pressures; and (4) a diminished sense of personal responsibility.

    3.   Tamotsu Shibutani stressed that dehumanization is helped along by the tendency for prolonged conflicts to be transformed into a struggle between good and evil.

    4.   Dehumanization does not always insulate the self from guilt; after the war ends, returning soldiers often find themselves disturbed by what they did during the war. Although most eventually adjust, some live with the guilt forever.

D.   Today, terrorism directed against civilian populations is a fact of life.

    1.   Suicide terrorism is one of the few options available to a weaker group that wants to retaliate against a powerful country.

    2.   The real danger is from nuclear, chemical, and biological weapons that could be unleashed against civilian populations.

THE ECONOMY: WORK IN THE GLOBAL VILLAGE
VI. The Transformation of Economic Systems

A.   The **economy** is a system of producing and distributing goods and services. It has evolved over time from preindustrial, to industrial, to postindustrial.

B.   The transformation of preindustrial societies, from hunting-and-gathering to agricultural, was accompanied by growing inequality.

    1.   Earliest hunting and gathering societies had subsistence economies characterized by little trade with other groups, and a high degree of social equality.

    2.   In pastoral and horticultural economies, people created more dependable food supplies. The creation of a surplus allowed groups to grow in size, settle in a single place, develop a specialized division of labor, and trade with other groups, all of which fostered social inequality.

    3.   Agricultural economies brought even greater surpluses, magnifying prior trends toward social, political and economic inequality. More people were freed from food production, a more specialized division of labor developed, and trade expanded.

C.   The surplus (and greater inequality) grew in industrial societies. As the surplus increased, emphasis changed from the production to the consumption of goods (**Thorstein Veblen** coined the term *conspicuous consumption*).

D.   The emergence of a new type of society, called the **postindustrial society,** was noted by **Daniel Bell** in 1973.

    1.   According to Bell, postindustrial economies have six traits: (1) a service sector so large that it employs the majority of workers; (2) a large surplus of goods; (3) even more extensive trade among nations; (4) a wide variety and amount of goods available to the average person; (5) an information explosion, and (6) a "global village" with instantaneous, worldwide communications.

    2.   The key to the postindustrial society is the "information explosion" with large numbers of people managing information and designing and servicing products.

    3.   The consequence of this explosion is that the transformation of the world is uneven; some live comfortably while others continue the struggle just to survive.

E.   In recent years some ominous economic trends have emerged within the United States.

    1.   To reduce costs, U.S. firms are downsizing. "Expensive" full-time workers are fired and temporary workers are hired in their place. Firms therefore do not have to spend money on expensive "frills" like vacation pay and retirement benefits.

    2.   Many Americans find their standard of living stagnating or even declining. There has been a net decline in wages and the standard of living (the Great American U-Turn) since the early 1970s.

    3.   Income inequalities continue to plague our society; the distribution of income resembles an inverted pyramid.

    4.   If these trends continue, the United States will become a "two-thirds society". At the top would be the one-third of the population that is well-educated and securely employed. The middle third would be the working class, insecure in their jobs, earning more-or-less adequate income. At the bottom would be the unemployed and the underemployed.

VII. World Economic Systems

A.   **Capitalism** has three essential features: (1) the private ownership of the means of production; (2) the pursuit of profit; and (3) market competition.

    1.   Pure (laissez-faire) capitalism exists only when market forces are able to operate without interference from the government.

    2.   The United States today has welfare (or state) capitalism. Private citizens own the means of production and pursue profits, but do so within a vast system of laws designed to protect the public welfare (market restraints).

B.   **Socialism** also has three essential features: (1) the public ownership of the means of production; (2) central planning; and (3) the distribution of goods without a profit motive.

    1.   Under socialism, the government owns the means of production, and a central committee determines what the country needs instead of allowing supply and demand to control production and prices.

    2.   Socialism is designed to eliminate competition, to produce goods for the general welfare, and to distribute them according to people's needs, not their ability to pay.

    3.   Socialism does not exist in pure form. Although the ideology of socialism calls for resources to be distributed according to need rather than position, socialist nations have found it necessary to offer higher salaries for some jobs in order to entice people to take greater responsibilities.

    4.   Some nations (e.g., Sweden and Denmark) have adopted democratic or welfare socialism: both the state and individuals engage in production and distribution

although the state owns certain industries (steel, mining, forestry, telephones, television stations, and airlines) while retail stores, farms, and most service industries remain in private hands.

C.   Capitalism and socialism represent distinct ideologies.

    1.   Capitalists believe that market forces should determine both products and prices, and that it is good for people to strive for profits.

    2.   Socialists believe that profit is immoral and represents excess value extracted from workers.

    3.   Each ideology sees the other as a system of exploitation: capitalists that socialists violate basic human rights (freedom of decision and opportunity); and socialists that capitalists violate basic human rights (freedom from poverty).

D.   The primary criticism of capitalism is that it leads to social inequality (a top layer of wealthy, powerful people, and a bottom layer of people who are unemployed or underemployed). Socialism has been criticized for not respecting individual rights, or being capable of producing much wealth (thus the greater equality of socialism is actually that almost everyone has an equal chance of being poor).

E.   As societies industrialize, they display comparable divisions of labor, emphasis on higher education, and a trend towards extensive urbanization. According to convergence theory, as both capitalists and socialist systems adopt features of the other, the result may be the emergence of a hybrid or mixed economy.

VIII.   Capitalism in a Global Economy

A.   The **corporation** (joint ownership of a business enterprise whose liabilities are separate from those of its owners) has changed the face of capitalism.

    1.   *Corporate capitalism* refers to the domination of the economic system by giant corporations. One of the most significant aspects of large corporations is the separation of ownership and management, producing ownership of wealth without appreciable control, and control of wealth without appreciable ownership.

    2.   Because of the dispersion of ownership, a power vacuum is created. Often, stockholders will simply rubber-stamp management's recommendations at annual stockholders' meetings. However, a stockholders' revolt (stockholders of a corporation refusing to rubber stamp decisions made by management) is likely to occur if the profits do not meet expectations.

B.   **Interlocking directorates** occur when individuals serve as directors of several companies, concentrating power and minimizing competition.

C.   As corporations outgrow national boundaries, the creation of **multinational corporations** results.

    1.   As multinationals move investments and production from one part of the globe to another in search of greater profits, there is a flood of low-priced consumer goods.

    2.   This comes at a cost as millions of U.S. jobs are lost, while workers in the Least Industrialized Nations are exploited and their environments polluted.

D.   A New World Order?

New technologies underlay the globalization of capitalism, creating a worldwide flow of information, capital, and goods. New alliances among nations have emerged, creating new possibilities for world peace.

    1.   As the power of multinationals continue to grow, their elites become more interconnected, forging partnerships with national elites. The end result may be that the multinationals and their new trade agreements will become a force for

peace, but the price may be high if it means that the new world order is dominated by a handful of the world's top corporate leaders.

KEY TERMS

After studying the chapter, review each of the following terms.

anarchy: a condition of lawlessness or political disorder caused by the absence or collapse of governmental authority (p. 300)

authority: power that people consider as legitimate, as rightly exercised over them; also called legitimate power (p. 292)

capitalism: an economic system characterized by the private ownership of the means of production, the pursuit of profit, and market competition (p. 313)

charismatic authority: authority based on an individual's outstanding traits, which attract followers (p. 293)

checks and balances: separation of powers among the three branches of U.S. government—legislative, executive, and judicial—so that each is able to nullify the actions of the others, thus preventing the domination of any single branch (p. 300)

citizenship: the concept that birth (and residence) in a country impart basic rights (p. 295)

city-state: an independent city whose power radiates outward, bringing the adjacent area under its rule (p. 295)

coercion: power that people do not accept as rightly exercised over them; also called illegitimate power (p. 292)

conspicuous consumption: Thorstein Veblen's term for a change from the Protestant ethic to an eagerness to show off wealth by the elaborate consumption of goods (p. 305)

convergence theory: the view that as both capitalist and socialist economic systems adopt features of the other, a hybrid (or mixed) economic system will emerge (p. 315)

corporate capitalism: the domination of the economic system by giant corporations (p. 316)

corporation; the joint ownership of a business enterprise whose liabilities and obligations are separate from those of its owners (p. 316)

dehumanization: the process of reducing people to objects that do not deserve to be treated as humans (p. 302)

democracy: a system of government in which authority derives from the people; the term comes from two Greek words that translate literally as "power to the people" (p. 295)

democratic socialism: a hybrid economic system in which capitalism is mixed with state ownership (p. 314)

dictatorship: a form of government in which power is seized by an individual (p. 296)

direct democracy: a form of democracy in which the eligible voters meet to discuss issues and make decisions (p. 295)

economy: a system of distribution of goods and services (p. 305)

interlocking directorates: individuals serving on the board of directors of several companies (p. 316)

laissez-faire capitalism: unrestrained manufacture and trade (literally "hands off" capitalism) (p. 313)

lobbyists; people who try to influence legislation on behalf of their clients or interest groups (p. 300)

market forces: the law of supply and demand (p. 313)

monarchy: a form of government headed by a king or a queen (p.295)

multinational corporations: companies that operate across many national boundaries, also called transnational corporations (p. 317)

oligarchy: a form of government in which power is held by a small group of individuals; the rule of the many by the few (p. 296)

pluralism: diffusion of power among many interest groups, preventing any single group from gaining control of the government (p. 300)

political action committees (PACs): an organization formed by one or more special-interest groups to solicit and spend funds for the purpose of influencing legislation (p. 300)

power: the ability to get your will, even over the resistance of others (p. 292)

power elite: C. Wright Mills' term for the top leaders of U.S. corporations, the military, and politics who make the nation's major decisions (p. 301)

rational-legal authority: authority based on law or written rules and regulations (also called bureaucratic authority) (p. 293)

representative democracy: a form of democracy in which voters elect representatives to govern and make decisions on their behalf (p. 295)

routinization of charisma: the transfer of authority from a charismatic leader to either a traditional or a rational-legal form of authority (p. 294)

socialism; an economic system characterized by the public ownership of the means of production, central planning, and the distribution of goods without a profit motive (p. 313)

special-interest group: a group of people who have a particular issue in common and can be mobilized for political action (p. 299)

state: a government; the political entity that claims a monopoly on the use of violence within a territory, commonly known as a country (p. 292)

stockholders' revolt: the refusal of a corporation's stockholders to rubber-stamp decisions made by its managers (p. 316)

subsistence economy: a type of economy in which human groups live off the land with little or no surplus (p. 305)

terrorism: the use of violence to produce fear in order to attain political objectives (p. 304)

totalitarianism: a form of government that exerts almost total control over the people (p. 296)

traditional authority: authority based on custom (p. 293)

universal citizenship: the idea that everyone has the same basic rights by virtue of being born in a country (or by immigrating and becoming a naturalized citizen) (p. 295)

voter apathy: indifference and inaction on the part of individuals or groups with respect to the political process (p. 299)

war: armed conflict between nations or politically distinct groups (p. 302)

welfare (or **state**) **capitalism**: an economic system in which individuals own the means of production but the state regulates many economic activities for the welfare of the population
(p. 313)

KEY PEOPLE

Review the major theoretical contributions or research findings of these theorists and thinkers.

Daniel Bell: Bell identified six characteristic of the postindustrial society.
Peter Berger: Berger argued that violence is the ultimate foundation of any political order.
William Domhoff: Like Mills, Domhoff saw that power resides in an elite—a group he referred to as the *ruling class*. He focused on the top one percent of Americans who belong to the super-rich, powerful capitalist class.
C.Wright Mills: Mills suggested that power resides in the hands of an elite made up of the top leaders of the largest corporations, the most powerful generals of the armed forces, and certain elite politicians.
Nicholas Timasheff: Sociologist who identified seven "fuels" for why countries go to war.
Michael Useem: Using a conflict perspective, Useem studied the activities of the "inner circle" of corporate executives.
Thorstein Veblen: Veblen created the term "conspicuous consumption" to refer to the eagerness to show off one's wealth through the elaborate consumption of material goods.

Max Weber: Weber identified three different types of authority: traditional, rational-legal, and charismatic.

SELF-TEST

After completing this self-test, check your answers in the Answer Key of this Study Guide.

MULTIPLE CHOICE QUESTIONS

1. Authority is:
   a. legitimate power.
   b. coercion.
   c. power.
   d. persuasion.

2. The ultimate foundation of any political order, according to Berger, is:
   a. lobbying.
   b. violence.
   c. patriarchy.
   d. matriarchy.

3. Traditional authority is based on:
   a. written rules.
   b. personality.
   c. custom.
   d. none of the above.

4. Rational-legal authority is based on:
   a. custom.
   b. personality.
   c. written rules.
   d. gender.

5. Rational-legal authority is sometimes called:
   a. custom.
   b. tradition.
   c. charisma.
   d. bureaucratic authority.

6. Which of the following types of authority is most likely to pose a threat to the established order?
   a. Charismatic
   b. Professorial
   c. Rational-legal
   d. Traditional

7. The transfer of authority from a charismatic leader to either traditional or rational-legal authority is:
   a. bureaucratic procession.
   b. routinization of charisma.

c. discussed by Weber.

d. both "b" and "c" are correct.

8. The political entity that claims a monopoly on the use of violence within a territory is known as a:
   a. city-state.
   b. state.
   c. region.
   d. society.

9. As a society gets more populous and geographically larger, what type of democracy most likely will come into being?
   a. Representative democracy
   b. Direct democracy
   c. A dictatorial democracy
   d. None of the above

10. The relatively new perspective that a person, by virtue of birth and residence, has basic rights is known as:
    a. charismatic authority.
    b. the right to free speech of any kind.
    c. citizenship.
    d. direct democracy.

11. If a small group seizes power, the type of government is called:
    a. a representative democracy.
    b. a dictatorship.
    c. a coup.
    d. an oligarchy.

12. What kind of government tolerates no opposing opinions?
    a. Representative democracy.
    b. Oligarchy.
    c. Totalitarian.
    d. Charismatic.

13. In the United States, in general, voting increases with:
    a. age.
    b. income.
    c. employment.
    d. education.
    e. all of the above.

14. In the United States, large percentages of people (regardless of personal characteristics) do not vote because of:
    a. voter apathy.
    b. lack of transportation to polls.
    c. radical views.
    d. fear of reprisals.

15. In a political system, people who are paid to influence legislation on behalf of their clients are called:

a. dictators.
b. lobbyists.
c. criminals.
d. agents.

16. The major criticism leveled against lobbyists and PACs is that their money, in effect:
a. is worthless.
b. represents totalitarianism.
c. buys votes.
d. enhances charismatic authority.

17. A condition of disorder and violence is:
a. fun.
b. anarchy.
c. democracy.
d. pluralism.

18. Diffusion of power among many interest groups is called:
a. checks and balances.
b. pluralism.
c. traditional authority.
d. both "a" and "b" are correct.

19. C. Wright Mills took the position that most important matters (in the United States) are decided by:
a. a power elite.
b. voters.
c. newly elected members of Congress.
d. only the President.

20. According to conflict theorists, the ruling class:
a. is a group that meets together and agrees on specific matters.
b. is a group which tends to have complete unity on issues.
c. is made up of people whose backgrounds and orientations to life are so similar that they automatically share the same goals.
d. a myth.

21. Which of the following is one of the essential conditions of war as identified by Timasheff?
a. A cultural condition of war
b. An antagonistic situation
c. A "fuel" that heats the antagonistic situation
d. A totalitarian regime

22. The use of violence to create fear to bring about political objectives is:
a. something that has never happened in the United States.
b. terrorism.
c. representative democracy.
d. not used by people who like to think of themselves as "victims".

23. Hunting and gathering societies are characterized by a :
a. market economy.

b. surplus economy.
c. subsistence economy.
d. maintenance economy.

24. The primary sociological significance of surplus and trade is/was to:
a. foster inequality.
b. foster equality.
c. foster terrorism.
d. foster oligarchies and monarchies.

25. Veblen labeled the lavishly wasteful spending of goods designed to enhance social prestige:
a. prestigious consumption.
b. wasteful consumption.
c. conspicuous prestige.
d. conspicuous consumption.

26. Which of the following is not a defining characteristic of postindustrial economies?
a. extensive trade among nations
b. machines powered by fuels
c. a global village
d. a large surplus of goods

27. Private ownership of the means of production is an essential feature of:
a. communism.
b. socialism.
c. democracy.
d. capitalism.

28. The theory that capitalism and socialism will grow more alike as they develop is called:
a. unity theory.
b. convergence theory.
c. amalgamation theory.
d. merger theory.

29. Jointly owning an enterprise, with liabilities and obligations independent of its owners is:
a. an oligopoly.
b. a monopoly.
c. a corporation.
d. an interlocking directorate.

30. The elites who sit on the boards of directors of multiple companies are referred to as:
a. vertical integrators.
b. interlocking trustees.
c. interlocking directorates.
d. oligopolies.

TRUE-FALSE QUESTIONS

T F 1. Coercion refers to legitimate power.
T F 2. The ability to get your own way, even over the resistance of others, is power.

T F   3.   Governments are also called "states."
T F   4.   Traditional authority is the hallmark of tribal groups.
T F   5.   Rational-legal authority is based on personality.
T F   6.   Charismatic authority always has "rules for succession."
T F   7.   Monarchies involve having kings and/or queens as rulers.
T F   8.   Power radiates outward from city-states.
T F   9.   In the past, small tribes and cities were able to practice representative democracy.
T F   10.   Coups are examples of oligarchies.
T F   11.   Food surpluses ushered in social inequality.
T F   12.   One major characteristic of the postindustrial society is the large service sector.
T F   13.   To increase costs, U.S. Firms are downsizing.
T F   14.   U.S. workers today can buy as much with $15 an hour as workers in 1970 could buy with $3 an hour.
T F   15.   The United States economy is an example of pure capitalism.
T F   16.   Profit is not the major goal of socialism.
T F   17.   Both capitalism and socialism do not exist in pure forms.
T F   18.   Stockholder revolts occur frequently in the United States.
T F   19.   Multinational corporations have little power in the global economy.
T F   20.   The world's nations seem to be embracing capitalism.

FILL-IN QUESTIONS

1.   _____, synonymous with government, is the source of legitimate violence in society.
2.   Berger stated that _____ is the ultimate foundation of any political order.
3.   _____ is a form of democracy in which the eligible voters meet to discuss issues and make decisions.
4.   _____ refers to indifference and inaction on the part of individuals or groups with respect to the political process in the United States.
5.   _____ refers to the top people in leading corporations, the most powerful generals and admirals in the armed forces, and certain highest-ranked politicians.
6.   One of the seven fuels for war includes saving the nation's honor, Timasheff identified this as_____.
7.   Exposure to brutality and killing in war often causes_____.
8.   _____ is the term for a system of distribution of goods and services.
9.   A "global village" is one of the most important characteristics of a _____ society.
10.   We may be on the verge of yet another new type of society—one being ushered in by advances in biology, especially the deciphering of the _____.
11.   To reduce costs, U.S. Firms are practicing_____.
12.   "Hands-off" capitalism is known as _____ capitalism.
13.   Unlike capitalism, in which market forces determine prices, a_____ determines supply and demand in a socialist economy.
14.   Sociologists use the term _____ to indicate how corporations now dominate the economy.
15.   The wealthy expand their power through_____; that is they serve as directors of several companies.

MATCH THESE THEORISTS/PHILOSOPHERS WITH THEIR CONTRIBUTIONS

1. Daniel Bell
2. Peter Berger
3. Michael Useem
4. William Domhoff
5. Thorstein Veblen
6. C. Wright Mills
7. Max Weber
8. Terrorism
9. Seymour Lipset
10. Nicholas Timasheff

a. *Use of violence to create fear for political objectives*
b. *created the term "conspicuous consumption"*
c. *the "ruling class"*
d. *three types of authority*
e. *studied activities of the "inner circle"*
f. *identified the characteristics of post-industrial societies*
g. *the "power elite"*
h. *violence is the foundation of the political order*
i. *defined the concept charismatic*
j. *studied the "conditions of war"*

ESSAY QUESTIONS

1. Summarize both the functionalist and the conflict theory views on who rules the United States and then state which you think is more accurate and why.
2. Discuss why wars happen.
3. Discuss what you see as the future of the New World Order.
4. Discuss the advantages and disadvantages of both capitalism and socialism both as ideologies and as economic systems.
5. The author suggests that the globalization of capitalism may be the most significant economic change of the last 100 years. Discuss the consequences of the change for our society and for nations around the globe.

STUDENT PROJECTS

1. Who do you think rules the United States? Do you agree with any particular perspective presented in this chapter? Explain.

2. What is meant by the new world order? Cite examples Do you think the world is moving in this direction? Do you see this as a positive or negative change? Explain.

CHAPTER 12

MARRIAGE AND FAMILY

CHAPTER SUMMARY

- Because there are so many cultural variations on family structure, it is hard to define. Nevertheless, **family** is defined broadly as two or more people who consider themselves related by blood, marriage, or adoption. Marriage and family patterns vary remarkably across cultures, but four universal themes in marriage are mate selection, descent, inheritance, and authority.

- According to the functionalist perspective, the family carries out important social functions. Conversely, conflict theorists focus on how families help perpetuate inequality, especially in gender relations. Symbolic interactionists focus on the meanings that people give their marital relationships, particularly in regard to the household division of labor.

- The family life cycle can be analyzed in terms of love and courtship, marriage, childbirth, child rearing, and the family in later life. In the United States, patterns of marriage vary by social class, age, religion, and race; patterns of childbearing and child rearing vary by social class.

- Family diversity in U.S. culture is related to social class rather than race or ethnicity. One-parent families, childless families, blended families, and gay families represent some of the different types of families today. Poverty is especially significant for one-parent families, most of which are headed by women.

- Major trends in U.S. families today include postponement of first marriage, cohabitation, unmarried mothers and the emergence of the "sandwich generation"—middle-aged couples who are caught between caring for their own children and caring for their elderly parents.

- Studies on divorce have focused on the problems in measuring the impact of divorce and remarriage on children and ex-spouses. Time seems to heal most children's wounds over the divorce of their parents, but research suggests that a minority carry the scars of divorce into adulthood. Men and women experience divorce differently; for men, this event often results in a weakening of their relationships with their children, while for women it means a decline in their standard of living. Although most divorced people do remarry, the rate of remarriage has slowed considerably.

- Violence and abuse—including battering, child abuse, and incest—are the "dark side" of family life. Researchers have identified variables that help marriages last and be happy.

- Trends for the future include a continued increase in cohabitation, births to unmarried mothers, and postponement of marriage. The continuing growth of the numbers of working wives will impact on the marital balance of power.

LEARNING OBJECTIVES

As you read Chapter 12, use these learning objectives to organize your notes. After completing your reading, you should be able to answer each of the objectives.

1. Explain why it is difficult to precisely define the term "family" and discuss some of the different ways that family systems can be organized and classified.
2. Identify the common cultural themes that run through marriage and the family.
3. Explain why the family is universal and list the basic societal needs that it fulfills.
4. Contrast the functionalist, conflict, and symbolic interaction perspectives regarding marriage and family and provide examples that illustrate each of their perspectives.

5. Identify the major elements of the family life cycle and discuss how these elements may be affected by age, education, social class, race and ethnicity, sex, and/or religion.

6. Describe the distinctive characteristics of family life in African American, Latino, Asian American, and Native American families, and discuss the role that social class and culture play in affecting these distinctions.

7. Talk about the characteristics — and concerns — of one-parent, childless, blended, and gay and lesbian families in the United States.

8. Identify the general patterns and trends in marriage and family life in the United States and discuss how these are reflected in postponement of marriage, cohabitation, single motherhood, the sandwich generation, divorce, and remarriage.

9. Talk about the different measures of divorce rates, the adverse effects of divorce on children, and the factors that most help children adjust to divorce in the United States. Explain how divorce affects men and women differently.

10. Describe the "dark side" of family life as it relates to battering, child abuse, marital rape, and incest.

11. Identify the characteristics that most contribute to happy marriages and happy families.

12. Talk about future patterns and trends in marriage and family life in the United States.

CHAPTER OUTLINE

I. Marriage and Family in Global Perspective

A. The term **family** is difficult to define since there are many types of families.

    1. In some societies men have more than one wife (polygyny) or women have more than one husband (polyandry).

    2. A broad definition of family is a group of two or more people who consider themselves related by blood marriage (or adoption) and lives together (or has lived together). A household, in contrast, consists of all people who occupy the same housing unit.

    3. A family is classified as a nuclear family (husband, wife, and children) or an extended family (a nuclear family plus other relatives who live together).

    4. The family of orientation is the family in which a person grows up, while the family of procreation is the family formed when a couple's first child is born.

    5. Marriage, usually marked by a ritual, is a group's approved mating arrangement.

B. Despite diversity, several common themes run through the concepts of marriage and family.

    1. Each group establishes norms to govern who can and cannot marry. *Endogamy* is the practice of marrying within one's own group, while *exogamy* is the practice of marrying outside one's own group; the incest taboo is the best example of a norm of exogamy. Some norms of mate selection are written into law, others are informal.

    2. Three major patterns of descent (tracing kinship over generations) are: (a) bilateral (descent traced on both the mother's and the father's side); (b) patrilineal (descent traced only on the father's side); and (c) matrilineal (descent traced only on the mother's side).

    3. Mate selection and a system of descent are regulated in all societies in order to provide an orderly way of passing property, kinship, etc., to the next generation. In a bilateral system, property passes to males and females; in a patrilineal system, property passes only to males; in a matrilineal system, property passes only to females.

4.   *Patriarchy*, found in all societies, is a social system in which men dominate women. No historical records exist of a true *matriarchy* (a system in which women as a group dominate men). In an *egalitarian* social system authority is more or less equally divided between men and women.

II.   Marriage and Family in Theoretical Perspective

A.   Functionalists stress that to survive, a society must meet certain basic needs; they examine how the family contributes to the well-being of society.

1.   The family is universal because it serves functions essential to the well-being of society: economic production, socialization of children, care of the sick and aged, recreation, sexual control, and reproduction.

2.   The incest taboo (rules specifying which people are too closely related to have sex or marry) helps the family avoid role confusion and forces people to look outside the family for marriage partners, creating an extended network of support.

3.   The nuclear family has few people it can depend on for material and emotional support; thus, the members of a nuclear family are vulnerable to "emotional overload." The relative isolation of the nuclear family makes it easier for the "dark side" of families (incest and other types of abuse) to emerge.

B.   To conflict theorists, the issue is the struggle over scarce resources; they argue that within the family, the conflict over housework is really about control over scarce resources—time, energy, and the leisure to pursue interesting activities.

1.   Most men resist doing housework and working wives end up doing almost all of it, even though men think that they are splitting the work equally.

2.   **Arlie Hochschild** found that after an 8-hour day at work, women typically work a "second shift" at home; this means that wives work an extra month of 24-hour days each year. The result is that working wives feel deep discontent.

C.   Symbolic interactionists look at the meanings people give to their experiences; they are interested in how husbands view housework.

1.   Research indicates that the less difference there is between a husband's and a wife's earnings, the more likely they are to share housework. When husbands are laid off from work, their contribution decreases, and husbands who earn less than their wives do the least housework.

2.   The key to understanding this pattern is gender role. When a wife earns more than her husband, his masculinity is threatened; to do housework is even more threatening. By not doing housework, he is able to "reclaim" his masculinity.

III.   The Family Life Cycle

A.   Romantic love provides the ideological context in which people in the U.S. seek mates and form families. Romantic love has two components: (1) **emotional**—a feeling of sexual attraction; and (2) **cognitive**— a feeling we describe as being "in love."

B.   The social channels of love and marriage in the United States include age, education, social class, race, and religion.

1.   *Homogamy* is the tendency of people with similar characteristics to marry one another, usually resulting from propinquity (spatial nearness). People living near one another tend to marry.

2.   Interracial marriage is an exception to these social patterns. In the U.S., about 6 percent of the population marries someone from a different race. At the same time, interracial marriages are becoming more acceptable.

C.   Marital satisfaction usually decreases with the birth of a child, according to **Martin Whyte**. **Lillian Rubin** found that social class influences how couples adjust to children. Working-class couples are more likely to have a baby nine months after marriage and have major interpersonal and financial problems; middle-class parents are more prepared because of more resources, postponement of the birth of the first child, and therefore more time to adjust to one another.

D.   Traditionally, child rearing automatically fell on the mother. As more mothers become employed outside the home, this has changed.

     1.   Overall, childcare arrangements appear to be quite similar for married couples and single mothers; the main difference is the role played by the child's father while the mother is at work. For married couples, almost one in four children is cared for by the father, while for single mothers this arrangement occurs for only one of fourteen children. Grandparents often help to fill the child care gap left by absent fathers.

     2.   One in six children is in day care. Only a minority of U.S. day care centers offer high-quality care, primarily due to the abysmal salaries paid to day care workers.

     3.   Social class is also important in child rearing. According to **Melvin Kohn**, parents socialize children into the norms of their respective work worlds. Working-class parents want their children to behave in conformity with social expectations, while middle-class parents are more concerned that their children develop curiosity, self-expression, and self-control.

     4.   Birth order is significant in child rearing: first-borns tend to be more disciplined than the children who follow, but also receive more attention; when the next child arrives, the fist born competes to maintain attention.

E.   The later stages of the family life cycle bring their own pleasures and problems.

     1.   The empty-nest syndrome is thought to signal a difficult adjustment for women; however **Lillian Rubin** argues that this is largely a myth because women's satisfaction generally increases when the last child leaves home. Most women feel relieved at being able to spend more time on themselves and many couples report a renewed sense of companionship. This closeness is related to four factors: freedom from the responsibilities of child rearing; increased leisure; higher incomes; and fewer financial obligations.

     2.   With prolonged education and the growing cost of establishing households, U.S. children are leaving home later, or returning after initially leaving home .

     3.   Women are more likely than men to face the problem of adjusting to widowhood; not only does the average women live longer than a man, but she has also usually married a man older than herself.

IV.   Diversity in U.S. Families

A.   As with other groups, the family life of African Americans differs with social class.

     1.   The upper class is concerned with maintaining family lineage and preserving their privilege and wealth; the middle-class focuses on achievement and respectability; poor African-American families face the problems that poverty brings — sharing scarce resources and "stretching kinship" are primary survival mechanisms for poor families. Sociologists use the term *fictive kin* to refer to the non-related individuals who help the family out in hard times.

     2.   A marriage squeeze (fewer unmarried males than unmarried females) exists among African Americans; thus these women are more likely to remain single, to marry men with less education or who are unemployed or divorced.

B.   The effects of social class on families also apply to Latinos, but these families differ by country of origin as well.

        1.   Latino families can be distinguished by the Spanish language, Roman Catholic religion, and strong family ties with a disapproval of divorce.

        2.   Machismo, the emphasis on male strength and dominance, also seems to be a characteristic of Latino families. As a result, the husband-father plays a stronger role than in white or African-American families, and the wife-mother deals with family and child-related decisions. Machismo decreases with each generation that lives in the U.S.

C.   While the structure of Asian-American families is almost identical to white families, there are still significant variations in family life because Asian Americans come from many different countries.

        1.   The family life of recent immigrants is closer to that in their country of origin.

        2.   **Bob Suzuki** points out that while Chinese-American and Japanese-American families have adopted the nuclear family pattern of the United States, they have retained Confucian values that provide a distinct framework to family life: humanism, collectivity, self-discipline, hierarchy, respect for the elderly, moderation, and obligation.

D.   Perhaps the most significant issue facing Native-American families is whether to follow traditional values or to assimilate; traditionals speak native languages and emphasize distinctive Native American values and beliefs, while those who have assimilated do not.

E.   There has been an increase in one-parent families.

        1.   This increase is due to both the high divorce rate and the sharp increase in unwed motherhood.

        2.   Most of these families are poor because they are headed by women who earn less than men.

        3.   Children from one-parent families are more likely to drop out of school, become delinquent, be poor as adults, divorce, and have children outside of marriage.

F.   F.   There are a growing number of families who are voluntarily childless. The percentage varies with the education of the woman; the more education she has, the more likely she expects not to bear children. Latinos are much less likely to remain childless than whites and African Americans.

        1.   There are different reasons why a couple chooses not to have a child: a weak relationship, financial constraints, or a demanding career are among the reasons identified.

        2.   More education, careers for women, effective contraception, abortion, the costs of rearing children, and changing attitudes toward children and life goals all contribute to the increase in childless and childfree marriages.

G.   A blended family is one whose members were once part of other families (i.e., two divorced persons marry and bring their children into a new family unit). Blended families are increasing in number and often experience complicated family relationships.

H.   Although marriage between homosexuals is illegal in most of the United States, many homosexual couples live in monogamous relationships that they refer to as marriage.

        1.   In 2004, Massachusetts became the first state to legalize same sex marriages.

        2.   Gay families have the same problems of heterosexual marriages: housework, money, careers, problems with relatives, and sexual adjustment.

V.   Trends in U.S. Families

A.   The average age of U.S. brides is the oldest it has been since records were first kept.

        1.   The percentage of unmarried women is now about double what it was in 1970.

2.   Many young people postpone marriage, but not cohabitation; if cohabitation were counted as marriage, rates of family formation and age at first marriage would show little change.

B.   Cohabitation, living together as an unmarried couple, is ten times more common today than 30 years ago. About 60 percent of the couples who marry have cohabited; this rate is lower in the United States than in Canada and most European countries. Commitment is the essential difference between cohabitation and marriage; marriage assumes permanence; cohabiting assumes remaining together "as long as it works out".

C.   As previously discussed, there has been an increase in the number of births to unmarried mothers.

    1.   In the ten industrialized nations for which data are available, all except Japan have experienced sharp increases in births to unmarried mothers—the U.S. rate falls in the middle third of these nations.

    2.   Industrialization alone is too simple an explanation for this increase. To more fully understand this trend, future research must focus on the customs and values embedded within particular cultures.

D.   The term "**sandwich generation**" refers to people who find themselves between two generations, responsible for the care of their children and for their aging parents.

    1.   These people are typically between the ages of 40 and 55.

    2.   More businesses offer elder care assistance to their employees. With people living longer, this issue is likely to become even more urgent in the future.

VI.   Divorce and Remarriage

A.   The United States has the highest divorce rate in the industrialized world; estimates suggest that half or more of all couples getting married today eventually divorce.

    1.   Although the divorce rate is reported at 50 percent, this statistic is misleading because with rare exceptions those who divorce do not come from the group who married that year.

    2.   An alternative is to compare the number of divorces in a given year to the entire group of married couples; this amounts to 2 percent of all married couples getting a divorce.

    3.   A third way is to calculate the percent of divorced persons among all US adults.

B.   Each year over one million children are in families affected by divorce. Divorce threatens a child's world.

    1.   Research has found that the grown children of divorce feel more distant from parents than children from intact families; they are less likely to marry and more likely to divorce.

    2.   Research shows that children's adjustment to divorce is affected by the relationship(s) their mothers form after divorce; those whose mothers entered into a single, stable relationship had the best adjustment.

    3.   Several factors help children adjust to divorce. Both parents expressing understanding and affection; the parent with whom the child lives is making a good adjustment; family routines are consistent; the family has adequate money for its needs; and, according to preliminary studies, the child lives with the parent of the same sex.

    4.   Children adjust better when a second adult can be counted on for support.

C.   A new fathering pattern, known as serial fatherhood, is beginning to emerge.

    1.   Divorced fathers tend to live with, support, and play an active fathering role with children of the woman to whom they are currently married or living.

    2.   Over time, contact with their children from a previous marriage diminishes; one study found that only about one-sixth of children who live apart from their

fathers see them as often as every week. Research suggests that most divorced fathers stop seeing their children altogether.

D.   Women are more likely than men to feel divorce gives them a new chance at life. Divorce most likely spells economic hardship for women, especially mothers of small children; in the first post-divorce year, the standard of living for women with dependent children declines significantly. The ex-husband's standard of living is likely to increase.

E.   Most divorced persons eventually remarry, with an average lapse between divorce and remarriage of about five years for women.

1.   Most divorced people remarry other divorced people.

2.   Women with small children, and women with less than a high school education, are more likely to remarry.

3.   Perhaps because they have a larger pool of potential mates from which to select, men are more likely than women to remarry.

4.   The divorce rate for remarried people without children is the same as that of first marriages. Those who bring children into their new marriage, however, are more likely to divorce again; this suggests that remarriages with children are more difficult because there are not yet norms governing these relationships.

VII.   Two Sides of Family Life

A.   The dark side of family life deals with events that people would rather keep in the dark—battering, child abuse, and incest.

1.   Although wives are about as likely to attack their husbands as husbands are to attack their wives, it is generally the husband who lands the last and most damaging blow. Living in a sexist society, some men who batter think they are superior and have a right to force their will on their wives.

2.   Child abuse is extensive. Each year, three million U.S. children are reported to the authorities as victims of abuse or neglect.

3.   *Incest* is sexual relations between relatives, such as brothers and sisters or parents and children. It occurs most frequently in families that are socially isolated. The most common offenders are uncles, followed by first cousins, fathers/stepfathers, brothers, and finally, other male relatives.

B.   There are a number of factors that make marriages work. Variables that produce happy marriages include: spending time together, appreciating one another, having a commitment to the marriage, using good communications, confronting and working through problems together, and putting more into the marriage than you take out.

VIII.   The Future of Marriage and Family

A.   Despite its problems, marriage is not likely to disappear as a social institution because it is functional; we see it as vital to our welfare.

B.   Certain trends appear firmly in place.

1.   It is likely that cohabitation will increase, as will the age at first marriage and the number of women joining the work force, with a resulting shift in marital power toward a more egalitarian norm.

2.   The number of elderly will continue to increase, with more and more middle-aged couples finding themselves part of the "sandwich generation."

C.   It is not clear what the long-term trend in divorce will be. The recent decline may be a prelude to a longer-term decline, or it could be a lull before the rate rises again.

D.   Sociology can play a role in correcting some of the distortions associated with marriage and family life, as well as help formulate social policy that will enhance family life.

KEY TERMS

After studying the chapter, review each of the following terms.

bilineal system: a system of reckoning descent that counts both the mothers and the father's side (p. 325)

blended family: a family whose members were once part of other families (p. 338)

cohabitation: unmarried people living together in a sexual relationship (p. 339)

egalitarian: authority more or less equally divided between people or groups. In this case between husband and wife (p. 325)

endogamy: the practice of marrying within one's own group (p. 324)

exogamy: the practice of marrying outside one's group (p. 325)

extended family: a nuclear family plus other relatives, such as grand parents, who live together (p. 324)

family: two or more people who consider themselves related by blood, marriage, or adoption (p. 324)

family of orientation; the family in which a person grows up (p. 324)

family of procreation: the family formed when a couple's first child is born (p. 324)

homogamy: the tendency of people with similar characteristics to marry one another (p. 331)

household: people who occupy the same housing unit (p. 324)

incest taboo: the rule that prohibits sex or marriage among designated relatives (p. 325)

machismo: an emphasis on male strength and dominance (p. 335)

marriage: a group's approved mating arrangements, usually marked by a ritual of some sort (p. 324)

matriarchy: a society in which women as a group dominate men as a group (p. 325)

matrilineal (system of descent): a system of reckoning descent that counts only the mother's side (p. 325)

nuclear family: a family consisting of a husband, wife, and child(ren) (p. 324)

patriarchy: a society or group in which men dominate women, authority is vested in males (p. 325)

patrilineal (system of descent): a system of reckoning descent that counts only the father's side (p. 325)

polyandry: a form of marriage in which a woman has more than one husband (p. 324)

polygyny: a form of marriage in which a man has more than one wife (p. 324)

romantic love: feelings of erotic attraction accompanied by an idealization of the other (p. 329)

serial fatherhood: a pattern of parenting in which a father, after divorce, reduces contact with his own children, serves as a father to the children of the woman he marries or lives with, then ignores his own children after moving in with or marrying another woman; this pattern repeats (p. 346)

system of descent: how kinship is traced over the generations (p. 325)

KEY PEOPLE

Review the major theoretical contributions or research findings of these theorists and thinkers.

Philip Blumstein and Pepper Schwartz: These two sociologists interviewed same-sex couples and found their main struggles were the same ones facing heterosexual couples.

Urie Bronfenbrenner: This sociologist studied the impact of divorce on children and found that children adjust better if there is a second adult who can be counted on for support.

Andrew Cherlin: Cherlin notes that our society has not yet developed adequate norms for remarriage.

Donald Dutton and Arthur Aron: These researchers compared the sexual arousal levels of men who are in dangerous situations with men in safe situations and found that the former were more sexually aroused than the latter.

Kathleen Gerson: Gerson found that there are different reasons why some couples choose not to have children—weak marriages, expenses associated with raising children, diminished career opportunities.

Alex Heckert, Thomas Nowak and Kay Snyder: These researchers did secondary analysis of data gathered on a nationally representative sample and found that divorce increases when women earn more than their husbands, the wife's health is poorer than her husband's, or the wife does less housework.

Arlie Hochschild: Hochschild conducted research on families in which both parents were employed full-time to find out how household tasks are divided. She found that women did more of the housework than their husbands, resulting in women putting in a *second shift* at home after their workday had ended.

William Jankowiak and Edward Fischer: These anthropologists surveyed data on 166 societies and found that the majority of them contained the ideal of romantic love.

Melvin Kohn: He studied the differences in social class and child rearing.

Jeanette & Robert Lauer: These sociologists interviewed couples who had been married fifteen years and longer in order to find out what makes a marriage successful.

Lillian Rubin: Rubin compared working and middle class couples and found the key to how well the couple adjusts to the arrival of children is social class. Rubin also interviewed both career women and homemakers found that the notion of the "empty-nest" as a difficult time for women is largely a myth and that most women's satisfaction increased when the last child left home.

Diana Russell: Russell found that incest victims who experience the most difficulty are those who have been victimized the most often, over longer periods of time, and whose incest was "more intrusive."

Nicholas Stinnett: Stinnett studied 660 families from all regions of the U.S. and parts of South America in order to find out what the characteristics of happy families are.

Murray Straus: This sociologist has studied domestic violence and found that, while husbands and wives are equally likely to attack one another, men inflict more damage on women than the reverse.

Bob Suzuki: This sociologist studied Chinese-American and Japanese-American families and identified several distinctive characteristics of these families.

SELF-TEST

After completing this self-test, check your answers in the Answer Key of this Study Guide.

MULTIPLE CHOICE QUESTIONS

1. Polyandry is:
    a. a marriage in which a woman has more than one husband.
    b. a marriage in which a man has more than one wife.
    c. male control of a society or group.
    d. female control of a society or group.

2. A household differs from a family in which of the following ways?
    a. It includes only those people who are related by blood.
    b. It is a broader definition because it includes people who support the family, such as housekeepers and nannies.
    c. It is only used by government agencies for statistical purposes.
    d. It pertains only to people who occupy the same housing unit or living quarters.

3. The family of orientation is:
    a. the family formed when a couple's first child is born.
    b. the same thing as an extended family.
    c. the same as the family of procreation.
    d. none of the above.

4. Endogamy is:
    a. the practice of marrying outside one's group.
    b. the practice of marrying within one's own group.
    c. the practice of marrying someone within one's own family.
    d. none of the above.

5. In a matrilineal system:
    a. descent is figured only on the mother's side.
    b. children are not considered related to their mother's relatives.

    c.   descent is traced on both the mother's and the father's side.

    d.   descent is figured only on the father's side.

6.   In terms of authority within the family, an increasing number of U.S. families are:

    a.   matriarchal.

    b.   patriarchal.

    c.   egalitarian.

    d.   without authority.

7.   The incest taboo:

    a.   ` is rules specifying the degrees of kinship that prohibit sex or marriage.

    b.   helps families avoid role confusion.

    c.   facilitates the socialization of children.

    d.   all of the above.

8.   According to functionalists, the family:

    a.   serves very different functions from society to society.

    b.   serves certain essential functions in all societies.

    c.   has very few functions left.

    d.   is no longer universal.

9.   According to the research findings, women average how many more hours each week on child care and housework than their husbands?

    a.   7.5

    b.   8

    c.   11

    d.   15

10.   According to Arlie Hochschild, most men engage in strategies of resistance when it comes to doing housework. Which of the following is *not* one of the strategies she identified?

    a.   *Playing dumb* — By withdrawing their mental attention from the task, men get credit for trying and being a good sport, but in such a way that they are not chosen the next time.

    b.   *Substitute labor* — By hiring someone else to do the work (a maid service, a lawn care company), they guarantee that the work gets done but that they're not the ones doing it.

    c.   *Waiting it out* — Some men never volunteer, thereby forcing their wives to ask them to do household chores. Wives sometimes don't ask, because they say it feels like "begging."

    d.   *Needs reduction* — The husband scales down his own housework "needs," forcing the wife to step in and do things herself because of her "greater need" to see them done right.

11.   According to research findings, which of the following feels most threatened by doing housework, and consequently does the least?

    a.   men who earn significantly more money than their wives

    b.   men who earn about the same amount of money as their wives

    c.   men who earn less money than their wives

    d.   men who are employed in occupations that are highly sex-typed as masculine

12.   According to research by Dutton and Aron, what does love usually start with?

    a.   sexual attraction

    b.   a commitment

    c.   a cognitive awareness of our feelings

    d.   a chance meeting

13. The tendency of people with similar characteristics to marry one another is:
    a. propinquity.
    b. erotic selection.
    c. homogamy.
    d. heterogamy.

14. What percentage of people marry outside their racial-ethnic identity?
    a. 20 percent
    b. 15 percent
    c. 10 percent
    d. 6 percent

15. In what ways do child care arrangements of married couples and single mothers differ?
    a. Single mothers are more likely to leave their children home alone.
    b. Single mothers are much less likely to rely on the child's father for help.
    c. Single mothers are much more likely to rely on the child's father for help.
    d. Single mothers are more likely to enroll their children in poor-quality child care.

16. In comparing child-rearing styles of middle and working class parents, Kohn concluded that:
    a. parents of all social classes socialize their children similarly.
    b. middle-class parents are more likely to use physical punishment.
    c. working-class parents are more likely to withdraw privileges or affection.
    d. none of the above.

17. The empty-nest syndrome:
    a. is not a reality for most parents.
    b. causes couples to feel a lack of companionship.
    c. is easier for women who have not worked outside the home.
    d. none of the above.

18. A major concern of upper-class African American families is:
    a. achievement and respectability.
    b. problems of poverty.
    c. maintaining family lineage.
    d. all of the above.

19. Machismo:
    a. distinguishes Latino families from other groups.
    b. is an emphasis on male strength and dominance.
    c. is seen in some Chicano families where the man has a strong role in his family.
    d. all of the above.

20. In what ways do Native American families differ from most other U.S. families?
    a. There are more single parent families.
    b. There is less nonmarital childbirth.
    c. Elders play a more active role in their children's families.
    d. They have higher rates of divorce and marital instability.

21. Since 1970, the number of children in the United States who live with both parents has:
    a. remained stable.

b.   dropped.

c.   increased.

22. Children from one-parent families are more likely to:
     a.   drop out of school.
     b.   become delinquent.
     c.   be poor as adults.
     d.   all of the above.

23. A family whose members were once part of other families is known as a:
     a.   reconstituted family.
     b.   mixed family.
     c.   blended family.
     d.   multiple nuclei family.

24. In 2004, what state in the United States became the first to legalize same sex marriages?
     a.   Hawaii
     b.   California
     c.   Massachusetts
     d.   New York

25. Cohabitation:
     a.   is the condition of living together as an unmarried couple.
     b.   has increased eight times in the past 25 years.
     c.   has occurred before about half of all couples marry.
     d.   all of the above.

26. The *sandwich generation* refers to:
     a.   stay-at-home moms who spend their days making sandwiches for their preschoolers.
     b.   people who are sandwiched between two sets of family relations because of the increase in divorce today.
     c.   young children who consume a lot of sandwiches and whose needs are often overlooked by parents whose time is stretched by work and household responsibilities.
     d.   people who find themselves caught between two generations, simultaneously responsible for the care of their children and their aging parents.

27. According to research, what percent of children who live apart from their fathers following a divorce continue to see their dads as often as every week?
     a.   one-half
     b.   one-third
     c.   one-quarter
     d.   one-sixth

28. Which statement about divorce and remarriage is *incorrect*?
     a.   The divorce rate of remarried people without children is the same as first marriages.
     b.   Divorced people tend to marry other divorced people.
     c.   The divorce rate of remarried couples with children is higher than that of first marriages.
     d.   The presence or absence of children makes no difference in a remarried couple's chances of divorce.

29. According to research by Diana Russell, who is most likely to be the offender in incest?
    a. brothers
    b. fathers/stepfathers
    c. first cousins
    d. uncles

30. According to the author, what trend(s) are likely to continue into the next century?
    a. increase in cohabitation
    b. increase in age at first marriage
    c. more equality in the husband-wife relationship
    d. all of the above.

TRUE-FALSE QUESTIONS

T F   1.   Polygyny is a marriage in which a man has more than one wife.
T F   2.   Families are people who live together in the same housing unit.
T F   3.   Laws of endogamy in the United States prohibit interracial marriages.
T F   4.   Today, family authority patterns in the United States are becoming egalitarian.
T F   5.   Functionalists believe that the incest taboo helps the family to avoid role confusion.
T F   6.   Conflict theorists believe that one of the consequences of married women working for pay is a reshuffling of power in the home.
T F   7.   Arlie Hochschild concluded that women are generally happy to work a second shift.
T F   8.   According to Hochschild, it is important for a husband to express appreciation to his wife when she juggles both work for wages and the second shift at home.
T F   9.   Gender role is the key to understanding why men who get laid off from their jobs would decrease the amount of work they do around the house.
T F   10.   Love and marriage include age, education, social class, race, and religion.
T F   11.   Social class does not affect the ways couples adjust to the arrival of children.
T F   12.   Middle class parents have more concern that their children develop curiosity and self expression.
T F   13.   Researchers have found that most husbands and wives experience the empty nest when their last child leaves home.
T F   14.   Women are about as likely as men to face the problem of adjusting to widowhood.
T F   15.   The structure of Asian American families is almost identical to that of white families.
T F   16.   Two divorced people who marry and each bring their children into a new family unit become a blended family.
T F   17.   Today's average first-time bride and groom are older than at any time in U.S. history.
T F   18.   U.S. rate of births to unmarried women is the highest among a group of ten industrialized nations for which there are accurate data.
T F   19.   The usual pattern of father-child contact following a divorce is for the contact to be fairly high for several years while the child is young but then to drop off significantly as the child moves through adolescence.
T F   20.   Russell found that uncles are the most common offenders of incest in families.

FILL-IN QUESTIONS

1. There are no historical records of a true _____.
2. The _____ forces people to look outside the family for marriage partners.
3. Husbands who earn less than their wives do the _____ housework.
4. Indian sociologists estimate that parents still arrange about _____ % of marriages.
5. _____ occurs largely as a result of propinquity, or spatial nearness.
6. _____ makes a huge difference in child rearing.
7. Sociologists use the term _____ kin to refer to the stretching of kinship.
8. The concern expressed over one-parent families may have more to do with _____ than with children being reared by one parent.
9. _____ became the first country to legalize marriage between people of the same sex.
10. Postponing _____ is today's norm.
11. _____ is the essential difference between cohabitation and marriage.
12. It is becoming increasingly common for _____ to rear their grandchildren.
13. The main reason for _____ families is that parents are incapable of caring for their children.
14. The _____ generation is the term for people responsible for both children and their parents.
15. The women who are most likely to remarry after a divorce are young mothers and those with less _____.

MATCH THESE THEORISTS/PHILOSOPHERS WITH THEIR CONTRIBUTIONS

1.	Blumstein and Schwartz	a.	*Factors associated with successful marriages*
2.	Dutton and Aron	b.	*Studied household issues of same-sex couples*
3.	Andrew Cherlin	c.	*Found women's satisfaction increased after last child moved out*
4.	Lauer and Lauer	d.	*Studied incest victims*
5.	Kathleen Gerson	e.	*Identified reasons why couples choose to be child-free*
6.	Arlie Hochschild		
7.	Melvin Kohn	f.	*Studied danger and sexual arousal*
8.	Lillian Rubin	g.	*Identified distinctive characteristics of Asian-American families*
9.	Diana Russell	h.	*Noted lack of norms regarding remarriage*
10.	Bob Suzuki	i.	*Studied social class differences in child-rearing*
		j.	*Identified the second shift*

ESSAY QUESTIONS

1. Discuss whether the family still provides a useful function.
2. Explain what the second shift is and consider whether it will disappear in the future.
3. Identify the stages in the family life cycle, discussing what tasks are accomplished in each stage and what event marks the transition from one stage to the next.

4. Identify the trends among U.S. families today and explain the social forces that have contributed to each of them.
5. Discuss the impact that divorce has on family members — men, women and children.

STUDENT PROJECTS

1. Do you think the "second-shift" is a temporary problem or a long-range problem   regarding family and marriage? How has the issue been dealt with in your family? How do you plan to resolve the potential issues caused by the "second shift" in your own marriage or family?

2. List the problems faced by American families. Given these problems, do you think marriage and family are worth the effort? Why or why not?

CHAPTER 13

EDUCATION AND RELIGION

CHAPTER SUMMARY

- Industrialized societies are **credential societies**; employers use diplomas and degrees to determine who is eligible for jobs. Educational certification provides evidence of a person's ability in societies that are large and anonymous and where people lack personal knowledge of one another.

- In general, formal education is more extensive in the Most Industrializes Nations, undergoing extensive change in the Industrializing Nations, and very spotty in the Least Industrialized Nations.

- Functionalists emphasize the functions of education, including teaching knowledge and skills, transmitting cultural values, bringing about social integration, and providing gatekeeping and mainstreaming.

- Conflict theorists view education as a mechanism for perpetuating social inequality and reproducing the social class system. Accordingly, they stress how unequal funding of schools, culturally biased IQ tests, tracking, and the hidden curriculum reinforce basic social inequality.

- Symbolic interactionists examine classroom interaction and study how teacher expectations cause a self-fulfilling prophecy, producing the very behavior the teacher is expecting.

- The problems facing the current U.S. educational system include violence, falling SAT scores, grade inflation, social promotion, and functional illiteracy. Suggestions for solving these problems include increasing academic standards and expectations for both students and teachers; however, these standards will not occur until students' basic security is guaranteed.

- Durkheim identified the essential elements of all religion: beliefs that separate the profane from the sacred, rituals, and a moral community that centers around both.

- According to the functionalist perspective, religion meets basic human needs such as answering questions about ultimate meaning, providing social solidarity, guidelines for everyday life, adapting to social change, and support for the government. Functionalists also believe religion has two main dysfunctions: war and terrorism and religious persecution.

- Symbolic interactionists focus on how religious symbols communicate meaning and how rituals, beliefs, and religious experiences unite people into a community.

- Conflict theorists see religion as a conservative force that serves the needs of the ruling class by reflecting and reinforcing social inequality.

- Unlike Marx, Weber saw religion as a powerful force for social change. He analyzed how Protestantism gave rise to an ethic that stimulated "the spirit of capitalism." The result was capitalism, which transformed society.

- Sociologists have identified cults, sects, churches, and ecclesia as distinct types of religious groups. All religions begin as cults and although most ultimately fail, those that survive become sects. As a sect grows and integrates into society it may change into a church. Ecclesiae, or state religions, are rare.

- Religion in the United States includes the following features: diversity, pluralism, competition for members, a revival among fundamentalist churches, and the development of the electronic church. Secularization, a shift from spiritual concerns to those of "this world," is the force behind the dynamics of many religious organizations. As a cult or sect evolves into a church, its teachings are adapted to reflect changes in the social status of its members. Dissatisfied members often break away to form new cults or sects.

LEARNING OBJECTIVES

As you read Chapter 13, use these learning objectives to organize your notes. After completing your reading, you should be able to answer each of the objectives.

1. Summarize the development of modern education and discuss the links between democracy, industrialization, and universal education.
2. Compare the education systems of Japan, Russia, and Egypt, and discuss how they represent the differences in education between the Most Industrialized, Industrializing, and Least Industrialized Nations.
3. From the functionalist perspective, identify and evaluate the manifest and latent functions of education.
4. From the conflict perspective, explain and discuss the different ways the education system reinforces basic social inequalities.
5. From the symbolic interactionist perspective, cite the research—and implications of — the effects of teachers' expectations on students' performances.
6. Identify the major problems that exist within the United States educational system and evaluate potential solutions.
7. Define religion and explain its essential elements.
8. Describe the functions and dysfunctions of religion from the functionalist perspective.
9. Apply the symbolic interactionist perspective to religious symbols, rituals, and beliefs, and discuss how each of these help to establish and/or maintain communities of like-minded people.
10. From the conflict perspective, discuss how religion supports the status quo, and reflects, reinforces, and legitimates social inequality.
11. Summarize Max Weber's analysis of religion and the spirit of capitalism; explain its significance.
12. Define cult, sect, church, and ecclesia and describe the process by which some groups move from one category to another.
13. Explain how religious membership in the United States varies by region, social class, age, race and ethnicity.
14. Describe and discuss the major features of religious groups in the United States.
15. Define secularization and distinguish between the secularization of religion and that of culture.
16. Explain the fundamental significance of religion in people's lives and why, in all likelihood, religion will remain a permanent fixture in human society.

CHAPTER OUTLINE

EDUCATION: TRANSFERRING KNOWLEDGE AND SKILLS
I. Education in Global Perspective

    A.   A **credential society** is one in which employers use diplomas and degrees when determining job eligibility.

            1.   The sheer size, urbanization and consequent anonymity of U.S. society is a major reason for the requirement of credentials. Diplomas/degrees often serge as sorting devices for employers; because they don't know the individual personally, they depend on schools to weed out the capable from the incapable.

            2.   As technology and knowledge change, simple on-the-job training is not enough; specific job skills must be mastered before an individual is hired.

B. Education in the Most Industrialized Nations: Japan
  1. Japanese education reflects a group-centered ethic. Children in grade school work as a group mastering the same skills/materials; cooperation and respect for elders (and those in positions of authority) is stressed.
  2. College admission procedures are based on test scores only; the top scorers are admitted, regardless of social class.
C. Education in the Industrializing Nations: Russia
  1. After the Revolution of 1917, the government insisted that socialist values dominate education as a means to undergird the new political system. Children were taught that capitalism was evil and communism was the salvation of the world.
  2. Education at all levels was free and centralized; all schools followed the same curriculum.
  3. Today, Russians are in the midst of "reinventing" education. Private, religious and even foreign-run schools are operating, and students are encouraged to think for themselves.
  4. The primary difficulty facing the post-Soviet educational system is the rapidly changing values and world view in Russia.
D. Education in the Least Industrialized Nations: Egypt
  1. Several centuries before the birth of Christ, Egypt was a world-renowned center of learning. Primary areas of study were physics, astronomy, geometry, geography, mathematics, philosophy, and medicine. After defeat in war, education declined, and has not risen to its former prominence.
  2. Today, education is free at all levels, including college; but qualified teachers are few and classrooms are crowded. Children of the wealthy are still more likely to get a college education.

II. The Functionalist Perspective: Providing Social Benefits
A. A central position of functionalism is that when the parts of society are working properly, each contributes to the stability of society. For education, both the manifest (intended) and latent (unintended but positive) functions can be identified.
B. The functions of education include: (1) teaching knowledge and skills; (2) cultural transmission of values (individualism, competition, and patriotism); (3) social integration (molding students into a more or less cohesive unit); and (4) gatekeeping (determining who will enter what occupations, through tracking and social placement).
C. Schools have also assumed many functions previously fulfilled by the family (e.g., child care and sex education).

III The Conflict Perspective: Perpetuating Social Inequality
A. The educational system is a tool used by those who control society to maintain their dominance. Education reproduces the social class structure, as well as society's divisions of race-ethnicity.
  1. Regardless of ability, children of the wealthy are usually placed in college-bound tracks and children of the poor in vocational tracks. The funneling effect of education is seen as whites are more likely to complete high school, go to college, and get a degree than are African Americans and Latinos.
  2. The education system helps pass privilege (or lack thereof) across generations.
B. In addition to the formal curriculum, the **hidden curriculum** is the unwritten rules of behavior and attitude (e.g., obedience to authority, conformity to cultural norms) taught in school.

C. Conflict theorists criticize IQ (intelligence quotient) testing because they measure not only intelligence but also culturally acquired knowledge. By focusing on these factors, IQ tests reflect a cultural bias that favors the middle class and discriminates against minority and lower class students.

D. Because public schools are largely financed by local property taxes, there are rich and poor school districts. Unequal funding stacks the deck against minorities and the poor.

IV. The Symbolic Interaction Perspective: Fulfilling Teacher Expectations

A. Symbolic interactionists study face-to-face interactions inside the classroom. They have found that the expectations of teachers are especially significant in determining what students learn.

B. The **Rist research** (participant observation in an African-American grade school with an African-American faculty) found tracking begins immediately with teachers' perceptions.
1. After eight days—and without testing for ability—teachers divided the class into fast, average, and slow learners; social class was the basis for the assignments.
2. Students from whom more was expected did the best; students in the slow group were ridiculed and disengaged themselves from classroom activities.
3. The labels applied in kindergarten followed the child through school.

C. **George Farkas** found that students scoring the same on course material receive different grades: female and Asian Americans get higher grades. Some students signal that they are interested in what the teacher is teaching and the teachers pick up these signals.

V. Problems in U.S. Education—and Their Solutions

A. Several factors have been identified as the major problems facing the U.S. educational system today, including the rising tide of mediocrity, grade inflation, and how it relates to social promotion and functional illiteracy, and violence in schools.

B. Solutions offered to address these problems include creating a secure learning environment and establishing higher academic standards and expectations.

RELIGION: ESTABLISHING MEANING
VI. What Is Religion?

A. According to Durkheim, all religions separate the profane from the sacred, Developing community around their beliefs and practices.
1. *Sacred* refers to aspects of life having to do with the supernatural that inspire awe, reference, deep respect, or deep fear.
2. *Profane* refers to the other more ordinary aspects of everyday life.

B. He found **religion** to be defined by three elements: (1) beliefs that some things are sacred (forbidden, set off from the profane); (2) practices (rituals) concerning things considered sacred; and (3) a moral community (a church) which results from a group's beliefs and practices.

VII. The Functionalist Perspective

A. Religion performs functions such as (1) answering questions about ultimate meaning (the purpose of life, why people suffer); (2) uniting believers into a community that shares values and perspectives; (3) providing guidelines for life; (4) controlling behavior; (5) providing support for the government; and (6) spearheading social change (on occasion, as in the case of the civil right movement in the 1960a).

B. War and religious persecution are dysfunctions of religion.

## VIII.	The Symbolic Interactionist Perspective

A.	Religions use symbols to provide identity and social solidarity for members. These are not ordinary symbols to members, but sacred symbols evoking awe and reverence, which become a condensed way of communicating with others.

B.	Rituals are ceremonies or repetitive practices that unite people into a moral community. Some are designed to create a feeling of closeness with God and unity with one another.

    1.	Symbols, including rituals, develop from beliefs. A belief may be vague ("God is") or specific ("God wants us to prostrate ourselves and face Mecca five times each day").

    2.	Religious beliefs provide values and a cosmology (unified picture of the world).

C.	Religious experience refers to a sudden awareness of the supernatural or a feeling of coming in contact with God. Some Protestants use the term "born again" to describe people who have undergone such a religious experience.

## IX.	The Conflict Perspective

A.	Conflict theorists are highly critical of religion. Karl Marx called religion the "opium of the people" because he believed that the workers find escape in religion. He argued that religion diverts the energies of the oppressed from changing their circumstances because they focus on the happiness they will have in the coming world rather than on their suffering in this world.

B.	Religious teachings and practices reflect a society's inequalities. Religion legitimates social inequality, reflecting the interests of those in power by teaching that the existing social arrangements of a society represent what God desires.

## X.	Religion and the Spirit of Capitalism

A.	Observing European countries industrializing under capitalism, Weber questioned why some societies embraced capitalism while others clung to traditional ways. He concluded that religion held the key to modernization (transformation of traditional societies into industrial societies).

B.	Weber concluded that:

    1.	Religion (including a Calvinistic belief in predestination and the need for reassurance as to one's fate) is the key to the development of capitalism in Europe.

    2.	A change in religion (from Catholicism to Protestantism) led to a change in thought and behavior. The result was the Protestant Ethic, a commitment to live a moral life, to work, and be frugal.

    3.	The spirit of capitalism (desire to accumulate capital as a duty, as an end in itself), resulted from this new ethic, and was a radical departure from the past.

C.	Today the spirit of capitalism and the Protestant ethic are by no means limited to Protestants; they have become cultural traits that have spread throughout the world.

## XI.	Types of Religious Groups

A.	A **cult** is a new religion with few followers, whose teachings and practices put it at odds with the dominant culture and religion.

    1.	All religions begin as cults and often emerge with the appearance of a charismatic leader who exerts extraordinary appeal to a group of followers.

    2.	Each cult meets with rejection from society since the message given by the cult is seen as a threat to the dominant culture.

B.   A **sect** is larger than a cult, but still feels substantial hostility from and toward society. If a sect grows, its members tend to become respectable in society, and the sect is changed into a church.

C.   A **church** is a large, highly organized religious group with formal, sedate services with less emphasis on personal conversion. The religious group becomes highly bureaucratized (including national and international offices that give directions to local congregations). Most new members come from children born to existing members, rather than from outside recruitment.

D.   An **ecclesia** is a religious group so integrated into the dominant culture that it is difficult to tell where one begins and the other ends. The government and religion work together to shape society; there is no recruitment of members since citizenship makes everyone a member. But the majority of people in the society belong in name only.

E.   Although religions begin as cults, not all religions have done so. A denomination—a "brand name" within a religion (e.g. Methodist) — begins as a splinter group. On occasion a large group within a church may disagree on some of the church's teachings (but not its major message) and break away to form its own organization.

XII.   Religion in the United States

A.   Characteristics of membership in U.S. churches:

    1.   Membership is highest in the South and Midwest, and not much lower in the East.

    2.   Each religious group draws members from all social classes, although some are more likely to draw members from the top of the social class system and others from the bottom. The most top-heavy are Episcopalians and Jews; the most bottom-heavy the Baptist and Evangelicals.

    3.   All major religious groups in the United States draw from various racial and ethnic groups: however, persons of Hispanic or Irish descent are likely to be Roman Catholics, those of Greek origin to belong to the Greek Orthodox Church, while African Americans are likely to be Protestants. Worship services tend to be highly segregated along racial lines.

    4.   Membership rate increases steadily with age.

B.   Characteristics of Religious Groups

    1.   There is a diversity of religious groups—no state church, no ecclesia, and no single denomination predominates.

    2.   These religions compete with one another for members.

    3.   Today there is a fundamentalist revival as mainstream churches fail to meet the basic religious needs of large numbers of people.

    4.   The electronic church, in which televangelists reach millions of viewers and raise millions of dollars, is growing. And recently, the electronic church has moved to the Internet. Some believe that the Internet may fundamentally change our ideas about God.

C.   The history of U.S. churches is marked by secularization and splintering of religious groups.

    1.   Initially, founders of religious sects feel alienated from the general culture, and their values; a lower social class position sets them apart.

    2.   As time passes, the members of the group become more successful, acquire more education, become middle class, and grow more respectable. They no longer feel alienated from the dominant culture and there is an attempt to harmonize religious beliefs with the new cultural orientation.

    3.   This process is the secularization of religion, of shifting the focus from religious matters to affairs of this world.

      4.   Those who have not achieved worldly success often feel betrayed and break away to form a new sect.

XIII. The Future of Religion

      A.   Science cannot answer questions about four concerns many people have: the existence of God; the purpose of life; morality; and the existence of an afterlife.

          1.   Neither science nor political systems can replace religion, and religion will last as long as humanity lasts.

KEY TERMS

After studying the chapter, review each of the following terms.

born again: term describing Christians who have undergone a life-transforming religious experience so radical that they feel they have become a new person (p. 371)

charisma: an extraordinary gift from God; more commonly, an outstanding, 'magnetic' personality (p. 374)

charismatic leader: someone to whom God has given an extraordinary gift; more commonly, someone who exerts extraordinary appeal to a group of followers (p. 374)

church: to Durkheim, one of the three essential elements of religion—a moral community of believers (p. 367)

cosmology: a unified picture of the world (p. 371)

credential society: a group that uses diplomas and degrees to determine who is eligible for jobs, even though the diploma or degree may be irrelevant to the actual work (p. 354)

cult: a new religion with few followers, whose teachings and practices put it at odds with the dominant culture and religion (p. 374)

cultural transmission of values: in reference to education, the ways by which schools transmit culture, especially its core values (p. 358)

denominations: "brand names" within a major religion (p. 374)

ecclesia: a religious group so integrated into the dominant culture that it is difficult to tell where the one begins and the other leaves off; also called a state religion (p. 374)

functional illiteracy: a high school graduate who has difficulty with basic reading and math (p. 365)

gatekeeping: a process by which education opens and closes doors of opportunity; another term for the social placement function of education (p. 360)

hidden curriculum: the unwritten goals of schools, such as teaching obedience to authority and conformity to cultural norms (p. 361)

latent functions: unintended beneficial consequences of people's actions that help to keep a social system in equilibrium (p. 358)

mainstreaming: helping people with disabilities become part of the mainstream of society (p. 360)

manifest functions: the intended consequences of people's actions, designed to help some part of a social system (p. 358)

profane: Durkheim's term for common elements of everyday life (p. 366)

Protestant ethic: Weber's term to describe the ideal of a self-denying moral life accompanied by hard work and frugality (p. 373)

religion: to Emile Durkheim, beliefs and practices that separate the profane from the sacred and unite its adherents into a moral community (p. 367)

religious experience: awareness of the supernatural or a feeling of coming in contact with God (p. 371)

sacred: Durkheim's term for things set apart or forbidden, that inspire fear, awe, reverence, or deep respect (p. 366)

sect: a group larger than a cult whose members still feel hostility from and toward society (p. 374)

secularization of religion: the replacement of a religion's 'other worldly' concerns with concerns about "this world" (p. 378)

self-fulfilling prophecy: a false assumption that something is going to happen and then comes true simply because it was predicted (p. 363)

social placement: a function of education; funneling people into a society's various positions (p. 360)

social promotion: promoting students to the next grade even though they have not mastered the basic materials (p. 365)

spirit of capitalism: Weber's term for the desire to accumulate capital as a duty—not to spend it, but as an end in itself—and to constantly reinvest it (p. 372)

tracking: sorting students into educational programs on the basis of real/perceived abilities (p. 360)

KEY PEOPLE

Review the major theoretical contributions or research findings of these theorists and thinkers.

James Coleman and Thomas Hoffer: A study of students in Catholic and public high schools by these two sociologists demonstrated that student performance was based on setting higher standards rather than on individual ability.

Randall Collins: Collins studied the credential society.

Kingsley Davis and Wilbert Moore: Davis and Moore argue that a major task of society is to fill social positions with capable people and that one of the functions of schools is gatekeeping—the funneling of people into these positions based on merit.

Emile Durkheim: Durkheim investigated world religions and identified elements that are common to all religions—beliefs about what is sacred, practices surrounded the sacred, and a moral community, all of which separate the sacred from the profane.

George Farkas: Farkas and a team of researchers investigated how teacher expectations affect student grades, finding that good students signal teachers that they are eager, cooperative and ready to work hard.

Benton Johnson: Johnson analyzed types of religious groups—cults, sects, churches, and ecclesia.

Karl Marx: Marx was critical of religion, calling it the opium of the masses.

Richard Niebuhr: This theologian suggested that the splintering of Christianity into numerous branches has more to do with social change than with religious conflict.

Talcott Parsons: A functionalist who suggested that a function of schools is to funnel people into social positions.

Liston Pope: Another sociologist who studied types of religious groups.

Ray Rist: This sociologist's classic study of an African-American grade school uncovered some of the dynamics of educational tracking.

Thomas Sowell: Sowell has studied international differences in student performance.

Ernst Troeltsch: Sociologist who is identified with types of religious groups from cults to ecclesia.

Max Weber: Weber studied the link between Protestantism and the rise of capitalism and found that the ethic associated with Protestant denominations was compatible with the needs of capitalism.

SELF-TEST

After completing this self-test, check your answers in the Answer Key of this Study Guide.

MULTIPLE CHOICE QUESTIONS

1. The positive things that people intend their actions to accomplish are known as:
    a. latent functions.
    b. manifest functions.
    c. mainstreaming.
    d. none of the above.

2. Functions of education, in the United States, include:
    a. teach knowledge and skills.
    b. child care.
    c. sex education.
    d. all of the above.

3.   A process by which schools pass a society's core values from one generation to the next is:
      a.   cultural transmission.
      b.   cultural assimilation.
      c.   cultural accommodation.
      d.   cultural diffusion.

4.   Schools help mold students into a more cohesive unit by stressing:
      a.   cultural diffusion.
      b.   conflict.
      c.   social integration.
      d.   political correctness.

5.   When schools try to incorporate students with disabilities into regular social activities it is called:
      a.   tracking.
      b.   social placement.
      c.   mainstreaming.
      d.   cultural transmission.

6.   Gatekeeping includes:
      a.   credentialing.
      b.   tracking.
      c.   social placement.
      d.   all of the above.

7.   Sorting students into different educational programs on the basis of their perceived abilities is:
      a.   tracking.
      b.   social placement.
      c.   cultural transmission.
      d.   a latent function of schools.

8.   From a conflict perspective, the real purpose of education is to:
      a.   perpetuate existing social inequalities.
      b.   provide educational opportunities for students from all types of backgrounds.
      c.   teach patriotism, teamwork, and cooperation.
      d.   replace family functions which most families no longer fulfill.

9.   The hidden curriculum is based on:
      a.   functionalism.
      b.   symbolic interactionism.
      c.   the conflict perspective.
      d.   ethnomethodology.

10.   Public schools are largely supported by:
      a.   state funding.
      b.   federal funding.
      c.   local property taxes.
      d.   state income taxes.

11.   Teacher expectations and face-to-face interactions are of interest to which theoretical perspective?
      a.   Functionalism

    b.   Conflict
    c.   Symbolic interactionism
    d.   Educational

12.   In his study of students in a large school district in the Southwestern United States, sociologist George Farkas found that females and Asian-Americans averaged higher course grades even though they had the same test scores as other students. He concluded that the reason for this finding is that female and Asian-American students were more likely to:
    a.   do more extra-credit work than other students.
    b.   ask more questions about the work they were doing.
    c.   show that they are good students by eagerly cooperating and quickly agreeing with the teacher.
    d.   stay after school and help the teacher clean up the room.

13.   The practice of passing students from one grade to the next even though they have not mastered basic materials is:
    a.   functional illiteracy.
    b.   social promotion.
    c.   tracking.
    d.   mainstreaming.

14.   High school graduates who have difficulty with basic reading and math are known as:
    a.   "boneheads."
    b.   functional illiterates.
    c.   functional literates.
    d.   underachievers.

15.   Sociologists James Coleman and Thomas Hoffer found that Catholic schools produce better results than public schools because the Catholic schools:
    a.   have higher standards.
    b.   have less parental interference.
    c.   attract better students.
    d.   are not hampered by educational bureaucracy.

16.   Called the best teacher in America, Jaime Escalante's approach to teaching illustrates that the problem with the United States educational system is the:
    a.   teachers.
    b.   structure of the learning setting.
    c.   students.
    d.   lack of funds.

17.   Sociologist Emile Durkheim found that all religions separate:
    a.   good and evil.
    b.   sins of omission and commission.
    c.   clergy and laity.
    d.   the sacred and the profane.

18.   Durkheim said a religion is defined by all the following elements *except*:
    a.   authoritarian personalities.
    b.   beliefs.

c. practices.
d. moral communities.

19. All of the following are functions of religion *except*:
    a. encouraging wars for holy causes.
    b. instilling the values of patriotism.
    c. spearheading social change.
    d. providing guidelines for daily life.

20. In 1692, Protestant leaders in Salem, Massachusetts, executed 21 men and women who were accused of being witches. According to the functionalist perspective, such persecution would be considered a:
    a. function of religion.
    b. dysfunction of religion.
    c. symbolic act of faith.
    d. ritual sacrifice.

21. Symbolic interactionists study religion to:
    a. analyze how it perpetuates the social structure.
    b. understand the meanings people give to their experiences.
    c. discover the major social functions it fills.
    d. uncover the social origins of religious faith.

22. Religious beliefs include not only values but a unified picture of the world, called a:
    a. theology.
    b. cosmology.
    c. cosmetology.
    d. superstition.

23. Karl Marx believed that religion:
    a. takes the minds of the oppressed workers off their misery.
    b. motivated the upper-middle class to become capitalists.
    c. was a major cause for the rise of capitalism.
    d. could not be proved or disproved.

24. The transformation of traditional societies into industrial societies, according to Weber, was called:
    a. the spirit of capitalism.
    b. sociology.
    c. modernization.
    d. cultural diffusion.

25. Weber saw religion's focus on the afterlife as a source of profound:
    a. social disorganization.
    b. social change.
    c. social and psychological superstitions.
    d. none of the above are correct.

26. A cult is best defined as:
    a. a new or different religion
    b. a group with a belief in the occult

    c.   a religion with bizarre practices

    d.   a simple faith system

27.   Which of the following tends to have the largest member base?

    a.   a cult

    b.   a sect

    c.   a church

    d.   an ecclesia

28.   State religions are also called:

    a.   sects.

    b.   churches.

    c.   ecclesia.

    d.   none of the above.

29.   Religion in the United States is stratified by_____ and race.

    a.   gender

    b.   social class

    c.   choice

    d.   residential location

30.   _____ is the shifting focus from spiritual matters to affairs of the world.

    a.   Fundamentalism

    b.   Secularization

    c.   Protestant ethnic

    d.   Ecclesia

TRUE-FALSE QUESTIONS

T F   1.   In the United States, employers use diplomas and degrees to determine who is eligible for a job.

T F   2.   In Russia, private, religious, and foreign-run schools are not allowed to operate.

T F   3.   Education's most obvious function is to teach knowledge and skills.

T F   4.   Students everywhere are taught that their country is the best country in the world.

T F   5.   Functionalists emphasize the importance of the "hidden curriculum" in their analysis of United States education.

T F   6.   Research by Rist concluded that the child's journey through school was preordained by the end of the first year in kindergarten.

T F   7.   Conflict theorists believe that intelligence tests in schools are not only positively useful but also free of graded judgments.

T F   8.   Conflict theorists stress that in all states the deck is stacked against the poor.

T F   9.   The "rising tide of mediocrity" is not linked to the educational dogma that students should, above all, feel good about themselves.

T F   10.   One-third of all college first-year students have an overall high school grade point average of "A".

T F   11.   Mediocrity in high-schools and colleges is enhanced by the "dumbing-down" of textbooks.

T F   12.   The goal of the sociological study of religion is to understand the role religion plays in people's lives.

T F 13. Two dysfunctions of religion are religious persecution and war.
T F 14. The term "born again" is a term used to describe the Hindu belief in reincarnation.
T F 15. The term "religious experience" refers to a sudden awareness of the supernatural or a feeling of coming in contact with God.
T F 16. According to Weber, capitalism developed in Europe because Protestantism came on the scene.
T F 17. Cults often begin with the appearance of a charismatic leader.
T F 18. All religions began as cults.
T F 19. According to your text, the Amish remain a cult.
T F 20. The chances that an American belongs to a church or synagogue generally increases with age.

FILL-IN QUESTIONS

1. Using diplomas and degrees to determine who is eligible for jobs, even though the diploma or degree may be irrelevant to the actual work, is a characteristic of _____.

2. _____ discourages competition between individuals in its school system.

3. In the _____ most people find little need for formal education.

4. Because most families in the United States have two wage earners, _____ has become a manifest function of the school system.

5. Many United States schools practice _____, the sorting of students into different educational programs based on their real or perceived abilities.

6. In the United States, a central issue in intelligence testing is the potential problem of _____ biases.

7. According to research done in California and Wisconsin, the _____ is the most important factor in how teenagers do in school.

8. The first step in offering a good education, according to your text's author, is to make students _____.

9. According to Durkheim, aspects of life that are not concerned with religion or religious purposes but, instead, are part of the ordinary aspects of everyday life are the_____.

10. One of the dysfunctions of religion, as illustrated by the Salem, MA, witchcraft trials, is _____.

11. For Muslims, the crescent moon and star, for Jews the Star of David, and for Christians the cross, all are examples of_____.

12. According to conflict theorists, religion is the _____.

13. _____ is Weber's term to describe the ideal of a highly moral life, hard work, industriousness, and frugality.

14. Most new members of a _____ have not joined through conversion, but are children born to existing members.

15. The _____ church began as a ministry to shut-ins and those not belonging to the church.

MATCH THESE THEORISTS/PHILOSOPHERS WITH THEIR CONTRIBUTIONS

1. Rist
2. Farkas
3. Durkheim
4. Weber
5. Marx

a. *The Protestant ethic*
b. *Religion is the opium of the people*
c. *Expectations of kindergarten teachers*
d. *Teacher expectations in grading students*
e. *The Elementary Forms of the Religious Life*

MATCH EACH CONCEPT WITH ITS DEFINITION

1. The Protestant ethic
2. Ecclesia
3. Charisma
4. Fundamentalism
5. Secularization

a. *Shifts focus from spiritual matters to the affairs of this world*
b. *Teaches that the bible is literally true*
c. *A state religion*
d. *Magnetic charm and leadership*
e. *Self-denying approach to life*

ESSAY QUESTIONS

1. Explain the link between democracy, industrialization, and universal education.
2. Explain what conflict theorists mean when they say that the deck is stacked against the poor when it comes to education. Offer a solution that might address this problem.
3. Select one of the three perspectives and design a research project to test its' claims about the nature of education.
4. The functionalists point out both the functions and dysfunctions of religion. Discuss both the functions and dysfunctions and consider whether it is possible for religion to fulfill its functions without producing dysfunctions.
5. Discuss the process by which a religion matures from a cult into a church.
6. Discuss whether secularization is inevitable.

STUDENT PROJECTS

1. Your text discusses research by Farkas in which he examined the process by which teacher expectations affect grades. Do you think teachers' expectations in college affect grades and if so, has it happened to you? Explain and offer illustrations.

2. What do you think about distance learning education? List the positive and negative benefits of distance learning. Have you or someone you know ever taken a class via the internet? Briefly summarize the experience. Do you think it is possible to learn the same material via the internet as in a classroom setting? Explain. What do you think the future holds for distance education?

CHAPTER 14

POPULATION AND URBANIZATION

CHAPTER SUMMARY

- Demography is the study of the size, composition, growth, and distribution of human populations. Over 200 years ago Thomas Malthus observed that populations grow geometrically while food supplies increase arithmetically; he argued that the population of the world would eventually outstrip its food supply. The debate between those who agree with this prediction (the New Malthusians) and those who disagree (the Anti-Malthusians) continues. Today, the basic cause of starvation is the global misdistribution of food rather than world overpopulation.

- Because children play a very different role in the cultures of the Least Industrialized Nations, people have large families. To project population trends, demographers use three demographic variables: fertility, mortality, and migration. A nation's growth rate is affected by unanticipated variables, such as war, plague, and famine, as well as government policies and industrialization.

- Urbanization is when an increasing proportion of a population lives in cities; it represents the greatest mass migration in human history. Cities can only develop if there is an agricultural surplus. Until the Industrial Revolution cities were small, but as transportation and communication systems grew , the infrastructure of modern cities developed and they grew larger.

- Urbanization today is so extensive that some cities have become metropolises; some times merging to form a megalopolis. Within the U.S., the trend is toward gentrification and regional migration.

- Three major models have been proposed to explain how cities expand: the concentric-zone, sector, and multiple-nuclei models. No one model is adequate in completely explaining the complexities of urban growth.

- Some people find a sense of community in cities, while others find alienation,   depending largely on their background and urban networks. Herbert Gans identified five types of city dwellers: cosmopolites, singles, ethnic villages, the deprived, and the trapped. To develop community in the city, people personalize their shopping, identify with sports teams, and even become sentimental about objects in the city. Noninvolvement is generally functional for urbanites, but impedes giving help in emergencies.

- Cities in the U.S. are subject to constant change, including disinvestment, suburbanization, and deindustrialization. Rural rebound refers to rural counties once again growing, reversing a trend that has been in place for a couple of hundred years. The guiding principles for developing social policy are scale, livability, and social justice.

LEARNING OBJECTIVES

As you read Chapter 14, use these learning objectives to organize your notes. After completing your reading, you should be able to answer each of the objectives.

1. Know what is meant by the Malthus theorem and state the major points and counterpoints in the debate between the New Malthusians and the Anti-Malthusians.
2. Identify the primary causes of famines and starvation.
3. Understand why people in the Least Industrialized Nations have so many children and discuss the implications of different rates of population growth.
4. Understand how to read a population pyramid.
5. Describe the three demographic variables used to estimate population growth and explain why it is difficult to forecast.
6. Define urbanization and trace the development of cities from ancient times through industrialization.
7. Discuss the trends contributing to the emergence of metropolises and megalopolises.
8. Identify urban patterns in the United States.
9. Describe and evaluate the four models of urban growth.
10. Discuss how some people find a sense of community in cities while others become alienated.
11. Describe the five types of urban dwellers identified by sociologist Herbert Gans.
12. Talk about the ways people who live in cities create a sense of intimacy.
13. Explain why many urban dwellers follow a norm of noninvolvement and how this norm contributes to a dysfunctional diffusion of responsibility.
14. Know why large numbers of Americans have begun moving from cities and suburbs to rural areas.
15. Identify the primary problems of urban life today and discuss how suburbanization, disinvestment, and deindustrialization contribute to these problems.
16. Evaluate current attempts to address urban problems in the United States and discuss the guiding principles for developing future policies to deal with these problems.

CHAPTER OUTLINE

POPULATION IN GLOBAL PERSPECTIVE
I.   A Planet with No Space to Enjoy Life?

    A.   **Demography** is the study of the size, composition, growth, and distribution of populations.

    B.   **Thomas Malthus** wrote *An Essay on the Principle of Population* (1798) and stated the *Malthus theorem*—that population grows geometrically while food supply increases arithmetically; thus, if births go unchecked, population will eventually outstrip food supply.

    C.   The **New Malthusians** believe Malthus was correct and the world's population is following an exponential growth curve (where numbers increase in extraordinary proportions): 1800, one billion; 1930, two billion; 1960, three billion; 1975, four billion; 1987, five billion; and 1999, six billion.

    D.   The **Anti-Malthusians** believe that people do not blindly reproduce until there is no room left.

        1.   They cite the three stages of the demographic transition in Europe as an example: Stage 1, a fairly stable population (high birth rates offset by high death rates);

Stage 2, "population explosion" (high birth rates and low death rates); Stage 3, population stability (low birth rates and low death rates).

2. They assert that the Least Industrialized Nations, which currently are in the second state, will follow this transition.

E. Who is correct?

1. There is no question that the Least Industrialized Nations are in Stage 2, but there is a question about when they will reach Stage 3. Death rates have dropped but birth rates remain high.

2. Leaders of the Most Industrialized Nations, fear that these growing nations will upset the international balance of power, and use the United Nations to spearhead global efforts to reduce world population growth.

3. The population of the Least Industrialized Nations is increasing, but at a slower rate. To the New Malthusians, the catastrophe is still coming; to Anti-Malthusians, this is a sign that the Least Industrialized Nations are approaching Stage 3.

4. The Anti-Malthusians argue that the world's problem will not be a population explosion but population shrinkage (when birth rate and immigration do not replace those who die and emigrate), as has occurred in Europe.

5. Some Anti-Malthusians even predict a "demographic free fall"—after peaking at 7–8 billion, the world's population will begin to grow smaller.

6. Only the future will prove the accuracy of either side's projections.

F. Why are people starving? Does the world produce enough food to feed everyone?

1. Anti-Malthusians note that the amount of food produced for each person in the world has increased: famines are not the result of too little food production, but from the global misdistribution of this food.

2. The New Malthusians counter that as the world's population continues to grow, the earth may not be able to continue to produce sufficient food.

3. Recent famines have been concentrated in Africa. However, these famines are not due to too many people living on too little land. Rather, these famines are due to outmoded farming techniques and ongoing political instability that disrupt harvests and food distribution.

II. Population Growth

A. There are different reasons why people in the Least Industrialized Nations have so many children.

1. Parenthood provides status. For women, motherhood is the most exalted status a woman can achieve—the more children, the higher the status. For men, their manhood is proven if they father many (and especially male) children.

2. The community supports this view by awarding or withholding status. Since children are considered to be a sign of God's blessing; couples are expected to have many children.

3. Children are considered economic assets since the parents rely on their children to take care of them in their old age.

4. The conflict perspective stresses that internalized values support the domination of females by males in all spheres of life, including reproduction. Male dominance includes fathering many children as a means of achieving status in the community.

B. Demographers use population pyramids (graphic representations of a population, divided into age and sex) to illustrate a country's population dynamics (e.g., Mexico's doubling rate is only 35 years).

1.   Different population growth rates have different implications. Countries with slow growth rates have fewer people on which to spend their resources, while countries with rapid growth rates have an increased number of people who must share resources.

2.   A declining standard of living may result in political instability followed by severe repression by the government.

C.   Estimated population growth is based on three demographic variables

1.   **Fertility**, measured by the fertility rate (number of children an average woman bears), is sometimes confused with **fecundity** (number of children a woman theoretically can bear). To compute a country's fertility rate, demographers look at the crude birth rate (annual number of births per 1,000 people).

2.   **Mortality** is measured by the crude death rate (number of deaths per 1,000 people).

3.   **Migration** is measured by the net migration rate (the number of immigrants moving in vs. the emigrants moving out per 1,000 population). **Push factors** make people want to leave where they are living (e.g., poverty, persecution, lack of economic opportunity); **pull factors** attract people (e.g., opportunities for higher wages or better jobs in the new locale). The flow of migration is from the Least Industrialized Nations to the industrialized countries, with the U.S. being the world's number one choice of immigrants.

D.   Demographers often encounter problems in forecasting population growth.

1.   The **growth rate** equals births minus deaths, plus net migration.

2.   Social factors—wars, economic booms and busts, plagues, and famines—push death and birth rates up and down.

3.   The primary factor that influences a country's growth rate is its rate of industrialization—as a country industrializes the growth rate declines. New economic opportunities open up, but having and raising children also becomes more expensive.

4.   Because of the difficulties in forecasting population growth, demographers formulate several predictions simultaneously, each depending on different assumptions.

URBANIZATION

III.   The Development of Cities

A.   A **city** is a place in which a large number of people are permanently based and do not produce their own food.

1.   Small cities with massive defensive walls existed as far back as 10,000 years ago; cities on a larger scale originated about 3500 B.C. as a result of the development of more efficient agriculture and the resulting food surplus.

2.   The Industrial Revolution drew people to cities to work.

3.   Urbanization today not only means that more people live in cities, but also that today's cities are larger; about 300 of the world's cities contain at least one million people.

B.   **Urbanization** is when an increasing proportion of a population lives in cities. There are specific characteristics of cities, such as size and anonymity that give them their unique urban flavor.

1.   A **metropolis** is a city that grows so large that it exerts influence over an entire region; the central city and surrounding smaller cities and suburbs are connected economically, politically, and socially.

2. **Megalopolis** refers to an overlapping area consisting of at least two metropolises and their suburbs which are connected economically, socially, and, sometimes, politically.

C. In 1790, only about 5 percent of Americans lived in cities; by 1920, 50 percent of the U.S. population lived in urban areas; today, between 75 and 80 percent of Americans live in urban areas.

1. The U.S. Census Bureau divided the country into 284 *metropolitan statistical areas (MSAs)*—a central city of at least 50,000 people and the urbanized counties that are linked to it.

2. About three in five Americans live in just 50 or so MSAs.

3. As Americans migrate in search of work and better life styles, distinct migration patterns appear. Urban growth today is fastest in the West and South, while urban decline is highest in the Northeast.

4. As Americans migrate and businesses move to serve them, edge cities (a clustering of service facilities and residential areas near highway intersections) have developed.

5. **Gentrification**, the movement of middle-class people into rundown areas of a city, is another major U.S. urban pattern.

D. **Robert Park** coined the term *human ecology* to describe how people adapt to their environment (also known as "urban ecology"); human ecologists have constructed three models which attempt to explain urban growth patterns.

1. **Ernest W. Burgess** proposed the concentric zone model, which views the city as a series of zones emanating from the center, each characterized by a different group of people and activity: Zone 1—central business district; Zone 2—in transition with deteriorating housing and rooming houses; Zone 3—area to which thrifty workers have moved to escape the zone in transition, yet maintain access to work; Zone 4—more expensive apartments, single-family dwellings, and exclusive areas where the wealthy live; and Zone 5—commuter zone consisting of suburban areas or cities that have developed around rapid transit routes.

2. The **sector model** sees urban zones as wedge-shaped sectors radiating out from the center. A zone might contain one sector of working-class housing, another sector of expensive housing, a third of businesses, and so on, all competing with one another for the same land. In an invasion-succession cycle, when poor immigrants move into a city, they settle in the lowest-rent area available and, as their numbers grow, begin to encroach on adjacent areas. As the poor move closer to the middle class, the middle class leave, expanding the sector of lower-cost housing.

3. The **multiple-nuclei** model views the city as comprised of multiple centers or nuclei, each of which focuses on a specialized activity (e.g., retail districts, automobile dealers, etc.).

4. More recently, the **peripheral model** was developed to reflect the impact of radial highways on the movement of people and services away from the central city to the city's periphery, or outskirts.

5. Cities are complex, and no single model yet developed does justice to this complexity; the models do not make allowances for the extent to which elites influence the development of cities. The models also fall short when it comes to explaining urbanization in the Least Industrialized Nations.

IV. City Life

A. For some, cities provide a sense of community—a feeling that people care about what happens to each other and depend upon one another. For others, the city is alienating.

B. **Louis Wirth** argued that the city undermines kinship and neighborhood, which are the traditional bases of social control and social solidarity.

    1. Urban dwellers live in anonymity; their lives marked by segmented and superficial encounters which make them grow aloof from one another and indifferent to other people's problems.

    2. This is similar to the idea that *Gemeinschaft* (a sense of community that comes from everyone knowing everyone else) disappears as a country industrializes, and *Gesellschaft* (a society characterized by secondary, impersonal relationships which result in alienation) replaces it.

C. **Herbert Gans** uses the term urban village to refer to an area of the city that people know well and in which they live, work, shop, and play.

D. Gans identified five types of people who live in the city.

    1. **Cosmopolites**—intellectuals and professionals, students, writers, and artists who live in the inner city to be near its conveniences and cultural benefits.

    2. **Singles**—young, unmarried people who come seeking jobs and entertainment.

    3. **Ethnic villagers**—live in tightly knit neighborhoods that resemble villages and small towns, united by race and social class.

    4. **The deprived**—the very poor, the emotionally disturbed, and the handicapped that live in neighborhoods more like urban jungles than urban villages.

    5. **The trapped**—consisting of four subtypes: those who cannot afford to move when their neighborhood is invaded by another ethnic group; downwardly mobile persons who have fallen from a higher social class; the elderly who have drifted into the slums because they are not wanted elsewhere and are powerless to prevent their downward slide; and alcoholics or drug addicts.

E. Sociologists have analyzed how urban dwellers build community in the city.

    1. City people create a sense of intimacy for themselves by personalizing their shopping (frequenting the same stores and restaurants, people become recognized as "regulars").

    2. Spectator sports also engender community identification.

F. Urban dwellers are careful to protect themselves from the unwanted intrusions of strangers.

    1. They follow a norm of noninvolvement—using a newspaper or a Walkman to indicate inaccessibility for interaction—to avoid encounters with people they do not know.

    2. The more bystanders there are to an incident, the less likely people are to help because people's sense of responsibility becomes diffused. The norm of noninvolvement and the diffusion of responsibility may help urban dwellers get through every day city life, but they are also dysfunctional because people do not provide assistance to others.

V. Urban Problems and Social Policy

A. **Suburbanization**—the movement from the city to the suburbs—has had a profound effect on U.S. cities.

    1. For over 100 years people have moved into towns next to the cities in which they worked; today the speed and extent which people are leaving the city is new.

2. Central cities have lost residents, businesses, and jobs, causing the cities' tax base (which supports essential city services and schools) to shrink; the people left behind are those with limited financial means.

3. According to **William Wilson**, the term *ghetto* reflects a social transformation; the groups represented in these areas today are more socially isolated than those who lived in these communities in the past.

4. Suburbanites prefer that the city keep its problems to itself; they fight movements to share suburbia's revenues with the city. The time may come, however, when suburbanites will have to "pay" for their uncaring attitudes toward the city's urban disadvantaged.

B. By the 1940's, the movement to the suburbs began to undermine the cities' tax base, a problem accelerated as huge numbers of poor rural migrants moved into northern cities.

1. As the tax base eroded, services declined, buildings deteriorated, and banks began redlining (drawing a line around problem areas and refusing to make loans to those living and working within these areas). This disinvestment pushed these areas into further decline.

2. The development of a global market has led to deindustrialization, as manufacturing firms have relocated from the inner city to areas where production costs are lower. The inner-city economies have not been able to provide alternative employment for poor residents, thereby locking them out of the economy.

C. Beginning in the 1970s, people began to move out of the cities and suburbs into rural areas and a new trend has emerged—the **rural rebound**.

1. During the 1990s, seven out of ten rural counties grew in population and little farming towns began making a comeback.

2. The "push" factors include fears of urban crime and violence; the "pull" factors are safety, lower costs of living, recreation, and more space.

3. Facilitating this movement are improvements in transportation and communications.

D. Social policy usually takes one of two forms.

1. **Urban renewal** involves tearing down and rebuilding the buildings in an area. As a result of urban renewal, the areas residents can no longer afford to live in the area and are displaced.

2. **Enterprise zones** are economic incentives to encourage businesses to move into the area. Most business, however, refuse to move into high-crime areas.

3. If U.S. cities are to change, adequate resources in terms of money and human talents focused on overcoming urban woes must become top agenda items for the U.S. government..

4. **William Flanagan** suggests three guiding principles for working out specific solutions to urban problems: (1) regional and national planning is necessary; (2) growth needs to be channeled to make city living attractive; and (3) social policy must be evaluated by its effects on people. Unless the root causes of urban problems—housing, education, and jobs—are addressed, solutions will only serve as band-aids that cover the real problems.

KEY TERMS

After studying the chapter, review each of the following terms.

alienation: Marx's term for workers' lack of connection to the product of their labor; caused by their being assigned repetitive tasks on a small part of a product; leading to a sense of powerlessness and normlessness; also used in the general sense of not feeling a part of something
(p. 406)

basic demographic equation: growth rate = births - deaths + net migration (p. 394)

city: a place in which a large number of people are permanently based and do not produce their own food
(p. 397)

crude birth rate: the annual number of births per 1,000 population (p. 393)

crude death rate: the annual number of deaths per 1,000 population (p. 393)

deindustrialization: a process by which fewer people work in manufacturing; one reason is automation, another is the globalization of capitalism, which moves manufacturing jobs to countries where labor costs less (p. 411)

demographic transition: a three-stage historical process of population growth: first, high birth rates and high death rates; second, high birth rates and low death rates; and third, low birth rates and low death rates; a fourth stage of population shrinkage may be emerging in the Most Industrialized Nations (p. 385)

demographic variables: the three factors that influence population growth: fertility, mortality, and net migration (p. 392)

disinvestment: the withdrawal of investments by banks, which seals the fate of an urban area
(p. 410)

edge city: a large clustering of service facilities and residences near a highway intersection that provides a sense of place to people who live, shop, and work there (p. 402)

enterprise zone: the use of economic incentives in a designated area with the intention of encouraging investment there (p. 411)

exponential growth curve: a pattern of growth in which numbers double during approximately equal intervals, thus accelerating in the latter stages (p. 384)

fecundity: the number of children that women are capable of bearing (p. 392)

fertility rate: the number of children that the average woman bears (p. 392)

gentrification: the displacement of the poor as the relatively affluent purchase and renovate their homes
(p. 402)

growth rate: the net change in a population after adding births, subtracting deaths, and either adding or subtracting net migration (p. 394)

human ecology: Robert Park's term for the relationship between people and their environment (natural resources, such as land); also called *urban ecology* (p. 404)

invasion-succession cycle: the process of one group of people displacing a group whose racial-ethnic or social class characteristics differ from their own (p. 404)

Malthus theorem: an observation by Thomas Malthus that although the food supply increases arithmetically (from 1 to 2 to 3 to 4 and so on) population grows geometrically (from 2 to 4 to 8 to 16 and so forth) (p. 384)

megagcity: a city of ten million or more residents (p. 401)

megalopolis: an urban area consisting of at least two metropolises and their many suburbs (p. 401)

metropolis: a central city surrounded by smaller cities and their suburbs (p. 400)

metropolitan statistical area (MSA): a central city and the urbanized counties adjacent to it (p. 401)

net migration rate: the difference between the number of immigrants and the number emigrants per 1,000 population (p. 393)

population pyramid: a graphic representation of a population, divided into age and sex (p. 391)

population shrinkage: the process by which a country's population becomes smaller because its birth rate and immigration are too low to replace those who die and emigrate (p. 387)

redlining: the officers of a bank refusing to make loans in a particular area (p. 410)

urban renewal: the rehabilitation of a rundown area of a city, which usually results in the displacement of the poor who are living there (p. 411)

zero population growth: a demographic condition in which women bear only enough children to reproduce the population (p. 394)

KEY PEOPLE

Review the major theoretical contributions or research findings of these theorists and thinkers.

Ernest Burgess: Burgess developed the concentric zone model of urban development.
John Darley and Bibb Latane: these social psychologists uncovered a *diffusion of responsibility*—the more bystanders there are to an incident, the less likely anyone is to help.
William Flanagan: Flanagan has suggested three guiding principles for finding solutions to pressing urban problems—use of regional planning, awareness of human needs, and equalizing the benefits as well as the impact of urban change.

Herbert Gans: Gans studied urban neighborhoods, with the result that he documented the existence of community within cities and identified the urban dwellers that live there.

Chauncey Harris and Edward Ullman: These two geographers developed the multiple-nuclei model of urban growth.

Homer Hoyt: Hoyt modified Burgess's model of urban development with his sector model.

Donald Huddle: This economist shows that immigrants are a drain on taxpayers.

David Karp and William Yoels: These sociologists note that identification with a city's sports teams can be so intense that even after an individual moves away from the city, he continues to root for the team.

Thomas Malthus: Malthus was an economist who made dire predictions about the future of population growth.

Robert Park: Park coined the term human ecology.

Julian Simon: Economist who claims that immigrants benefit the economy.

Louis Wirth: Wirth wrote a classic essay, "Urbanism as a Way of Life," in which he argued that city life undermines kinship and neighborhood.

SELF-TEST

After completing this self-test, check your answers in the Answer Key of this Study Guide.

MULTIPLE CHOICE QUESTIONS

1. Who studies the size, composition, growth, and distribution of human population?
   a. population experts
   b. growth specialists
   c. demographers
   d. social development professionals

2. The proposition that the population grows geometrically while the food supply increases arithmetically is known as the:
   a. food surplus equation.
   b. Malthus theorem.
   c. exponential growth curve.
   d. demographic transition.

3. Which of the following statements is consistent with beliefs of the Anti-Malthusians?
   a. People will blindly reproduce until there is no room left on earth.
   b. It is possible to project the world's current population growth into the indefinite future.
   c. Most people do not use intelligence and rational planning when it comes to having children.
   d. The demographic transition provides an accurate picture of what the future looks like.

4. The three-stage historical process of population growth is known as the:
   a. demographic equation.
   b. demographic transition.
   c. exponential growth curve.
   d. implosion growth curve.

5. The process by which a country's population becomes smaller because its birth rate and immigration are too low to replace those who die and emigrate is:
    a. population transfer.
    b. population annihilation.
    c. population shrinkage.
    d. population depletion.

6. Starvation occurs because:
    a. there is not enough fertile land worldwide on which to grow food.
    b. some parts of the world lack food while other parts of the world produce more than they can consume.
    c. population is growing at a faster rate than the world's ability to produce food.
    d. people do not eat a well-balanced diet.

7. People in the Least Industrialized Nations have so many children because:
    a. parenthood provides status.
    b. children are considered to be an economic asset.
    c. the community encourages people to have children.
    d. all of the above.

8. For conflict theorists, the explanation for why women in poor nations have so many children is that:
    a. women derive special meaning from children.
    b. children's labor can be exploited by their parents.
    c. men control women's reproductive choices.
    d. women use sex as a means of control over men.

9. Mexico's current population will double in _____ years.
    a. 18
    b. 42
    c. 58
    d. 78

10. To illustrate population dynamics, demographers use:
    a. population growth charts.
    b. population pyramids.
    c. fertility rates.
    d. demographic models.

11. The factors that influence population growth are called:
    a. demographic variables.
    b. demographic transitions.
    c. demographic equations.
    d. demographic constants.

12. _____ refers to the number of children the average woman bears.
    a. Fertility rate
    b. Fecundity
    c. Crude birth rate
    d. Real birth rate

13. The annual number of deaths per 1,000 population is the:
    a. crude death rate.
    b. crude mortality rate.
    c. crude life expectancy rate.
    d. net death rate.

14. What factors might push someone to migrate?
    a. poverty
    b. lack of religious and political freedom
    c. political persecution
    d. all of the above.

15. Around the globe, the flow of migration is generally from:
    a. Most Industrialized Nations to Least Industrialized Nations
    b. one of the Least Industrialized Nation to another one.
    c. Least Industrialized Nations to Industrializing Nations.
    d. Least Industrialized Nations to Most Industrialized Nations.

16. According to your text, why is it difficult to forecast population growth?
    a. Government programs may encourage or discourage women from having children.
    b. Government bureaus may be dishonest in reporting data.
    c. There is a lack of computer programs to deal with data adequately.
    d. Births, deaths, and migration are human behaviors and thus impossible to predict.

17. China's practice of female infanticide is rooted in:
    a. sexism.
    b. economics.
    c. traditions that go back centuries.
    d. all of the above.

18. The process by which an increasing proportion of a population lives in cities is:
    a. suburbanization.
    b. gentrification.
    c. megalopolitanism.
    d. urbanization.

19. What does today's rapid urbanization mean?
    a. More people live in cities.
    b. Today's cities are larger.
    c. About 300 of the world's cities contain at least one million people.
    d. All of the above.

20. The area that extends from Maine along the coast to Virginia is an example of:
    a. urban sprawl.
    b. population congestion.
    c. megalopolis.
    d. metropolis.

21. What is a megacity?
    a. A city of 10 million or more residents
    b. A city that is at the center of a megalopolis.

    c.   A city with a multitude of problems.

    d.   A central city of at least 50,000 people and the urbanized areas linked to it.

22.   Edge cities:

    a.   consist of a clustering of shopping malls, hotels, office parks, and residential areas near the intersection of major highways.

    b.   overlap political boundaries and include parts of several cities or towns.

    c.   provide a sense of place to those who live there.

    d.   all of the above.

23.   Who first proposed the concentric-zone model?

    a.   Herbert Gans

    b.   Ernest Burgess

    c.   Robert Park

    d.   Homer Hoyt

24.   When a new group of immigrants enter a city, they tend to settle in low-rent areas. As their numbers increase, those already living in the area begin to move out; their departure creates more low-cost housing for the immigrants. Sociologists refer to this process as:

    a.   progressive population replacement.

    b.   reverse gentrification.

    c.   cycle of assimilation.

    d.   invasion-succession cycle.

25.   The model that suggests that land use in cities is based on several centers, such as a clustering of restaurants or automobile dealerships is the:

    a.   sector model.

    b.   concentric-zone model.

    c.   multiple-nuclei model.

    d.   commerce model.

26.   Louis Wirth argued that city undermines:

    a.   kinship and neighborhood.

    b.   economy and politics.

    c.   religion.

    d.   police.

27.   According to Gans' typology, the trapped include:

    a.   downwardly mobile persons.

    b.   elderly persons.

    c.   alcoholics and drug addicts.

    d.   all of the above.

28.   The Kitty Genovese case in an example of:

    a.   ethnic villagers.

    b.   cosmopolites.

    c.   diffusion of responsibility.

    d.   community.

29.   What is suburbanization?

    a.   movement from the suburbs to edge cities

b.   movement from the city to the suburbs
c.   movement from rural areas to suburbs
d.   displacement of the poor by the relatively affluent who renovate the farmer's homes

30.   What has facilitated the rural rebound?
a.   inflation
b.   globalization
c.   improvements in transportation and communications
d.   divorce

TRUE-FALSE QUESTIONS

T F   1.   Thomas Malthus said that population grows arithmetically and the food supply grows geometrically.

T F   2.   The exponential growth curve is based on the idea that if growth doubles during approximately equal intervals of time, it accelerates in the later stages.

T F   3.   Stage 2 of the demographic transition involves a "population explosion."

T F   4.   The major reason why people in the Least Industrialized Nations have so many children is because they do not know how to prevent conception.

T F   5.   Anti-Malthusians say, just as they predicted, that birth rates are falling.

T F   6.   Machismo is the emphasis on femininity and submissiveness.

T F   7.   Population pyramids represent a population, divided into race, age, and sex.

T F   8.   Demographers study fertility, mortality, and migration to predict population trends.

T F   9.   The fecundity rate is the number of children the average woman bears.

T F   10.   The rate and extent of urbanization in recent years is new to the world scene.

T F   11.   In 2007, more than ½ of the world's populations will live in cities.

T F   12.   A megacity is a city of 1 million or more residents.

T F   13.   About 3 in 5 Americans live in just fifty or so metropolitan statistical areas.

T F   14.   The concentric-zone model is based on the idea that cities expand from their central business district outward.

T F   15.   The multiple-nuclei model is the most accurate model of urban growth.

T F   16.   *The Urban Villagers* was written by Herbert Gans.

T F   17.   The norms of noninvolvement and the diffusion of responsibility can be dysfunction in some critical situations.

T F   18.   The Suburban Rebound is due to the desire to retreat to a safe haven.

T F   19.   When banks redline, the quality of life in the neighborhoods generally improves.

T F   20.   Enterprise zones tend to be very successful for cities.

FILL-IN QUESTIONS

1.   _____ is the study of the size, composition, growth, and distribution of human populations.

2.   A(n) _____ is a graphic presentation of a population, divided into age and sex.

3.   Conflict theorists point out that a declining standard of living often poses the threat of _____ instability.

4.   Three oil-rich countries of the world—Kuwait, Qatar, and United Arab Emirates—have the _____ death rate.

5. The higher the level of education that an immigrant has, the more likely he/she will _____ more than he/she _____ regarding the economy.
6. To reduce the number of children, China has a _____ national policy.
7. A demographic condition in which women bear only enough children to reproduce the population is _____.
8. _____ refers to masses of people moving to cities and to these cities having a growing influence in society.
9. An overlapping area consisting of at least two metropolises and their many suburbs is a _____.
10. Robert Park coined the term _____ to describe how people adapt to their environment.
11. The _____ model can exist within the concentric-zone model of urban growth.
12. The urban growth model that portrays the impact of radial highways on the movement of people and services away from the central city to its outskirts is the _____ model.
13. _____ is a sense of not belonging and a feeling that no one cares what happens to you.
14. _____ are a city's students, intellectuals, professionals, musicians, artists, and entertainers.
15. Darley and Latane uncovered, in their research that the more bystanders there are in a situation the _____ likely people are to offer help.

MATCH THESE THEORISTS/PHILOSOPHERS WITH THEIR CONTRIBUTIONS

1. Thomas Malthus   *a.* *Theorem on population growth*
2. Ernest Burgess   *b.* *Human ecology*
3. Herbert Gans   *c.* *Concentric-zone model*
4. Homer Hoyt   *d.* *Urban villagers*
5. Robert Park   *e.* *Sector model*

MATCH EACH CONCEPT WITH ITS DEFINITION

1. Urban renewal   *a.* *Avoiding intrusions by strangers*
2. Enterprise zone   *b.* *Banks' refusing to make loans in certain city areas*
3. Redlining
4. Deindustrialization   *c.* *Eliminates millions of U.S. manufacturing jobs*
5. Norm of noninvolvement
    d. *Replacing run-down, cheap housing with a new football stadium*
    e. *A designated area of a city that offers economic incentives to businesses*

ESSAY QUESTIONS

1. State the positions of the New Malthusians and the Anti-Malthusians and discuss which view you think is more accurate, based on the information provided about each position.
2. Identify and provide explanations for some of the population challenges that affect the Most Industrialized and the Least Industrialized Nations.
3. Identify the problems associated with forecasting population growth.
4. Discuss whether cities are impersonal *Gesellschafts* or communal *Gemeinshafts*.
5. Discuss the factors that fuel suburbanization and consider the impact this population shift has had on cities.

STUDENT PROJECTS

1. Map out where you currently live, or have lived, in terms of one or more of the models of urban growth. Even if you live in "rural" area, which one of the models can you envision your "rural" area eventually becoming? Explain and illustrate.

2. List the ways your college campus is similar to and different from living in a large urban environment. Why do many college students feel alienated and isolated? Explain. Do you think many college students follow a norm of noninvolvement? Why or why not? Explain what steps could be taken to reduce alienation on college campuses.

CHAPTER 15

SOCIAL CHANGE:
TECHNOLOGY, SOCIAL MOVEMENTS, AND THE ENVIRONMENT

CHAPTER SUMMARY

- **Social change**, the alteration of culture and society over time, is a vital part of social life. Social change has included four social revolutions, a change from *Gemeinschaft* to *Gesellschaft* societies, capitalism and industrialization, modernization, and global stratification. Ethnic conflicts and social movements indicate cutting edges of social change.

- Theories of social change include evolutionary theories, cyclical theories, and conflict theories. **William Ogburn** identified technology as the basis for social change. The processes of social change are innovation, discovery, and diffusion. **Cultural lag** refers to how some elements of a culture lags behind technological changes.

- **Technology** is a driving force behind social change and can shape an entire society. This become evident when analyzing the impact the computer has had on American society. The information superhighway is also likely to perpetuate social inequalities both nationally and globally.

- Social movements involve a large number of people who organize to promote or resist social change. Social movements can be classified as alterative, redemptive, reformative, or transformative depending on whether their target is individuals or society and whether the amount of change desired is partial or complete.

- Because the mass media are the gatekeepers for social movements, their favorable or unfavorable coverage greatly affects a social movement; tactics are chosen with this in mind.

- Social movements go through distinct stages: initial unrest, mobilization, organization, institutionalization, and decline.

- **Environmental problems** affect nations at all levels of industrialization. Due to the widespread burning of fossil fuels in internal combustion engines, the Most Industrialized Nations face problems as smog, acid rain, global warming, and the greenhouse effect. Currently the worst environmental problems are found in the former Soviet Union, in part due to the Communist Party's unrestrained exploitation of natural resources. And the rush of the Least Industrialized Nations to industrialize is adding to global environmental decay.

- The world is facing a basic conflict between lust for profits through exploitation of the earth's resources and the need to maintain a sustainable environment.

- In response, a worldwide environmental movement has emerged seeking to restore a healthy environment for the world's people. The solutions to environmental problems range from education, legislation, and political activism to ecosabotage—sabotaging the efforts of people thought to be legally harming the environment.

- Environmental sociologists attempt to study the relationship between humans and the environment. but at the same time are generally also environmental activists themselves.

LEARNING OBJECTIVES

As you read Chapter 15, use these learning objectives to organize your notes. After completing your reading, briefly state an answer to each of the objectives.

1.   Define social change and describe the four major social revolutions.

2.   Describe the shift from *Gemeinschaft* and *Gesellschaft* societies and explain the relationship between capitalism, modernization, and industrialization.
3.   Identify the relationship between conflict, power, and Global politics.
4.   Explain evolutionary, cyclical, and conflict theories of social change, noting the advantages and disadvantages of each.
5.   Identify and define Ogburn's three processes of social change. Explain what is meant by "cultural lag."
6.   Explain the double meaning of technology and discuss technology's sociological significance.
7.   Discuss the impact of computers on our society, including both the advances and the concerns that we have about them.
8.   Describe the impact of computers on education, medicine, business, war, and terrorism.
9.   Explain the relationship between new technology and global stratification.
10.   State the major reasons why social movements exist; compare and contrast proactive and reactive social movements.
11.   List the four types of social movements.
12.   Define propaganda and discuss the role of the mass media in social movements.
13.   Identify the five stages that social movements go through as they grow and mature.
14.   Describe the environmental problems facing the world today, noting differences between the Most Industrialized, the Industrializing, and the Least Industrialized Nations. State the ways in which capitalism may have contributed to these problems.
15.   Discuss the goals and activities of the environmental movement.
16.   List the assumptions of environmental sociology.
17.   Describe some of the actions necessary to reach the goal of harmony between technology and the environment.

CHAPTER OUTLINE

I.   How Social Change Transforms Social Life

    A.   **Social change** is a shift in the characteristics of culture and societies over time.

    B.   There have been four social revolutions: (1) the domestication of plants and animals, from which pastoral and horticultural societies arose; (2) the invention of the plow, leading to agricultural societies; (3) the industrial revolution; and (4) the information revolution, resulting in postindustrial societies.

    C.   The shift from **agricultural** to **industrial** economic activity was accompanied by a change from *Gemeinschaft* (daily life centers on intimate and personal relationships) to *Gesellschaft* (fleeting, impersonal relationships) societies.

    D.   Different explanations have been offered as to why societies changed from *Gemeinschaft* to *Gesellschaft*.

         1.   **Karl Marx** identified capitalism as the basic reason behind the breakup of feudal (agricultural) societies. As people were thrown off the land, they moved to cities, where they were exploited by the owners of the means of production.

         2.   **Max Weber** saw religion as the core reason for the development of capitalism; as a result of the Reformation, Protestants no longer felt assured that they were saved by virtue of church membership and concluded that through prosperity God would show visible favor to the elect.

         3.   **Modernization** (the change from agricultural to industrial societies) produced sweeping changes in societies. Modern societies are larger, more urbanized, and

subject to faster change. They stress formal education and the future and are less religiously oriented. Families are smaller, infant mortality rates lower, and life expectancy higher, as are income and material possessions.

    4.   When technology changes, societies change. Today, traditional societies are being changed by the technology of the industrialized world. For example, the export of Western medicine to the Least Industrialized Nations has reduced death rates but has not affected the high birth rates. Rapidly increasing populations strain the resources of the Least Industrialized Nations, leading to widespread hunger and starvation, and the mass migration to cities and to the Most Industrialized Nations.

  E.   Today's global divisions had already begun to emerge in the sixteenth century. As capitalism developed, the industrialized nations exploited the resources of those nations that did not industrialize.

    1.   **Dependency theory** asserts that because the Least Industrialized Nations have become dependent on the Most Industrialized Nations, they are unable to develop their own resources.

    2.   The G8, the world's industrial giants (the United States, Canada, Great Britain, France, Germany, Italy, Japan and Russia have decided how they will share the world's markets; by regulating global economic and industrial policy they guarantee their own dominance, and continued access to cheap raw materials from the Least Industrialized Nations.

    3.   The growing wealth and power of China poses another threat to the G8 as China attempts to recapture its glory from centuries past and expand its domain of influence.

    4.   The resurgence of ethnic conflicts, for example the conflict in Bosnia, threatens the global map as conceived by the G8.

II.   Theories and Processes of Social Change

  A.   Evolutionary theories are **unilinear** and **multilinear**.

    1.   Unilinear theories assume that all societies follow the same path, evolving from simple to complex through uniform sequences.

    2.   Multilinear theories assume that different routes can lead to a similar stage of development; societies need not pass through the same sequence of stages to become industrialized.

    3.   Both unilinear and multilinear theories assume the idea that societies progress toward a higher state. Because of the crises in Western culture today, these theories are now being discredited and these assumptions and evolutionary theories have been rejected.

  B.   **Cyclical theories** examine great civilizations, not just a particular society, presuming that societies are like organisms, and are born, reach adolescence, grow old, and die.

    1.   **Toynbee** proposed that initially a civilization is able to meet challenges, but as it becomes an empire, the ruling elite loses its capacity to keep the masses in line "by charm rather than by force," and the fabric of society is ripped apart.

    2.   **Oswald Spengler** proposed that Western civilization was on the wane; some analysts think the crisis in Western civilization may indicate he was right.

  C.   Marx's conflict theory viewed social change as a dialectical process, in which a *thesis* (the status quo) contains its own *antithesis* (opposition). The resulting struggle leads to a new state, or *synthesis* and the history of a society is thus a series of confrontations in which each ruling group creates the seeds of its own destruction (e.g., capitalism sets workers and capitalists on a collision course).

D. **William Ogburn** identified three processes of social change: (1) inventions, which can be either material (computers) or social (capitalism); (2) discovery, which is a new way of seeing things; and (3) diffusion, which is the spread of an invention, discovery, or idea from one area to another. Ogburn coined the term cultural lag to describe the situation in which some elements of a culture adapt to an invention or discovery more rapidly than others.

III. How Technology Changes Society

A. **Technology** refers to both the tools—items used to accomplish tasks—and the skills or procedures to make and use those tools. The chief characteristic of postindustrial societies is technology that extends our abilities to analyze information, to communicate, and to travel.

1. These new technologies allow us to probe space and other planets, to communicate instantaneously anywhere on the globe, to travel great distances in a shorter period of time, and to store, retrieve, and analyze vast amounts of information.

2. The sociological significance of technology is that it is not simply apparatus; it changes a people's way of life.

B. The computer, with its capacity to improve the quality of life, is an example. Currently, it is changing medicine, education, the workplace, and the world of business and finance.

1. The microchip is bringing even more technological wonders; with telemedicine, data are transmitted by fiber-optic cable to remote locations. Although computers can outperform doctors in diagnosis, physicians will resist challenges to their expertise and patients will resist the loss of human interaction.

2. The computer is transforming education and producing a technology gap between rich and poor schools.

3. The computer is altering the way work is organized, the nature of work relationships, and even the location of work. It also makes possible increased surveillance and depersonalization of workers.

4. Computers have impacted the way business is carried out. Businesses are "wired" to suppliers, salespeople and clients around the country and the globe. National boundaries now mean nothing, as computers instantaneously transfer billions of dollars from one country to another. This also makes it difficult for governments to trace the transfer of funds.

C. The term **information superhighway** carries the idea of information traveling at a high rate of speed around the world.

1. Currently, about 200 million people around the world are able to communicate by Internet.

2. The implications of the information superhighway are enormous; nationally a new dimension of existing inequality can emerge as inner city and rural residents become the information "have-nots."

3. Internationally the question is "who will control the information superhighway?" If the Most Industrialized Nations control the information superhighway the Least Industrialized Nations will be destined to a perpetual pauper status.

IV. Social Movements as a Source of Social Change

    A.   Social movements consist of large numbers of people, who, through deliberate and sustained efforts, organize to promote or resist social change. Grievances and dissatisfactions lie at the heart of social movements.

        1.   Proactive social movements promote social change because a current condition of society is intolerable. In contrast, reactive social movements resist changes they perceive as threatening.

        2.   To further their goals, people often develop social movement organizations. An example of a proactive social movement is the National Association for the Advancement of Colored People (NAACP); an example of reactive social movements is the Ku Klux Klan (KKK)

        3.   **Mayer Zald** suggests that a cultural crisis can give birth to a wave of social movements. According to Zald, when a society's institutions fail to keep up with social changes, many people's needs go unfulfilled, massive unrest follows, and social movements develop to bridge the gap.

    B.   **David Aberle** classified social movements into four broad categories according to the type and amount of social change they seek.

        1.   Two types seek to change people but differ in terms of the amount of change desired: alterative social movements seek to alter only a particular aspect of people (e.g., the Women's Christian Temperance Union); while redemptive social movements seek to change people totally; (e.g., a religious social movement that stresses conversion such as fundamental Christianity).

        2.   Two types seek to change society but differ in terms of the amount of change desired: reformative social movements seek to reform only one part of society (e.g., animal rights or the environment); transformative social movements seek to change the social order itself and replace it with their own version of the ideal society (e.g., revolutions in the American colonies, France, Russia, and Cuba).

    C.   Leaders of social movements try to manipulate the media in order to influence public opinion.

        1.   Propaganda is a key to understanding social movements. Propaganda simply means the presentation of information in an attempt to influence people.

        2.   The mass media play a critical role in social movements. It has become, in effect, the gatekeepers of social movements: If those who control and work in the mass media are sympathetic to a "cause," it will receive sympathetic treatment. If the social movement goes against their own biases, it will either be ignored or receive unfavorable treatment.

    D.   Social movements have a life course, that is, they go through five states as they grow and mature.

        1.   Unrest and agitation grow because people are upset about some social condition; at this stage leaders emerge who verbalize people's feelings.

        2.   Leaders mobilize a relative large number of people who demand that something be done about the problem; charismatic leaders emerge during this state.

        3.   An organization emerges with a leadership that makes policy decisions and a rank and file that actively supports the movement.

        4.   Institutionalization occurs as the movement becomes bureaucratized and leadership passes to career officials who may care more about their position in the organization than about the movement itself.

        5.   The organization declines, but there is a possibility of resurgence. Some movements cease to exist; others become reinvigorated with new leadership from within or comes into conflict with other social movements fighting for the opposite side of the issue, (e.g., social movements relating to abortion).

V. The Growth Machine Versus the Earth

A. **Globalization of capitalism** is responsible for today's environmental decay.

1. Economic production caused by the Industrialized Nations pushing for economic growth, the Industrializing Nations playing catch-up, and the Least Industrialized Nations trying to enter the competition means a faster-paced destruction of our environment.

2. Global economic production creates extensive pollution; as the pace of economic production increases, so does the destruction of our environment.

3. In order to achieve the goal of a sustainable environment, we must stop trashing the earth.

4. The ecological message is incompatible with an economic message.

B. **Industrialization**, while viewed as good for a nation's welfare, has led to a major assault on the environment.

1. Many of today's problems—ozone layer depletion, acid rain, the greenhouse effect, and global warming—are linked to our dependence of fossil fuels.

2. Contrary to what we are led to believe, there is an abundant source of natural energy that would provide low-cost power and help raise the living standards of humans across the globe. Better technology is needed to harness this energy supply.

3. From a conflict perspective, such abundant sources of energy present a threat to the energy monopoly ruled by multinationals. We cannot expect the practical development and widespread use of alternative sources of power until the multinationals have cornered the market on the technology that will harness them.

4. Racial minorities and the poor are disproportionately exposed to air pollution, hazardous waste, pesticides and the like. A new specialty known as environmental poverty law is developing to deal with these issues.

C. Environmental degradation is also a problem in the Industrializing and Least Industrialized Nations.

1. The rush to compete globally, the lack of funds to purchase expensive pollution controls, and few anti-pollution laws have all produced environmental problems in the Industrializing Nations.

2. Pollution was treated as a state secret in the former Soviet Union. With protest stifled, no environmental protection laws to inhibit pollution, and production quotas to be met, environmental pollution was rampant. Pollution is so severe that the life expectancy of Russians has dropped.

3. The combined pressures of population growth and the almost nonexistent environmental regulations destine the Least Industrialized Nations to be the earth's major source of pollution. Some companies in the Most Industrialized Nations use the Least Industrialized Nations as dumping sites for hazardous wastes; they build facilities to produce chemicals no longer tolerated in their own countries.

4. The consequences for humanity of the destruction of the tropical rain forests are unknown. With rain forests disappearing at a rate of 2500 acres every hour, it is estimated that 10,000 species are becoming extinct every year.

D. Concern about the world's environmental problems has produced a worldwide social movement.

1. In some countries, the environment has become a major issue in local and national elections (e.g., Germany, Great Britain, and Switzerland).

2.   This movement generally seeks solutions in education, legislation, and political activism. However, some in the movement choose a more radical course, and use extreme tactics to gain support.

E.   Environmental sociology examines the relationship between human societies and the environment.

      1.   Its basic assumptions include: (1) the physical environment is a significant variable in sociological investigation; (2) humans are but one species among many that are dependent on the environment; (3) because of intricate feedbacks to nature, human actions have many unintended consequences; (4) the world is finite, so there are potential physical limits to economic growth; (5) economic expansion requires increased extraction of resources from the environment; (6) increased extraction of resources leads to ecological problems; (7) these ecological problems place restrictions on economic expansion; and (8) the state creates environmental problems by trying to create conditions for the profitable accumulation of capital.

      2.   If we are to have a world that is worth passing on to coming generations, we must seek harmony between technology and the natural environment. As a parallel to the development of technologies, we must develop a greater awareness of their harmful effects on the planet, systems of control that give more weight to reducing technologies' harm to the environment than to lowering costs, and mechanisms to enforce rules for the production, use, and disposal of technology.

KEY TERMS

After studying the chapter, review each of the following terms.

alterative social movement: a social movement that seeks to alter only specific aspects of people's behavior (p. 425)

corporate welfare: the gifts or financial incentives (tax breaks, subsidies, and even lands and stadiums) given to corporations in order to attract them to an area or induce them to remain in an area (p. 431)

cultural lag: William Ogburn's term for human behavior lagging behind technological innovations (p.421)

dialectical process: a view of history and power in which each arrangement, or thesis, contains contradictions, or antitheses, which must be resolved; the new arrangement, or synthesis, contains its own contradictions; and so on (p. 419)

diffusion: the spread of an invention or discovery from one area to another; identified by William Ogburn as a major process of social change (p. 420)

discovery: a new way of seeing reality; identified by William Ogburn as a major process of social change (p.420)

ecosabotage: actions taken to sabotage the efforts of people thought to be legally harming the environment (p. 433)

environmental injustice: the greater impact of pollution on the poor and racial minorities (p. 432)

environmental sociology: a subdiscipline of sociology that examines how human activities affect the physical environment and how the physical environment affects human activities (p. 435)

global warming: an increase in the earth's temperature due to the greenhouse effect (p. 432)

greenhouse effect: the buildup of carbon dioxide in the earth's atmosphere that allows light to enter but inhibits the release of heat; believed to cause global warming (p. 432)

metaformative social movement: goal to change the social order itself—to change an entire civilization (p. 426)

modernization: the transformation of traditional societies into industrial societies (p. 417)

postmodern society: another term for postindustrial society; the use of tools to extend human abilities to gather and analyze information, to communicate, and to travel (p. 421)

proactive social movement: a social movement that promotes social change regarding some specific condition (p. 424)

propaganda: in its broad sense, the presentation of information in an attempt to influence people; in its narrow sense, one-sided information used to try to influence people (p. 426)

public opinion: how people think about some issue (p. 426)

reactive social movement: a social movement that reacts to and resists some social change (p. 424)

redemptive social movement: a social movement that seeks to change people totally (p. 426)

reformative social movement: a social movement that seeks to reform some specific aspect of society (p. 426)

resource mobilization: the mobilization of resources — time, money, information, and skills (p. 427)

social change: the alteration of culture and societies over time (p. 416)

social movement: a group of people who are organized to promote or resist social change (p. 424)

social movement organization: an organization developed to further the goals of a social movement (p. 424)

sustainable environment: a world system that takes into accounts the limits of the environment; produces enough material goods for everyone's needs, and leave the heritage of a sound environment to the next generation (p. 430)

technology: in its narrow sense, tools; in its broader sense, the skills or procedures necessary to make and use those tools (p. 421)

transformative social movement: a social movement that seeks to change society totally (p. 426)

transnational social movement: social movements with an emphasis on a global condition, instead of a condition on a specific country; also known as a new social movement (p. 426)

KEY PEOPLE

Review the major theoretical contributions or research findings of these theorists and thinkers.

Alfred & Elizabeth Lee: These sociologists found that propaganda relies on seven basic techniques, which they labeled "tricks of the trade."

Karl Marx: Marx analyzed the emergence of capitalism and developed the theory of dialectical materialism.

John McCarthy and Mayer Zald: These sociologists investigated the resource mobilization of social movements and found that, although there may be a group of angry and agitated people, without mobilization they will never become a social movement.

Lewis Henry Morgan: Morgan's theory of social development once dominated Western thought. He suggested that societies pass through three stages: savagery, barbarism, and civilization.

William Ogburn: Ogburn identified three processes of social change: invention, discovery, and diffusion. He also coined the term "cultural lag" to describe a situation in which some elements of culture adapt to an invention or discovery more rapidly than others.

Oswald Spengler: Spengler wrote *The Decline of the West* in which he proposed that Western civilization was declining.

Arnold Toynbee: This historian suggests that each time a civilization successfully meets a challenge, oppositional forces are set up. Eventually, the oppositional forces are set loose, and the fabric of society is ripped apart.

Max Weber: Weber argued that capitalism grew out of the Protestant Reformation.

Mayer Zald: In analyzing social movements, Zald suggested that they were like a rolling sea, hitting society like a wave.

SELF-TEST

After completing this self-test, check your answers in the Answer Key of this Study Guide.

MULTIPLE CHOICE QUESTIONS

1.   A shift in the characteristics of culture and society over time is:
     a.   social transformation.
     b.   social metamorphose.
     c.   social alternation.
     d.   social change.

2.   According to your text, the fourth revolution is:
     a.   the invention of the microchip.
     b.   the industrial revolution.

c.   the emergence of agricultural societies.

d.   none of the above.

3.   Paid work, contracts, and especially money are all characteristic of:

a.   farming societies.

b.   *Gemeinschaft*.

c.   *Gesellschaft*.

d.   capitalism.

4.   The sweeping changes ushered in by the Industrial Revolution are called:

a.   social alternation.

b.   social metamorphose.

c.   modernization.

d.   determinism.

5.   The "G8", in order to perpetuate their global dominance, rely very much on:

a.   cheap oil.

b.   social change.

c.   religion.

d.   cyclical social movements.

6.   A theorist believes that human societies begin in a primitive, lawless state and inevitably evolve into societies ruled by civilization and intellect. This view would be classified as an example of:

a.   disengagement theory.

b.   multilinear evolutionary theory.

c.   unilinear evolutionary theory.

d.   functionalist theory.

7.   _____ theories assume that all societies follow the same path.

a.   Unilinear

b.   Multilinear

c.   Cultural hegemony

d.   Protestant ethic

8.   Karl Marx identified a recurring process in human history that involved:

a.   a thesis.

b.   an antithesis.

c.   a synthesis.

d.   all of the above.

9.   Ogburn proposed a view of social change that is based on technology. Technology changes society in all the following ways *except*:

a.   invention.

b.   discovery.

c.   diffusion.

d.   cultural innovation.

10.   The idea of citizenship is an example of:

a.   invention.

b.   discovery.

    c.   diffusion.
    d.   innovation.

11.   Many Middle Eastern countries have used their great oil wealth to build new hospitals and equip them with the most modern equipment that money can buy. However, they have a shortage of individuals (i.e., doctors and nurses) who are capable of using this equipment. This situation would be an example of:
    a.   culture lag.
    b.   culture shock.
    c.   cultural integration.
    d.   cultural relativity.

13.   "Technology" refers to:
    a.   artificial means of extending human abilities.
    b.   tools as simple as a comb and as complicated as a computer.
    c.   the skills or procedures to make and use tools.
    d.   all of the above.

13.   Medical data transmitted by fiber-optic cable to remote locations is called:
    a.   managed care.
    b.   computer-assisted diagnosis.
    c.   remote-site care.
    d.   telemedicine.

14.   Which of the following aspects of the workplace has *not* been transformed by computers?
    a.   The way in which salaries/pay scales are calculated.
    e.   The way in which work is done.
    f.   The location where work is carried out.
    g.   The nature of social relationships in the workplace.

15.   Large numbers of people who organize to promote or resist social change are:
    a.   propaganda proponents.
    b.   social movements.
    c.   name-callers.
    d.   demonstrating cultural shock.

16.   People who feel threatened because some condition of society is changing and organize to *resist* that change are engaging in a:
    a.   proactive social movement.
    b.   reactive social movement.
    c.   redemptive social movement.
    d.   transformative social movement.

17.   Social movements that seek to change people totally are:
    a.   alterative social movements.
    b.   redemptive social movements.
    c.   reformative social movements.
    d.   transformative social movements.

18.   A social movement that seeks to change society totally is a(n):
    a.   alterative social movement.

    b.   redemptive social movement.
    c.   reformative social movement.
    d.   transformative social movement.

19.   Advertising is:
    a.   a type of propaganda.
    b.   an organized attempt to manipulate public opinion.
    c.   a one-sided presentation of information that distorts reality.
    d.   all of the above.

20.   Which one of the following is *not* one of the stages of a social movement, as identified by various sociologists?
    a.   initial unrest and agitation
    b.   disorganization
    c.   resource mobilization
    d.   institutionalization

21.   Technology and mailing lists are key factors in:
    a.   resource mobilization.
    b.   institutionalization.
    c.   resurgence.
    d.   none of the above.

22.   Fossil fuel burning releases sulfur dioxide and nitrogen oxide, which are essential to the development of:
    a.   global warming.
    b.   the greenhouse effect.
    c.   acid rain.
    d.   oil reserves.

23.   Which groups in United States society are disproportionately exposed to environmental hazards?
    a.   Office workers and factory workers
    b.   Racial minorities and the poor
    c.   Farm workers and lumberjacks
    d.   Racial and ethnic groups

24.   Conflict theorists would say that unequal power between groups can lead to _____ injustice.
    a.   warfare and
    b.   environmental
    c.   bureaucratic
    d.   ecosabotage

25.   One result of the concern about the environment has been the development of _____ parties.
    a.   environment
    b.   green
    c.   democratic
    d.   political anarchist

26. Actions taken to sabotage the efforts of people thought to be legally harming the environment are known as:
    a. ecosabotage.
    b. environmental terrorism.
    c. anarchy.
    d. none of the above.

27. Which of the following is not one of the assumptions of environmental sociology?
    a. The physical environment should be part of a sociological investigation.
    b. Human beings are but one species among many that depend on the environment.
    c. The world's resources are finite.
    d. All of the above.

28. The goal of environmental sociology is:
    a. to stop pollution.
    b. to stop nuclear power.
    c. to study the relationships between humans and the natural environment.
    d. to join the green party movement.

29. It is not unusual to see that environmental sociologists are also:
    a. terrorists
    b. bureaucrats
    c. activists
    d. members of ecosabotage groups

30. According to your textbook, which of the following is inevitable?
    a. Humans will continue to invent new technologies.
    b. Humans will continue to abuse the environment.
    c. Humans will continue to use technology to the detriment of natural environment.
    d. Industrialization will continue to be destructive.

TRUE-FALSE QUESTIONS

T F 1. All societies change, but rapid, visible change is comparatively "new" in world history.

T F 2. The social changes that the world is currently experiencing are a random event.

T F 3. The first social revolution involved agricultural societies developing as a result of the plow being invented.

T F 4. According to Marx, societies changed from *Gemeinschaft* to *Gesellschaft* because of the social invention of capitalism.

T F 5. Max Weber traced capitalism to the development of the Catholic Church.

T F 6. Realignment of the world's powers since World War II involves the continuing processes of geopolitics.

T F 7. Central to evolutionary theories, whether unilinear or multilinear, is the assumption of cultural progress.

T F 8. Cyclical theories assume that not all civilizations are like organisms—some are born and then die prematurely.

T F 9. Ogburn defined invention as a combining of existing elements and materials to form new ones.

T F 10. Diffusion includes the spread of an invention or discovery, or the spread of ideas.

T F   11.   Postindustrial societies are also called postmodern societies.
T F   12.   In the future, it will be the current Least Industrialized Nations who will control computer technology and other sophisticated information systems.
T F   13.   The use of computers in education, especially, will significantly reduce existing social inequalities between school districts.
T F   14.   A reactive social movement resists change.
T F   15.   The Women's Christian Temperance Union is an example of an alterative social movement.
T F   16.   Reformative and Transformative social movements target individuals and change.
T F   17.   An example of a Metaformative social movement would be animal-rights social movements.
T F   18.   Resource mobilization does not, in itself, guarantee a social movement's success.
T F   19.   There is a strong consensus among scientists that the greenhouse effect is the cause of global warming and represents a very serious threat to our natural environment.
T F   20.   There is no real energy shortage.

FILL-IN QUESTIONS

1.   The transformation of agricultural societies into industrial societies is the outcome of _____.

2.   The third social revolution involved the invention of the _____.
3.   _____ theories of change assume that all societies follow the same evolutionary path.
4.   Ogburn coined the term _____ to refer to how some elements of culture lag behind the changes that come from invention, discovery, and diffusion.
5.   Another term for postindustrial society is _____ society.
6.   Technology is more than an apparatus; it changes our way of _____.
7.   _____ are large numbers of people who organize to promote or resist social change.
8.   A group that seeks to resist change is known as a _____.
9.   Alcoholics Anonymous would be an example of a _____ social movement.
10.   The presentation of information in an attempt to influence people is _____.
11.   In the _____ stage of the potential development of a social movement, a division of labor and leadership occurs with the leaders making policy decisions.
12.   _____ is created when sulfur dioxide and nitrogen dioxide, released as a result of burning fossil fuels, react with moisture in the air.
13.   Political parties whose central issue is the environment are usually known as _____ parties.
14.   Actions taken to undermine the efforts of people thought to be legally harming the environment are known as _____.
15.   We will have achieved a _____ when we are able to use our physical environment to meet the needs of humanity without destroying our environment.

MATCH THESE SOCIOLOGICAL CONCEPTS WITH THEIR DEFINITIONS

1. acid rain   a. *change the entire social order of the world*
2. diffusion   b. *human behavior lagging behind technological innovation*
3. discovery   c. *another term for post-industrial*
4. invention   d. *sulfuric and nitric acid combined with moisture*
5. global warming   e. *spread of invention or discovery from one place to another*

6.	ecosabotage	f.	*process of change from traditional to contemporary society*
7.	metaformative	g.	*a new way of seeing reality*
8.	cultural lag	h.	*combining existing elements to form new ones*
9.	modernization	i.	*increase in the earth's temperature*
10.	postmodern	j.	*undermining efforts harmful to the environment*

ESSAY QUESTIONS

1. According to your text, social change is such a vital part of social life that any significant shift in the characteristics of culture and society warrants notice. Discuss how social change has affected social life (e.g., regarding social revolutions, capitalism, etc.).

2. Why do societies change? Discuss the attempts to explain the phenomenon of change, and give at least one illustration of each attempt.

3. Choose a particular technology and discuss the impact that the technology has had, and will have, on United States society.

4. What is a "social movement?" List the types of social movements and give an example of each. Discuss and explain the various stages in the development of social movements.

5. Why is there said to be an "environmental movement" around the world? What type of social movement would you call the "environmental movement" and why? What is environmental sociology, and what link(s) do you find between this relatively new field of sociology and the "environmental movement?"

STUDENT PROJECTS

1. In the last one hundred years, what technological invention do you think has had the greatest impact on the world and why? In what ways did society change due to this technological invention? Explain which technological invention has had the greatest impact on your everyday life. In what ways did you change due to this technology? Overall, how much of social change is due to technological change?

2. List the environmental problems that most concern you? In what ways, if any, do you actively strive to reduce these problems in your community? Explain. Do you think there can be harmony between technology and the environment? Explain.

CHAPTER 1
THE SOCIOLOGICAL PERSPECTIVE

ANSWER KEY

MULTIPLE CHOICE

1. a	6. b	11. b	16. b	21. a	26. b
2. c	7. c	12. b	17. c	22. d	27. b
3. c	8. c	13. b	18. b	23. d	28. c
4. d	9. a	14. a	19. a	24. c	29. a
5. b	10. c	15. c	20. c	25. d	30. a

TRUE-FALSE QUESTIONS

1. T	5. T	9. F	13. T	17. T
2. T	6. T	10. F	14. T	18. T
3. T	7. F	11. T	15. T	19. T
4. F	8. T	12. F	16. F	20. F

FILL-IN QUESTIONS

1. sociological perspective
2. scientific method
3. Herbert Spencer
4. bourgeoisie
5. Karl Marx
6. social Reform
7. theory
8. symbolic interactionism
9. Functional (Structural-functional)
10. manifest
11. close
12. a research method
13. sample
14. control group; experimental group
15. value free

MATCHING

MATCH THESE THEORISTS/PHILOSOPHERS WITH THEIR CONTRIBUTIONS		MATCH EACH CONCEPT WITH ITS DEFINITION	
1.	b	1.	c
2.	c	2.	e
3.	d	3.	a
4.	e	4.	d
5.	a	5.	b

ESSAYS

1. *Explain what the sociological perspective encompasses and then, using that perspective, discuss the forces that shaped the discipline of sociology.*

There are two parts to this question. First, you are asked to define the sociological perspective. As you define this, mention the idea of social location, perhaps by bringing into your essay C. Wright Mills' observations on the connection between biography and history. Another way to explain the perspective would be to contrast sociology with other disciplines, talking about what sociology is and what it isn't.

The second part of the essay involves discussing the forces that shaped sociology and its early followers. You are being asked to think about what was going on in the social world in the early nineteenth century that might have led to the birth of this new discipline. Refer back to the book identify four: (1) the Industrial Revolution; (2) the political revolutions of America and France; (3) imperialism; and (4) the emergence of the scientific method. You would conclude by discussing how each of the early sociologists — Auguste Comte, Herbert Spencer, Karl Marx, Emile Durkheim, and Max Weber — were influenced by these broader forces in making a contribution to sociology. Consider bringing into the discussion some of the material on sexism in early sociology, noting how the ideas about the appropriate role for women in society functioned to exclude women like Harriet Martineau and Jane Addams from the discipline, or you could talk about the emergence of sociology in North America.

2. *Explain why there has been a continuing tension between analyzing society and working toward reforming society since the very beginning of society.*

Referring to the work of such early sociologists as Auguste Comte and Emile Durkheim, you could begin by noting that, from its inception, sociology has had twin goals — the scientific study of society and the application of scientific knowledge to social reform. When sociology was transplanted to the United States at the end of the nineteenth century, this society was undergoing significant changes, with industrialization, urbanization, and immigration among them. The earliest North American sociologists, like their European predecessors, defined the sociologist's role as both social scientist and social reformer. At the same time, the record suggests that the primary emphasis had generally been on the sociologist's work as social scientist. For example, women who had been trained as sociologists but then excluded from the universities, turned to social reform and were denied the title of sociologist; instead, they were called social workers by male sociologists working from within academic departments of universities.

At this point you could draw on material in the text about the development of North American sociology, as well as the discussion of its different phases. From the 1920s through the early post-World War II era, as departments of sociology became more widely established, the emphasis was on sociological research rather than social reform. Sociologists like Talcott Parsons, whose work was primarily theoretical in nature, came to dominate the field. While the early part of this period was one of significant turmoil (with the Great Depression and World War II), at the end of this phase, given the general prosperity of the immediate post-World War II era, social problems were largely "invisible."

One option could be to point out that people like C. Wright Mills kept the tradition of social reform alive during these years. And with the social upheavals of the 1950s and 1960s — the civil rights movement, the women's movement, and the anti-war movement but to name a few — the focus once again shifted back to social reform.

Talking about applied sociology, a recent development that attempts to blend these two traditions would provide a conclusion. While it has gained legitimacy within the discipline, there are still those on both sides of this debate who reject applied sociology. For those whose emphasis is on pure sociology, this smacks of social reform, while for those who believe sociology should be working to reform society, it doesn't go far enough. The debate over the appropriate focus of sociological inquiry is unlikely to be resolved any time soon, because it reflects traditions that go back to the very origins of the discipline. Both sides can find ample support for their positions within the work and writings of earlier sociologists.

3. *Explain each of the theoretical perspectives that are used in sociology and describe how a sociologist affiliated with one or another of the perspectives might undertake a study of gangs. Discuss how all three can be used in research.*

There are three major perspectives in sociology: symbolic interactionism, functional analysis, and conflict theory. The first step is to explain the essential nature of each perspective and propose a research topic that would be consistent with each perspective. Because a symbolic interactionist focuses on the symbols that people use to establish meaning, develop their views of the world, and communicate with one another, to design a research project on gangs, he or she would want to find out what meaning gangs and gang membership have for the individuals who belong to them, as well as those who live in the communities in which they operate. A functionalist, who identifies with the functions of a particular social pattern, would choose to study what contributions gangs make within the fabric of social life, and also the dysfunctions of gangs. Finally, a conflict theorist would study the competition for scarce resources among gangs and between gangs and the larger society because he or she is interested in struggles over power and control within social groups. You would conclude by noting that each perspective provides an answer to an important question about the social order and by combining them, you arrive at a more complete picture.

4. *Choose a topic and explain how you would go through the different steps in the research model.*

In order to answer this question, you must select a topic and develop it from the beginning to the end of the research process, identifying all eight steps and explaining what tasks are carried out each step of the way. Your answer should make reference to variables, hypothesis, operational definitions, the different research methods, validity and reliability, different ways of analyzing the data, and replication.

5. *The author of your text discusses six different research methods. Pick a research topic of interest to you and discuss how you might try to investigate this topic using these different methods. In your answer, consider how a particular method may or may not be suitable for the topic under consideration.*

To review, the different methods discussed in the text are (1) surveys; (2) participant observation; (3) secondary analysis; (4) documents; (5) unobtrusive measures; and (6) experiments. Your first step is to pick a potential research topic. Let's say you decide to research homeless women. You could do a survey, developing a questionnaire that would be either self-administered or completed through an interview. This would use either closed-ended or open-ended questions, or a combination of both. You would discuss some of the problems that you might encounter in trying to define the homeless population or in attempting to draw a random sample. You could point out that while this method would allow you to sample a large number of people at a relatively low cost, there might be difficulties with rapport.

Using participant observation might be more suitable for the topic under consideration. You could spend time in a homeless shelter, getting to know the women who live there. Hopefully, over time you will have some rapport with the clients and be able to learn more about their lives and the reasons why they are homeless. You'll want to note that this method may make it difficult for you to generalize your findings.

As you proceed through the essay, you might consider the other methods. You could make an argument about using secondary analysis, documents, and unobtrusive measures. In all three instances, you'll want to note how these could be used and the limitations each presents. The only method you might find difficult to apply to this topic would be experiments.

Your conclusion would summarize what factors influence the researcher's choice of a method: available resources, degree of access to respondents, the purpose of the research, and the background of the researcher. You could also talk about the differences between quantitative and qualitative research.

CHAPTER 2
CULTURE

ANSWER KEY

MULTIPLE CHOICE

1. e	6. d	11. a	16. a	21. b	26. c
2. b	7. b	12. b	17. a	22. c	27. c
3. b	8. c	13. d	18. a	23. c	28. c
4. d	9. b	14. d	19. b	24. b	29. b
5. d	10. b	15. a	20. d	25. a	30. d

TRUE-FALSE QUESTIONS

1. F	5. T	9. T	13. T	17. T
2. T	6. T	10. T	14. T	18. F
3. T	7. T	11. T	15. T	19. T
4. T	8. T	12. T	16. T	20. F

FILL-IN QUESTIONS

1. material culture
2. ethnocentrism
3. cultural relativity
4. symbol
5. Language
6. language
7. norms
8. folkways
9. subcultures
10. Value clusters
11. culture wars
12. real culture
13. new technology
14. culture lag
15. cultural leveling

MATCHING

MATCH THESE
THEORISTS/PHILOSOPHERS
WITH THEIR
CONTRIBUTIONS

1. a
2. e
3. b
4. d
5. c

MATCH EACH CONCEPT
WITH ITS DEFINITION

1. b
2. a
3. d
4. c
5. e

ESSAYS

1. *Explain cultural relativism and discuss both the advantages and disadvantages of practicing it.*

Begin your essay by defining cultural relativism and explaining that it developed in reaction to ethnocentrism. The primary advantage of this approach to looking at other cultures is that we are able to appreciate another way of life without making judgments, thereby reducing the possibilities for conflict between cultures. The primary disadvantage is that it can be used to justify any cultural practice and especially those that endanger people's health, happiness, and survival. You could conclude with a reference to Robert Edgerton's proposed "quality of life" scale.

2. *As the author points out, the United States is a pluralistic society, made up of many different groups. Having read this chapter about culture, now discuss some of the things that are gained by living in such a society, as well as some of the problems that are created.*

The first thing to think about is how our national culture has been shaped by all of the different subcultures that exist within it. Consider aspects of both material culture and nonmaterial culture that have been influenced by youth subculture, by ethnic and racial subcultures, and by occupational subcultures, to name but a few. At the same time, note that the presence of so many different subcultures creates the possibility for ethnocentrism and misunderstandings and that, additionally, when the values of the subculture are too different from the mainstream culture, culture wars can develop.

3. *Consider the degree to which the real culture of the United States falls short of the ideal culture. Provide concrete examples to support your essay.*

First define what real and ideal culture mean. Then refer to the core values that are identified in the text as reflective of the ideal culture and discuss the ways in which Americans fall far short of upholding these values in their everyday. An interesting example of the difference between ideal and real culture is the increasing value we place on leisure, and yet we are working more hours than ever before, or the value we place on physical fitness and yet we are more obese and less physically fit than ever.

4. *Evaluate what is gained and lost as technology advances in society.*

One way to frame a response to this is to identify a specific technology that has had a significant impact on our society and discuss both the gains and losses. For example, the automobile provided us with new opportunities for mobility, freeing us from the constraints of public transportation. It created economic opportunities, as new industries and services opened up — car dealerships, gas stations, fast food restaurants, and malls are just a few examples. But at the same time, automobiles have contributed to urban sprawl and the decline of downtown shopping areas. We have become more isolated as we travel around in our cars rather than meeting and traveling with others on public transportation. The use of automobiles has contributed to increased congestion and air pollution. Finally, you could make the argument that the automobile has contributed to cultural leveling within the U.S., as regional differences have disappeared under the spread of national businesses in malls and food chains.

5. *Discuss whether or not cultural leveling is a positive or negative process.*

Like the previous question, this one also asks you to consider both sides of the cultural leveling process. Begin your answer by defining cultural leveling — a process by which cultures become similar to one another; present both sides of the cultural leveling argument. In some respects, this can be seen as positive, because it has the potential of fostering a greater understanding of different cultures. However, with the globalization of capitalism, what seems to be happening today is that aspects of Western culture, especially U.S. culture, are being exported around the world, which many see as negative. As your textbook notes, the Golden Arches of McDonald's can be seen around the globe, and U.S. cartoon icons like Mickey Mouse are popular with children internationally. The cultures of the world increasingly reflect U.S. culture with some national accents, resulting in a loss of distinctive cultural traditions. You would conclude with your own statement of which side you think is stronger.

CHAPTER 3
SOCIALIZATION

ANSWER KEY

MULTIPLE CHOICE

1. b	6. a	11. b	16. b	21. c	26. b
2. d	7. b	12. a	17. d	22. b	27. d
3. b	8. a	13. b	18. b	23. d	28. a
4. a	9. c	14. c	19. d	24. d	29. c
5. b	10. c	15. b	20. b	25. b	30. b

TRUE-FALSE QUESTIONS

1. F	5. F	9. T	13. T	17. T
2. F	6. T	10. F	14. T	18. T
3. T	7. F	11. F	15. F	19. F
4. T	8. T	12. T	16. T	20. T

FILL-IN QUESTIONS

1. nature vs. nurture
2. early learning
3. looking-glass self
4. take the role of the other
5. generalized other
6. Significant other
7. id
8. passive and dependent
9. social class
10. resocialization
11. degradation ceremony
12. life course
13. adolescence
14. the early middle years
15. 40

MATCHING

MATCH THESE THEORISTS/PHILOSOPHERS WITH THEIR CONTRIBUTIONS		MATCH EACH CONCEPT WITH ITS DEFINITION	
1.	b	1.	b
2.	c	2.	a
3.	a	3.	c
4.	d	4.	d
5.	e	5.	e

ESSAYS

1. *Explain what is necessary in order for us to develop into full human beings.*

You might begin by stating that in order for us to become full human beings, we need language and intimate social connections to others. Draw on the information presented in the previous chapter as to what language enables us to do: grasp relationships to others, think in terms of a shared past and future, and make shared plans. Our knowledge of language, and our ability to use it, develops out of social interaction, as evidenced by those children raised in isolation. Furthermore, we learn how to get along with others only through close personal experiences. The experience of Isabelle and the children raised in institutionalized settings confirms this.

The importance of social interaction and close social contact for our development is underscored by the work of a number of social psychologists. Mead and Piaget suggest that our mind and our ability to reason develop out of social interactions, while Kohlberg and Gilligan argue that our sense of right and wrong develop in the same way. Finally, even our expression of emotions comes out of our contact with others in our society.

2. *Why do sociologists argue that socialization is a process and not a product?*

Sociologists argue that socialization is a process rather than a product because there is no end to socialization. It begins at birth and continues throughout one's life, as you take on new roles. Cooley was the first to note that we are continually modifying our sense of self depending on our reading of other's reactions to us. Mead's work on taking the role of the other in the development of the self also suggests that socialization is a process. Researchers have identified a series of stages through which we pass as we age; at each stage we are confronted by new demands and new challenges to be mastered.

3. *Having read about how the family, the media, and peers all influence our gender socialization, discuss why gender roles tend to remain unchanged from one generation to the next.*

You could begin your essay by defining gender socialization, the process of learning what is expected of us from society because we are born either male or female. You could then note that this socialization is so complete that, as adults, most of us act, think, and even feel according to our particular culture's guidelines of what is appropriate for our sex. We do not question the way in which gender roles are defined — we have come to see the way we behave as natural and normal. Consequently, when we have children, we set out to socialize them into the same set of gender roles. You could incorporate some discussion of the research by Susan Goldberg and Michael Lewis about child rearing, as well as the fact that children are generally provided with gender-appropriate toys and subject to different parental expectations.

The ways in which the media perpetuate traditional gender roles should also be noted. Talk about gender stereotypes that show up in advertising, television, and video games, for example, and include a reference to studies that show the more television people watch, the more they tend to have restrictive views about women's role in society. Milkie's research on peer groups also demonstrates how media images contribute to gender socialization; boys used the media images to discover who they are as males.

4. *As the text points out, the stages of the life course are influenced by the biological clock, but they also reflect broader social factors. Identify the stages of the life course and indicate how social factors have contributed to the definition of each of these stages.*

Begin your essay by noting that the stages of the life course are shaped by both biological and social factors. Begin with childhood (from birth to age 12) and discuss how this stage extends over our earliest years as our bodies and minds are developing; at the same time, our understanding of childhood has been transformed by broader social factors like industrialization. The impact of social factors is even more apparent in the second stage, adolescence, which goes from ages 13 to 17. Biologically, our bodies are changing, but this stage is a total social invention, the result of the Industrial Revolution and the growing importance of education.

It used to be that most people, upon graduation from high school, immediately assumed adult responsibilities: jobs, marriages and children. A growing number of young people today, however, are postponing this next step as they acquire the additional education and training called for in our modern world. Consequently, we are witnessing the birth of a new stage: young adulthood. By the end of their 20s, most people are ready to launch their careers and their families, leading to the next stage, the middle years. But because the middle years are such a long stage, spanning from 30 to 65, it is generally divided into two stages — early and later. Even though the life expectancy of people in U.S. society has been extended, during the later middle years issues of health and mortality are important. As their own parents die, there is a fundamental shift in their orientation to life. This stage ends at 65, a time when most people are retiring, or have retired.

The final stage, the older years, is again divided into early and later. A few generations ago life expectancy ran to the late 60s or early 70s and this was a relatively short stage, characterized by preparations for one's own death. Today, because we enjoy longer lives, the early part of this stage is often experienced as an extension of the middle years. People are unlikely to see themselves as old and continue to be socially active. As health declines, and friends and spouses die, they move into the final years.

5. *How would you answer the question, "Are we prisoners of socialization?"*

From reading this chapter and learning more about socialization you have hopefully learned that the self is dynamic, interacting with the social environment and being affected by, and in turn, affecting it. We are involved in constructing our sense of self as active players rather than passive recipients. In answering this question, you should also refer to the work of Cooley and Mead, as well as Piaget, Kohlberg, Gilligan, and Freud, which demonstrates the role we play in the development of our own sense of self.

CHAPTER 4
SOCIAL STRUCTURE AND SOCIAL INTERACTION

ANSWER KEY

MULTIPLE CHOICE

1. d	6. b	11. c	16. c	21. a	26. b
2. a	7. c	12. d	17. b	22. d	27. b
3. a	8. a	13. b	18. d	23. a	28. a
4. b	9. c	14. b	19. c	24. a	29. c
5. c	10. c	15. a	20. a	25. b	30. a

TRUE-FALSE QUESTIONS

1. T	5. F	9. T	13. F	17. F
2. T	6. T	10. T	14. F	18. T
3. T	7. T	11. T	15. T	19. T
4. T	8. F	12. T	16. F	20. T

FILL-IN QUESTIONS

1. Macrosociology	9. division of labor
2. Social interaction	10. gesellschaft
3. structure	11. Role strain
4. social class	12. teamwork
5. master status	13. face-saving behavior
6. Roles	14. background
7. Social Institution	15. Thomas theorem
8. Social cohesion	

MATCHING

MATCH THESE THEORISTS/PHILOSOPHERS WITH THEIR CONTRIBUTIONS		MATCH EACH CONCEPT WITH ITS DEFINITION	
1.	b	1.	e
2.	a	2.	a
3.	d	3.	b
4.	c	4.	d
5.	e	5.	e

ESSAYS

1. *Choose a research topic and discuss how you approach this topic using both macrosociological and microsociological approaches.*

First select a topic; I've chosen the topic of labor unions. Remember that the macrosociological level focuses on the broad features of society. From this level, I might research the role that unions play within the economy or the political system, what types of workers are organized into unions, the level of union organization among workers, or the level of union activity. Shifting to a microsociological level of analysis, I would look at what happens within unions or between unions and management in terms of social interaction. From this perspective, I might investigate the behavior of union members and leaders at a union meeting, or the behavior of union and management negotiators at a bargaining session. By combining both perspectives, I have achieved a much broader understanding of the role of unions within society.

2. *The concept of a social structure is often difficult to grasp. Yet the social structure is a central organizing feature of social life. Identify the ways in which it takes shape in our society and in our lives.*

You will begin with the definition of social structure as the framework for society that establishes the typical patterns for the society. Then identify the major components of it: culture, social class, social status, roles, groups and social institutions. It is these components that give social structure shape and substance. The rest of your essay would focus on discussing the contribution that each of these components makes to the overall social structure. Conclude with the observation that when we are born into a society, we are immediately located within the social structure, based on the culture, the social class of our parents, and our ascribed statuses. As we grow and function within different groups and social institutions, we learn to perform roles that are consistent with our culture and our status. We may eventually acquire achieved statuses. All of this gives shape and meaning to our lives, which in turn gives shape and meaning to social life.

3. *Today we can see many examples of people wanting to recreate a simpler way of life. Using Tönnies' framework, analyze this tendency.*

Begin by describing Tönnies' framework of *Gemeinshaft* and *Gesellschaft*, and discussing the characteristics of each. Using these concepts, indicate that individuals' search for community reflects a rejection of the ever-increasing impersonality and formality of modern society. In their actions, people are trying to re-create a social world where everyone knows each other within the context of intimate groups. Some sociologists use the term "pseudo-*Gemeinshaft*" to describe the attractiveness of the past — people building colonial homes and decorating them with antiques.

4. *Assume that you have been asked to give a presentation to your sociology class on Goffman's dramaturgy approach. Describe what information you would want to include in such a presentation.*

One possibility would be to begin by explaining how Goffman saw life as a drama acted out on a stage. This would lead you to making a distinction between front stage and back stage. You might even want to provide some examples. For instance, you are presenting on a front stage, but you practiced for this presentation in your bedroom without an audience. Because dramaturgy focuses on the performances we give when we assume different roles, you might also talk about the problems of role conflict and role strain and the fact that we tend to become the roles we play. An important contribution of Goffman's was his insights into impression management. Explain what that is and how it involves the use of three different types of sign-vehicles: social setting, appearance, and manner. Finally, you could conclude with his concept of teamwork, especially as it relates to face-saving behavior. Remember to include examples of all of these concepts as you proceed.

5. *Explain what sociologists mean by "the social construction of reality."*

The first thing you want to explain is the distinction between the objective existence of something and our subjective interpretation of it. Include some mention of W. I. Thomas and his famous statement, "If people define situations as real, they are real in their consequences". In making your point, you could use the example from the textbook of the street vendors and germs (although it can be proven objectively that germs exist, but unless you have learned to perceive them, they do not exist), or you could use your own example. Your conclusion would be that, based on our social experiences, we construct reality.

CHAPTER 5
SOCIAL GROUPS AND FORMAL ORGANIZATIONS

ANSWER KEY

MULTIPLE CHOICE

1. a	6. b	11. c	16. a	21. c	26. d
2. a	7. c	12. b	17. c	22. d	27. d
3. d	8. b	13. c	18. b	23. a	28. a
4. c	9. c	14. c	19. b	24. c	29. c
5. c	10. b	15. d	20. c	25. c	30. a

TRUE-FALSE QUESTIONS

1. T	5. F	9. T	13. F	17. T
2. F	6. T	10. F	14. T	18. T
3. F	7. F	11. T	15. F	19. F
4. F	8. T	12. F	16. F	20. T

FILL-IN QUESTIONS

1. an aggregate
2. secondary
3. The Iron Law of Oligarchy
4. In-groups; out-groups
5. Reference
6. social networks
7. electronic
8. Goal displacement
9. the rationalization of society
10. Alienation
11. myth
12. group dynamics
13. small group
14. instrumental leader
15. Groupthink

MATCHING

MATCH THESE THEORISTS/PHILOSOPHERS WITH THEIR CONTRIBUTIONS		MATCH EACH CONCEPT WITH ITS DEFINITION	
1.	c	1.	b
2.	d	2.	d
3.	b	3.	c
4.	e	4.	e
5.	a	5.	a

ESSAYS

1. *Define the concept of primary group, and the concept of secondary group. Discuss how the two are linked in the workplace.*

Begin you answer by explaining the differences between primary and secondary groups including the issues of formality and size. The second part of the question would include a discussion about how many workplaces tend to be more of a secondary group but that within workplaces there are usually primary groups of co-workers.

2. *Define the iron law of oligarchy and discuss why this problem occurs in voluntary associations.*

Begin this answer by explaining that the iron law of oligarchy is the tendency within organizations for the leadership to become self-perpetuating. Although this problem occurs in all types of organizations, it is particularly evident in voluntary associations. A major reason for this is the nature of membership in this type of organization; it tends to be passive, varying in its degree of commitment to and involvement in the organization. The elite keep themselves in power by passing leadership positions from one member of the clique to another. If the leadership is not responsive to the membership, it runs the risk of being removed from office by a grassroots rebellion.

3. Explain the three different leadership styles and suggest reasons why the democratic leader is the best style of leader for most situations.

You begin by identifying the three styles of leadership and listing the characteristics of each. Then evaluate how characteristics of a democratic leader, such as holding group discussions, outlining the steps necessary to reach goals, suggesting alternatives, and allowing group members to work at their own pace, all contribute to outcomes like greater friendliness, group-mindedness, and mutual respect, and ability to work without supervision. Finally, consider why those qualities and outcomes are judged to be the best under most circumstances.

4. Discuss and compare Japanese and American Corporations. What are the myths and realities?

Begin by comparing the two types of corporations using information provided in the textbook including differences on hiring and promoting teams, lifetime security, almost total involvement, broad training, and decision making by consensus. In the second part of the question, examine some of the myths including life time job security, decision making, and how Japanese corporations also use information from U. S. corporations.

5. Explore the factors that influence the emergence of groupthink and consider strategies for minimizing the development of this collective tunnel vision.

There are several factors you could discuss. First, you could bring in the findings of the Asch experiment about the influence of peer pressure in individual and group decision-making. You could include reference to the Milgram experiment about obedience to authority. There is also strong pressure on members of a group to think alike, since voicing opposition can be viewed as a sign of disloyalty; one's role as a "team player" may even be questioned. Within groups, there is also a tendency to put aside moral judgments for the sake of the group.

The author of your text suggests that groupthink develops when leaders and members of groups are isolated and become cut off from information sources that do not fit with their own views. His suggestion is for leaders to have the widest possible access to research findings of social scientists and information freely gathered by media sources. You could also discuss how groupthink might be reduced by being sensitive to the size of the group and the nature of leadership — two factors that play a role in overall group dynamics.

CHAPTER 6
DEVIANCE AND SOCIAL CONTROL

ANSWER KEY

MULTIPLE CHOICE

1. b	6. a	11. c	16. d	21. c	26. b
2. b	7. c	12. b	17. b	22. d	27. a
3. c	8. d	13. d	18. a	23. b	28. b
4. c	9. c	14. a	19. d	24. c	29. c
5. c	10. c	15. d	20. c	25. b	30. d

TRUE-FALSE QUESTIONS

1. F	5. F	9. F	13. F	17. F
2. F	6. T	10. T	14. T	18. T
3. T	7. T	11. T	15. T	19. T
4. T	8. F	12. T	16. F	20. F

FILL-IN QUESTIONS

1. deviance
2. negative
3. individual
4. learn
5. families
6. inner
7. anomie
8. white-collar
9. female
10. marginal working class
11. recidivism
12. problem

MATCHING

MATCH THESE THEORISTS/PHILOSOPHERS WITH THEIR CONTRIBUTIONS

1.	c	6.	e
2.	a	7.	g
3.	f	8.	b
4.	h	9.	j
5.	d	10.	i

ESSAYS

1. *Discuss how the different sociological perspectives could be combined to provide a more complete picture of deviance.*

You would first identify the strengths of each perspective. Symbolic interactionism focuses on group membership and interaction within and between groups, functionalism focuses on how deviance is a part of the social order, and conflict theory focuses on how social inequality affects definitions of and reactions to acts of deviance. Combining perspectives is reflected in the work of William Chambliss on the Saints and the Roughnecks; he looked at patterns of inequality and different interaction styles to explain the different treatment the two groups received. Another example is Cloward and Ohlin's work on illegitimate opportunity structures; they added the concept of social class inequality to the notion of the strain between institutionalized means and cultural goals to explain patterns of lower class deviance.

2.   *Explain how forms of deviance such as street gangs can be both functional and dysfunctional at the same time.*

Your discussion could begin by making reference to Durkheim's views on the functionality of deviance. In particular, the presence of street gangs may serve to affirm normative boundaries and to promote social unity, both within society and within the neighborhoods where gangs operate. In this context, think about the dominant views we have of gang members and gang activity.

You would also want to make reference to Jankowski's research. Jankowski studied street gangs and discovered they function within low-income neighborhoods as sources of employment (often the *only* source), recreation, and protection. In a few cases the gangs were involved in legitimate activities such as running small groceries and renovating and renting abandoned apartment buildings. All of these demonstrate the functional nature of gangs, but at the same time, gangs generate most of their income through illegal activities, a dysfunctional aspect. Another dysfunctional aspect is the violence that accompanies gangs; violence that is not confined to gangs but often spills over into the neighborhood as a whole.

3.   *Using any one of the different sociological perspectives, develop an explanation for why white-collar crime is generally treated as less serious crime in our society.*

First, define white-collar crime. According to Edwin Sutherland, it is crime that people of respectable and high social status commit in the course of their occupations. Use the different perspectives to discuss why it is viewed as less serious a threat to our society than is street crime. You could include a discussion of labeling theory, especially the work of Sykes and Matza regarding techniques of neutralization. Given the nature of work and corporate life today, it is possible that those responsible for the crimes not see themselves as deviant, nor does society as a whole see corporate employees as deviant. In addition, much of the crime that is committed is largely invisible and indirect — we may not even be aware that we have been victimized.

The functionalist explanation for this type of crime could be included here. Specifically, you could begin with Merton's strain theory and then make reference to Cloward and Ohlin's discussion of illegitimate opportunity structures.

Perhaps it is easiest to apply conflict theory in trying to answer this question. White-collar crime is typically crime committed by those in power. As the conflict theorists point out, the law is an instrument of oppression; it does not operate impartially and directs its energies against the violations of the law by the working class.

4.   *Answer the question, "Is the criminal justice system biased?"*

This chapter provides a great deal of evidence that the criminal justice system is indeed biased. The differences in the ways in which our system views street crime, which is mostly committed by the lower class, and white-collar crime, which is mostly committed by the middle and upper classes could be discussed. Finally, you could reference the statistics that are provided regarding the inmate population and the racial/ethnic composition of prisoners on death row.

4.   *Obesity could be viewed as deviance because it is a condition that violates our cultural norms, regarding appearance. Develop an explanation for how this type of deviance is increasingly subject to medicalization.*

Your textbook has a discussion of how certain types of deviance have been medicalized — redefined so they are viewed as external symptoms of internal disorders. Subsequently, they become medical matters and subject to the care of physicians. For a long time, overweight people were considered weak and unable to control their eating; it was a commonly held view that they were responsible for their condition. The standard treatment for them was to go on a diet to limit their intake of calories. In the last several years, a different view of obesity has begun to emerge. The individual is no longer viewed as responsible for his or her deviant behavior. Excess weight (the external symptom) is seen as due to some medical problem (internal disorder). Today it is increasingly common for obese people to be treated with medications or medical procedures.

CHAPTER 7
GLOBAL STRATIFICATION

ANSWER KEY

MULTIPLE CHOICE

1. a	6. b	11. c	16. a	21. a	26. d
2. a	7. b	12. a	17. c	22. c	27. b
3. d	8. a	13. b	18. c	23. a	28. b
4. d	9. b	14. c	19. c	24. b	29. d
5. b	10. a	15. d	20. c	25. a	30. c

TRUE-FALSE QUESTIONS

1. T	5. F	9. F	13. T	17. T
2. T	6. F	10. T	14. T	18. F
3. T	7. T	11. T	15. F	19. T
4. F	8. T	12. F	16. F	20. F

FILL-IN QUESTIONS

1. Social stratification
2. indentured
3. caste
4. India
5. gender
6. false consciousness
7. meritocracy
8. ideology
9. Education
10. Colonialism
11. core
12. maquiladoras
13. culture
14. debt
15. elite

MATCHING

MATCH THESE THEORISTS/PHILOSOPHERS WITH THEIR CONTRIBUTIONS		MATCH EACH CONCEPT WITH ITS DEFINITION	
1.	c	1.	d
2.	a	2.	b
3.	e	3.	a
4.	d	4.	e
5.	b	5.	c

ESSAYS

1. *Compare Marx's theory of stratification with Weber's theory. Discuss why Weber's is more widely accepted by sociologists.*

The first task is to summarize these two perspectives, pointing out similarities and differences between the two. Then consider the advantages offered by Weber's theory. You could mention that Weber's concept of property (or wealth) was broadened to include *control* over decision making and ownership; that prestige and power can both be based on factors other than wealth; and that these three dimensions are interrelated but can, and do, operate independently. Your conclusion should be that

Weber's theory offers sociologists a more complete framework for understanding and analyzing systems of stratification.

2. *Using the different theories presented in this chapter, answer the question, "Why is stratification universal?"*

There are two competing views on why stratification is universal. Begin by discussing the Davis and Moore thesis that stratification is functional for society. Elaborate on their argument, pointing out that society has certain important positions that need to be filled by the most qualified people; to motivate the most talented to fill these positions, society offers them greater rewards. Provide some examples — college professors, military generals, doctors.

The alternative explanation is offered by the conflict theorists. Begin by noting that groups compete for control over society's resources. The "winners" use their position to keep other groups weak, thereby maintaining their own position. For conflict theorists, this arrangement is inevitable once society begins to produce a surplus. You could also include Mosa's argument about the need for leadership that comes with social organization and how leadership creates inequalities.

Your concluding paragraph could focus on Lenski and his efforts to reconcile these two views. Lenski focused on the level of social development and found that functionalism made sense in societies without any surplus resources, but once a surplus emerges, conflict theory is better at explaining why stratification emerges and persists.

3. *Consider why ideology is a more effective way of maintaining stratification than brute force.*

Begin by considering why it is even necessary to "maintain stratification." On the surface, the idea that some people get more than other people should produce widespread instability — after all, isn't it natural for those without to do whatever they can to take some away from those with? However, this doesn't often happen because the elites have a number of methods for maintaining stratification, ranging from ideology to force. Without question, ideology is the most effective. Once a system of beliefs develops and people accept that a particular system of stratification is right or just, they will go along with the status quo.

4. *In the 1960s, most former colonies around the globe won their political independence. Since that time the position of these countries has remained largely unchanged within the global system of stratification. Provide some explanation as to why political independence alone was not enough to alter their status.*

In order to answer this question review the different explanations aabout the forces that led to the initial system of global stratification. Two of the three theories presented in your book focus on *economic* forces. The only one that does not is the culture of poverty explanation; therefore the initial system of global stratification was most certainly based on economic relationships. Even after the Least Industrialized Nations won their political independence, they were still intimately linked with the Most Industrialized Nations in economic terms. Therefore, the explanation as to why so little has changed continues to be economic. Explain this by referring to neocolonialism, the development of multinational corporations, and the role of technology.

5. *Within a society, the elite rely on ideology, control of information, and use of force, to maintain stratification. Develop an explanation for how the Most Industrialized Nations maintain their status at the top of the global system of stratification.*

In the contemporary world, the Most Industrialized Nations maintain control of the global system of stratification by controlling the economic markets of the Least Industrialized Nations (neocolonialism), by expanding corporate activities into these areas of the world (multinational corporations), and by developing and applying new technologies.

Just as national elites use ideology to justify their position at the top, so do the nations of the Most Industrialized sector. While ideology is the most effective way of maintaining control, national elites can, and do, use force when necessary. Globally, the Most Industrialized Nations generally rely on the elites of the Least Industrialized Nations to maintain control through their own military forces, but there have been many instances where the military of the Most Industrialized Nations has intervened in order to protect economic interest.

CHAPTER 8
SOCIAL CLASS IN THE UNITED STATES

ANSWER KEY

MULTIPLE CHOICE

1. c	6. b	11. b	16. a	21. a	26. a
2. c	7. c	12. d	17. a	22. a	27. d
3. c	8. c	13. d	18. d	23. c	28. a
4. d	9. d	14. c	19. c	24. b	29. d
5. c	10. b	15. c	20. a	25. c	30. d

TRUE-FALSE QUESTIONS

1. T	5. F	9. F	13. F	17. F
2. F	6. T	10. T	14. F	18. T
3. T	7. T	11. F	15. T	19. F
4. T	8. T	12. T	16. F	20. F

FILL-IN QUESTIONS

1. wealth; power; prestige
2. larger
3. power elite
4. income examples
5. 10%
6. power
7. contradictory class location
8. status
9. super-rich (capitalist-elite)
10. underclass
11. Upward mobility
12. a method for advancement
13. old
14. the poverty line
15. women

MATCHING

MATCH THESE THEORISTS/PHILOSOPHERS WITH THEIR CONTRIBUTIONS		MATCH EACH SOCIAL CLASS WITH ITS DESCRIPTION	
1.	a	1.	b
2.	b	2.	a
3.	d	3.	e
4.	e	4.	d
5.	c	5.	d

ESSAYS

1. *Identify the three dimensions of social class and discuss their consequences.*

You could begin your essay by discussing how sociologists define wealth and income, power, and privilege. You might talk about how each is unevenly distributed within American society. Finally, you should discuss the consequences of this uneven distribution in terms of physical and mental health, family life, education, religion, politics, crime and the criminal justice system, and access to new technology.

2. *Discuss why you think women have been largely ignored in studies of mobility.*

Point out that most studies of mobility have focused on occupational mobility; until quite recently, most women did not have continuous occupational careers because of the nature of traditional gender roles. They derived their status from their fathers and their husbands. Therefore, studies of

Point out that most studies of mobility have focused on occupational mobility; until quite recently, most women did not have continuous occupational careers because of the nature of traditional gender roles. They derived their status from their fathers and their husbands. Therefore, studies of intergenerational mobility, excluded women because they did not have work histories that spanned their lifetime. As women's roles have changed, so has researchers' awareness of them as research subjects. Additionally, because of structural changes in the economy, employment opportunities for women have opened up; this reflects structural mobility.

3. *Describe which groups are at the greatest risk of poverty and then suggest ways in which poverty can be reduced by targeting these populations.*

Begin by identifying those groups that are at greater risk — the rural poor, minorities, the undereducated, female heads of household, and children, and then discuss specific ideas for overcoming some of the conditions that place these groups at greater risk. These could include possible programs for improvements in education, including more funding for college and technical training, increases in minimum wage, more increases in the number of jobs that pay a living wage, and more aggressive enforcement of anti-discrimination laws.

4. *Explore why individual explanations of poverty are easier for the average American to accept than structural explanations.*

When most Americans see or hear about poor people, the immediate response is that they are lazy and/or stupid. In trying to explain this response, refer back to the earlier discussion about American values, particularly the values of individualism and hard work. Given these values, it is understandable why people would draw this conclusion. Likewise, because we believe in the existence of a meritocracy, most people assume that they deserve the place they have earned in society. Therefore, if someone is poor, it must be because they don't deserve better.

You could also discuss the idea of the Horatio Alger myth. We grow up believing that if we only work hard (a core value), we will be rewarded with success. Obviously, those who don't achieve success haven't tried hard enough. Finally, point out that it is much easier to connect individual decisions to outcomes than it is to see broader social forces at work.

5. *Given what you have learned in this chapter about stratification, what do you think are the chances that welfare reform will ultimately be successful in moving people out of poverty?*

This question asks you to consider the structural explanations for poverty, that as long as the structure is not changed, people will remain poor. With welfare reform, the only thing that has changed is that the poor can no longer count on the federal government to provide them with some minimal assistance. Begin by summarizing the structural explanation for poverty and the features of society that deny some access to education and the learning of job skills. The structural explanation also emphasizes how discrimination based on race, ethnicity, age, and gender, as well as changes in the job market can all contribute to poverty.

Once you have done this, describe who makes up the poor population: racial and ethnic minorities, women, and people with low levels of education. In particular, discuss the feminization of poverty. You would conclude by arguing that it is not welfare that has made people poor, but factors like inferior education, discrimination, and especially divorce, nonmarital childbearing, and low wages. Until society begins to address these underlying factors, people will still be poor; they just won't be supported by the government.

CHAPTER 9
INEQUALITIES OF RACE AND ETHNICITY

ANSWER KEY

MULTIPLE CHOICE

1. b	6. c	11. c	16. d	21. d	26. c
2. b	7. a	12. a	17. c	22. b	27. a
3. a	8. c	13. d	18. d	23. b	28. c
4. a	9. d	14. b	19. b	24. a	29. d
5. d	10. d	15. c	20. c	25. a	30. b

TRUE-FALSE QUESTIONS

1. F	5. T	9. T	13. T	17. T
2. F	6. T	10. T	14. T	18. T
3. T	7. T	11. F	15. F	19. T
4. F	8. F	12. T	16. T	20. F

FILL-IN QUESTIONS

1. homogenous
2. idea
3. minority group
4. ethnic work
5. tossed salad
6. result
7. deliberate
8. age
9. Rwanda
10. Latinos
11. quadrupled
12. west
13. invisible minority
14. separatism
15. California

MATCHING

MATCH EACH CONCEPT WITH ITS DESCRIPTION		MATCH THESE THEORISTS/PHILOSOPHERS WITH THEIR CONTRIBUTIONS	
1.	e	1.	c
2.	c	2.	b
3.	b	3.	d
4.	a	4.	a
5.	d	5.	e

ESSAYS

1. *Explain what the author means when he says that race is both a myth and a reality.*

Begin by defining the concept of race, and then move on to talking about the myth of race, or how there is no universal agreement as to how many races there are and how a system of racial classification is more a reflection of the society than any underlying biological bases. At the same time, race is a reality in terms of people's subjective feelings about it, the superiority of some and the inferiority of others. You should bring Thomas's observations into the essay; that is, if people believe something is real, then it is real in its consequences.

2. *Using the experiences of different racial and ethnic groups in the U.S., identify and discuss the six patterns of intergroup relations.*

The book identifies six different patterns of intergroup relations — genocide, population transfer, internal colonialism, segregation, assimilation, and multiculturalism. You could begin by mentioning how these are arranged along a continuum from rejection and inhumanity to acceptance and humanity. Then define each pattern and bring into your discussion an example, or examples, from the history of the United States. For example, in discussing genocide mention the treatment of Native Americans by the U.S. military. For population transfer you could discuss the movement of Native Americans to reservations or the relocation of Japanese Americans to internment camps during World War II. In explaining internal colonialism you could mention the economic exploitation of Latino farm workers; an example of segregation would be the Jim Crow South, and the experiences of European immigrants would reflect assimilation. As the textbook notes, it is difficult to find an example of multiculturalism in the history of our nation; perhaps one example might be religious pluralism.

3. *Explore how both psychological and sociological theories can be used together to gain a deeper understanding of prejudice and discrimination.*

Your essay should discuss how psychological theories provide us with a deeper understanding of individual behavior, while sociological theories provide insights into the societal framework of prejudice and discrimination. The work of Theodor Adorno on the authoritarian personality or Dollard's work on individual frustration and the role of scapegoats could be discussed. However, without an understanding of the social environment, this work is incomplete. Bridging the two perspectives is symbolic interactionism and the analysis of the role of labels, selective perception, and the self-fulfilling prophecy in maintaining prejudice. But your essay should also include some reference to the functionalist analysis and the work of Muzafer and Carolyn Sherif, as well as to the conflict theorists and how the capitalist class exploits racial and ethnic strife to retain power and control in society.

4. *Summarize the arguments on both sides of the reparations debate and then analyze what factors influence your own views on this subject.*

Begin by explaining reparations (payment for past injustices) and state both sides of the argument. Those who support this argue believe that white America's wealth is built on centuries of unpaid labor of black slaves. Further, they suggest that the inequality in social conditions between African Americans and whites is the legacy of slavery.

Opponents counter that slavery was not a simple black/white issue; many Africans were sold into slavery by African slave traders. Second, many white Americans are descendants of immigrants who arrived here after slavery ended. Finally, they suggest that members of other ethnic and racial minorities, such as Latinos, Asian Americans, and Native Americans would also end up paying for the past injustice of slavery.

Now try to make sense of your own position on this issue; decide how you feel and then think about the basis for this view. As the author of your text noted, ideas, including opinions, are rooted in history and social location. What is your own race and ethnicity? Are you a member of a group that has experienced widespread discrimination in the past? Do you think the particular history of your racial or ethnic group has shaped your perception of this issue? When did your family arrive in this country? Is this an issue that you have talked about with family or friends? How do their positions on the issue affect your own views?

5. *What would have to change in our society in order for us to truly be a multicultural society?*

Start your essay by defining multiculturalism — the encouragement of racial and ethnic variation. In a pluralistic society, minority groups are able to maintain their separate identities, and still participate in their society's institutions. In a sense, minority groups no longer exist, since they are no longer singled out for unequal treatment, nor do they regard themselves as objects of collective discrimination.

Before we can claim to be a multicultural society, we have to attack the racism that continues. While we have eliminated many of the most blatant forms of racism, there is still much to be done. As the chapter points out, minorities still face prejudice and discrimination in terms of banking practices, real estate transactions, health care, employment, and education. Much of today's discrimination is institutionalized, which makes it much harder to see and to fight.

CHAPTER 10
INEQUALITIES OF GENDER AND AGE

ANSWER KEY

MULTIPLE CHOICE

1. b	6. d	11. a	16. d	21. d	26. a
2. b	7. d	12. d	17. c	22. b	27. a
3. b	8. b	13. b	18. b	23. a	28. b
4. b	9. d	14. d	19. d	24. c	29. a
5. c	10. c	15. a	20. c	25. b	30. b

TRUE-FALSE QUESTIONS

1. F	5. F	9. T	13. T	17. T
2. F	6. T	10. F	14. F	18. F
3. T	7. T	11. T	15. T	19. T
4. T	8. F	12. F	16. T	20. T

FILL-IN QUESTIONS

1. Sex
2. gender
3. biological
4. socialization; life goals; self-definitions
5. Marvin Harris
6. 1920
7. glass escalator
8. 69
9. lifespan
10. graying
11. Ageism
12. age cohort
13. 65
14. four
15. Medicare

MATCHING

MATCH EACH CONCEPT WITH ITS DEFINITION

1.	j		6.	i
2.	g		7.	d
3.	h		8.	b
4.	f		9.	c
5.	e		10.	a

ESSAYS

1. *Summarize the sociobiology argument concerning behavioral differences between men and women. Explain which position most closely reflects your own: biological, sociological, or sociobiological.*

Begin by stating how sociologists and biologists each explain the basis for differences in gendered behavior and discuss how sociobiology tries to bridge the gap between these two disciplines' views. In discussing sociobiology you might refer to Alice Rossi's suggestion concerning the biological basis for mothering and the connection between biological predispositions and cultural norms. As further evidence of the relationship between biology and social forces, you could discuss the two studies cited in the text: the case of the young boy whose sex was changed and the study of Vietnam veterans. Finally state which view you think is most consistent with what you have learned about gender inequality and explain why.

2. *Compare and contrast the two waves of the feminist movement in this country by identifying the forces that contributed to both waves.*

You could begin by noting that both waves of the feminist movement were committed to ending gender stratification and both met with strong opposition from both males and females. In each case, two different branches emerged — a liberal and a conservative branch — and within these branches, radical wings developed. The major difference between the two had to do with goals. The first wave was characterized by rather narrow goals; this movement focused on winning the vote for women. The second wave was broader and wanted to address issues ranging from changing work roles to changing policies on violence against women.

3. *Discuss why women are so often the victims of violence.*

That women are often victims of violence is true not only in the United States, but globally. As your text points out, this has become a global human rights issue. Historically, women have been victims of foot binding (China), witch burning (Europe and the United States), and *suttee* (in India). Women around the globe continue to face the risk of rape, wife beating, female infanticide, and forced prostitution. In some areas of the world, young women are still being subjected to female genital mutilation.

In this country, women face the risk of becoming victims of rape, especially date rape, and of violence in the home. In trying to understand why this happens, you could explore either symbolic interactionism or conflict theory. For symbolic interactionists, part of the explanation lies in the way in which our culture defines male and female roles. Men are expected to be strong and virile, while women are expected to be weak and submissive. Strength and virility are associated with violence, and both boys and girls learn this message as they grow up and are socialized into their respective gender roles.

For conflict theorists, the key lies in the changing nature of men's and women's roles in society. For the past century, women have slowly gained power and status in society. Because these are scarce and finite resources, women's gains translate into men's losses; for some men, the way to reassert their declining power and status is by becoming violent against women.

4. *Explain why sociologists say that aging is socially constructed.*

Begin your essay by explaining that "social construction of aging" means that there is nothing in the biological nature of aging that contributes to a particular set of attitudes either in the person who is aging or in others who surround him/her. Rather, attitudes toward aging develop out of society and are shaped by the particular context of the society. Consequently, attitudes vary from one social group to another. Discussions could include how the Industrial Revolution and the emergence of industrial societies affected the size of the aged population, social attitudes about aging, and the role of the aged in society.

In the context of this question it is important to mention the symbolic interactionists' views on aging. In particular, discuss the fact that social factors influence individuals' perceptions about the aging process. These factors include biology, personal history, gender age, and timetables.

5. *Choose one of the three different sociological perspectives and discuss how that perspective approaches the subject of aging. Consider both the strengths and weaknesses of the perspective you choose.*

In this question, you have the option of writing about symbolic interactionism, functionalism, or conflict theory. If you choose symbolic interactionism, talk about the process of labeling — both the cultural labels and factors that affect the individual's adoption of those labels. Bring up the concept of "ageism," the role of the media in defining images, and how the labels change over time. In particular, discuss how these labels changed with industrialization and how they are once again changing with the advent of a postindustrial society. The strength of this perspective is that it provides us with insights into the social nature of a biological process; a weakness is that it does not consider the conflict that may surround the labeling process.

If you choose to write about functionalism, remember that this perspective focuses on how the different parts of society work together. Two important theories associated with this perspective are disengagement theory and activity theory. Strengths might be the focus on adjustment and the smooth transitioning from one generation to the next. Weaknesses are tied to the theories; disengagement theory overlooks the possibility that the elderly disengage from one set of roles (work-related) but may engage in another set of roles (friendship); activity theory does not identify the key variables that underlie people's activities.

Finally, if you choose conflict theory, focus on the conflict that is generated between different age groups in society as they compete for scarce resources. As an example, discuss the controversy over social security, from its birth to the present time. A strength of this perspective is that it provides an understanding of why the elderly have reduced their level of poverty over time; a weakness might be that it tends to emphasize conflict to the extent that cooperation between generations is overlooked.

CHAPTER 11

POLITICS AND THE ECONOMY

ANSWER KEY

MULTIPLE CHOICE

1. a	6. a	11. d	16. c	21. d	26. b
2. b	7. b	12. c	17. b	22. b	27. d
3. c	8. b	13. e	18. b	23. c	28. b
4. c	9. a	14. a	19. a	24. a	29. c
5. d	10. c	15. b	20. c	25. d	30. c

TRUE-FALSE QUESTIONS

1. F	5. F	9. F	13. F	17. T
2. T	6. F	10. T	14. T	18. F
3. T	7. T	11. T	15. F	19. F
4. T	8. T	12. T	16. T	20. T

FILL-IN QUESTIONS

1. State	9. postindustrial
2. violence	10. human genome
3. Direct democracy	11. downsizing
4. Voter apathy	12. laissez-faire capitalism
5. Power elite	13. central committee
6. prestige	14. corporate capitalism
7. dehumanization	15. interlocking directorates
8. Economy	

MATCHING

MATCH THESE THEORISTS/PHILOSOPHERS WITH THEIR CONTRIBUTIONS

1.	f	6.	g
2.	h	7.	d
3.	e	8.	a
4.	c	9.	i
5.	b	10.	j

ESSAYS

1. *Summarize both the functionalist and the conflict theory views on who rules the United States and then state which you think is more accurate and why.*

Functionalists and conflict theorists have very different views on who rules the United States. Begin by noting that functionalists view the state as necessary for the overall operation of society; it is a balanced system that protects its citizens from one another and from government. At this point, discuss the notion of pluralism, which is at the root of the functionalist argument. Power is diffused among many different groups in society, which has the consequence of allowing no one group to amass too much. The founders of our government established a system of checks and balances that also functions to keep power diffused. Given this structural arrangement, power is shared by many and the government remains responsive to all. For the functionalist, the United States is ruled by its people.

Conflict theorists take a different view. For them, power is concentrated in the hands of a small group, the power elite. This group, made up of representatives of the largest corporations, the most powerful generals of the military, and a few elite politicians, makes the decisions for the nation. C. Wright Mills argued that the most powerful members of this elite are the corporate heads, who play the biggest role in setting national policy. They do not operate in secret to control the nation; rather, decisions flow from their mutual interests in solving the problems that face big business.

The final part of your essay is to decide which argument is closest to your views. You could follow the discussion that was presented in the book that both arguments make sense, depending on which level of government you focus your attention, or you could develop your own analysis.

2. *Discuss why wars happen.*

As the book states, war is not universal. Rather, it is simply one option that groups may choose when dealing with disagreements. As the record indicates, not all societies choose this option. At the same time, it would appear that war is rather common, both across history and in our own time. The question then is, *why*?

In trying to answer this, bring up the work of Nicholas Timasheff. He identified three essential conditions of war: (1) cultural traditions; (2) an antagonistic situation; (3) a fuel that heats the situation to a boiling point. You could also discuss the different fuels and the fact that leaders often see war as an opportunity to achieve certain objectives.

Finally, there is the issue of dehumanization. You could argue that just as experience in war can lead those who are fighting to see the enemy as less than human, a history or culture of warfare can contribute to an entire society viewing its enemies as less than fully human. In addition, as sociologist Tamotsu Shibutani stresses, dehumanization is aided by the tendency for prolonged conflicts to be transformed into struggles between good and evil. In our own history, many of the wars we have fought have been framed exactly this way. Wars exalt killing and those who fight and kill are often given metals that glorify their actions.

3. *Discuss what you see as the future of the New World Order.*

The author poses alternatives such as the development of a world order that transcends national boundaries or the fracturing of the globe into warring factions based on national identities. You have your choice as to which alternative you want to support; whichever you choose must be grounded in solid arguments. On the one hand, you could discuss how the globalization of capital, as well as recent attempts at multinational associations like NAFTA or the EU, support the first alternative. On the other hand, the continuing tensions between national groups — Arabs and Israelis, Indians and Pakistanis, Serbs, Croatians, and Muslims in the former Yugoslavia to name a few — suggest that national identities continue to be an extremely important source of conflict and division rather than peace and unity. You should also consider which of these two trends is stronger, economic globalization or political nationalism.

4. *Discuss the advantages and disadvantages of capitalism and socialism both as ideologies and as economic systems.*

This is a difficult question to answer because it is laden with social values. In this country we have been taught that capitalism is good and socialism is bad. Nevertheless, try to approach this from as objective a position as possible. You would want to begin by discussing the advantages and disadvantages of capitalism. For advantages, you could mention the idea of private ownership and the pursuit of profits, the motivation among workers to work hard, and the vast array of goods that are available in the marketplace. Among the disadvantages you could note the possibility for monopoly, the creation of constant discontent through advertising, and the violation of certain basic human rights like freedom from poverty. Turning to socialism, you could note that advantages include production for the general welfare rather than individual enrichment and the distribution of goods and services according to need rather than ability to pay. Critics point out that socialism violates basic human rights such as individual freedom of decision and opportunity.

5. *The author suggests that the globalization of capitalism may be the most significant economic change of the last 100 years. Discuss the consequences of the change for our society and for nations around the globe.*

In answering this question, combine both functionalist and conflict views on globalization. You could begin by talking about the role of corporations in the new global marketplace and how corporations today are multinationals that are committed first and foremost to profits and market shares, not to any nation. Another major development is the emerging global division of labor and increased global trade, which are together redefining how work is organized. Functionalists argue that these changes will lead to greater competition, increased productivity, lower prices and a higher standard of living for us all. Conflict theorists, on the other hand, look at these same trends and argue that some will benefit from them while others will suffer. They see increased corporate power as well as less protection for workers from unemployment. You could conclude by discussing the future: are we headed for utopia or a nightmare?

CHAPTER 12
MARRIAGE AND FAMILY

ANSWER KEY

MULTIPLE CHOICE

1. a	6. c	11. c	16. d	21. b	26. d
2. d	7. d	12. a	17. a	22. d	27. d
3. d	8. b	13. c	18. c	23. c	28. d
4. b	9. a	14. d	19. d	24. c	29. d
5. a	10. b	15. b	20. c	25. d	30. d

TRUE-FALSE QUESTIONS

1. T	5. T	9. T	13. F	17. T
2. F	6. T	10. T	14. F	18. F
3. F	7. F	11. F	15. T	19. F
4. T	8. F	12. T	16. T	20. T

FILL-IN QUESTIONS

1. matriarchy
2. incest taboo
3. least
4. 95
5. Homogamy
6. Social class
7. fictive
8. poverty
9. Denmark
10. marriage
11. Commitment
12. grandparents
13. skipped generation
14. sandwich
15. education

MATCHING

MATCH THESE THEORISTS/PHILOSOPHERS WITH THEIR CONTRIBUTIONS

1.	b	6.	j	
2.	f	7.	i	
3.	h	8.	c	
4.	a	9.	d	
5.	e	10.	g	

ESSAYS

1. *Discuss whether the family still provides a useful function.*

This is a rather straightforward question. Refer to the functionalist explanation regarding the functions that the family performs. These include (1) economic production, (2) socialization of children, (3) care of the sick and aged, (4) recreation, (5) sexual control, and (6) reproduction. Then, consider the degree to which families in this country still fulfill all of these functions. If they don't, which ones do they still fulfill? Are there other institutions that could do the job as well? Given your answers to these questions, construct an argument as to the continued usefulness of the family.

2. *Explain what the second shift is and consider whether or not it will disappear in the future.*

The second shift is a term Arlie Hochschild used to describe the work that full-time working women do at home. In her research she found that most men engage in "strategies of resistance". You could identify these different strategies in your response, and also discuss the research on the relationship between women's wages and men's willingness to do housework.

The second part of the essay is to consider whether the second shift can be eliminated. Hochschild believes that it can be. One factor to consider is how gender roles, especially as they relate to housework, have changed. As both men and women alter their views on what is appropriate for men and women, this could have an impact on the household division of labor. A second factor to consider is the changing pattern of women's employment outside the home; as more women work, and more work full-time, arrangements around the house may be forced to change. Finally, you could consider changing marriage patterns. As the age of first marriage continues to increase, men may have more experience taking care of a household on their own. They may be more comfortable with cooking, cleaning and laundry and cannot get by playing dumb.

3. *Identify the stages in the family life cycle, discussing what tasks are accomplished in each stage and what event marks that transition from one stage to the next.*

Discuss each of the several stages in sequence: love and courtship, marriage, childbirth, child rearing, the empty nest, and widowhood. For each stage, include the work that takes place and the events that mark the beginning and end of that stage. For example, the first stage is love and courtship. In our culture, this involves romantic love, with individuals being sexually attracted to one another and idealizing the other. Love actually has two components: one is emotion, related to feelings of sexual attraction, and the other is cognitive, attaching labels to our feelings. The stage begins with our meeting and being attracted to another person, and ends when we decide to get engaged to be married.

4. *Identify the trends among U.S. families today and explain the social forces that have contributed to each of them.*

This chapter identifies five trends in U.S. families: postponement of marriage, cohabitation, unmarried mothers, the sandwich generation, and elder care. Take each trend in turn, identifying and explaining the pattern. For example, for the first half of the twentieth century, the age at first marriage steadily declined, so that by 1950, women married at about age 20. For the next 20 years, this figure remained unchanged. Then, beginning in 1970, the average age began to climb. In 2000, women were waiting until they are almost 26 to marry. Now that you have described the pattern, try and explain it. Here's where you want to apply what you have learned previously about changing norms: Talk about how women's roles have changed tremendously since 1970 affecting women's lives and decisions on when to marry. You could also talk about attitudes about premarital sex, which began to change in the 1960s and 1970s. More liberal attitudes about premarital sex and cohabitation have also affected young people's decisions about when to marry: Research on changes in marriage and cohabitation supports this idea. Once you have described and analyzed this first trend, go on to do the same with the other three trends.

5. *Discuss the impact that divorce has on family members — men, women and children.*

Discuss each family role separately — children, wives and husbands. In your response, be sure to talk about the research on the impact on children, both short-term and long-term. In the short-term, this includes hostility, anxiety, nightmares, and poor school performance. In the long-term, it includes a loss of connection to parents, and difficulties forming intimate relations.

For spouses, there is anger, depression and anxiety following a divorce, but each also experiences unique problems related to their gender. For women, there is often a decrease in the standard of living, although the impact varies by social class. For men, there is a loss of connection to their children and the possible development into a series of families.

CHAPTER 13
EDUCATION AND RELIGION

ANSWER KEY

MULTIPLE CHOICE

1. b	6. d	11. c	16. b	21. b	26. a
2. d	7. a	12. c	17. d	22. b	27. d
3. a	8. a	13. b	18. a	23. a	28. c
4. c	9. c	14. b	19. a	24. c	29. b
5. c	10. c	15. a	20. b	25. b	30. b

TRUE-FALSE QUESTIONS

1. T	5. F	9. F	13. T	17. T
2. F	6. F	10. T	14. F	18. T
3. T	7. F	11. T	15. T	19. F
4. T	8. T	12. T	16. T	20. T

FILL-IN QUESTIONS

1. credentialing society
2. Japan
3. least industrialized nations
4. child care
5. tracking
6. cultural
7. peer group
8. safe and free from fear
9. profane
10. persecution
11. religious symbols
12. opium of the masses
13. The Protestant ethic
14. church
15. electronic

MATCHING

MATCH THESE THEORISTS/PHILOSOPHERS WITH THEIR CONTRIBUTIONS

1. c
2. d
3. e
4. a
5. b

MATCH EACH CONCEPT WITH ITS DEFINITION

1. e
2. c
3. d
4. b
5. a

ESSAYS

1. *Explain the link between democracy, industrialization and universal education.*

For this question, there are two strains of thought to be developed. The first is the link between democracy and universal education. Here you will want to talk about the need for voters who are knowledgeable about the issues and are capable of making sound decisions; it is necessary that they read and understand the news that is published in newspapers. In addition, the political culture is maintained through the educational system, as children learn patriotism and facts about the political process.

The second strain is to connect industrialization and universal education. Here you want to talk about the need for an educated workforce that is able to read instructions and learn how to use increasingly more complex machines. The work force must also be able to move from job to job, learning new skills as the work requires. The most efficient way in which to train workers, both to have the specific skills needed for a particular job and the general skills needed to survive in a constantly changing workplace, is through universal education For these two reasons, universal education developed in the United States, as well as other industrialized nations.

2.   *Explain what conflict theorists mean when they say that the deck is stacked against the poor when it comes to education. Offer a solution that might address this problem.*

Begin by noting that the basis for educational funding is largely local property taxes. Richer communities, where property values are higher, will have more money to spend on their children's education while poorer communities, where property values are lower, will have less. Schools in richer communities can pay better salaries for teachers and administrators and can afford to provide the most up-to-date resources. They can also offer a wider range of classes for their students. Obviously, schools in poorer districts don't have the tax revenue to do as much with the consequence that the quality of education suffers. It is not too hard to see why the conflict theorists say the deck is stacked against the poor.

Beyond this, wealthier families can provide more out-of-school opportunities for their children, contributing to their overall educational experience. These families have computers, encyclopedias, and magazines in their homes. They take advantage of the educational and cultural events offered in their communities. They may take trips to other parts of the country, or even to other countries, providing enriching experiences for their children. If their children need additional instruction, they can afford to hire tutors.

While it is difficult to address the inequities that stem directly from differences in family income, it is possible to find a solution to the inequities in funding education. Your final part of the essay is to discuss alternative ways that our communities and society could pay the bill for education. Equalizing the amount spent on local education would do a great deal to level the playing field. Some states have already adopted statewide funding and others have established minimum levels. You could explore some of these ideas, as well as others you might think of, for changing the current situation.

3.   *Select one of the three perspectives and design a research project to test its claims about the nature of education.*

In order to answer this question you must first choose one of the three perspectives. For example, you might choose the conflict perspective and decide to do a research project on the relationship between ethnicity and individual educational achievement and goals. Your research will involve an analysis of student choices of curricula, their grades, retention rates, and graduation from a large racially/ethnically diverse high school. Through access to student records you can collect data on students in one class as it moves through high school. You will compare white students' records to those of African-American and Hispanic students to test whether the conflict theorists are correct in their assertion that the educational system reproduces the students' class background.

4.   *The functionalists point out both the functions and dysfunctions of religion. Discuss both the functions and dysfunctions and consider whether it is possible for religion to fulfill its functions without producing dysfunctions.*

At the end of the chapter, Henslin notes that people have four major concerns. These are (1) the existence of God, (2) the purpose of life, (3) the existence of an afterlife, and (4) morality. In his discussion of the functionalist perspective, Henslin outlines several important functions of religion that address these concerns. Religion provides answers to their questions about the ultimate meaning of life, which in turn comforts people. People find community among others who share their values and beliefs. Religion also sets out guidelines for everyday living — what we should and should not do — thereby setting limits and establishing morality. Having connections to a community and guidelines for living also help in adapting to new environments and social change.

Despite the fact that there are several major religions around the globe, people tend to see their religion as being the only true religion. This is understandable, given the nature of religion. At the same time, this orientation can produce dysfunctions. The author discusses two: (1) war and terrorism; and (2) religious persecution.

The final part of the essay is to consider whether religions can exist and be functional without producing dysfunctions. In answering this, you need to consider the nature of the world today. If contact between people of different religions could be minimized, these dysfunctions would not be problematic. However, today, people of different faiths are drawn even closer together because of globalization. To avoid the dysfunctional side of religion, a way needs to be found for everyone with different belief systems to live together in harmony. So far, we have few examples of this, but we can think of many examples of war and religious persecution.

5.   *Discuss the process by which a religion matures from a cult into a church.*

This is a pretty straightforward question. All you are asked to do is to discuss the process by which a religion moves from cult to sect to church. You want to talk about what each is, how they range along a continuum, and what events mark the shift from one type to the next.

6.   *Discuss whether secularization is inevitable.*

For this answer, explain what secularization is. You could distinguish between the secularization of religion and that of culture and what forces contribute to each. Then, in order to answer the question of whether secularization is inevitable, you need to consider whether the forces can be resisted. For example, the major force behind the secularization of culture is modernization (538). Modernization involves industrialization, urbanization, the development of mass education, and the adoption of science and technology. Assuming that modernization is inevitable, and most say that it is, particularly today with the increasingly global connections, then secularization of culture must also be inevitable. In your response consider these types of issues.

CHAPTER 14

POPULATION AND URBANIZATION

ANSWER KEY

MULTIPLE CHOICE

1. c	6. b	11. a	16. a	21. a	26. a
2. b	7. d	12. a	17. d	22. d	27. d
3. d	8. c	13. a	18. d	23. b	28. c
4. b	9. b	14. d	19. d	24. d	29. b
5. c	10. b	15. d	20. c	25. c	30. c

TRUE-FALSE QUESTIONS

1. F	5. T	9. F	13. T	17. T
2. T	6. F	10. F	14. T	18. F
3. T	7. F	11. T	15. F	19. F
4. F	8. T	12. F	16. T	20. F

FILL-IN QUESTIONS

1. Demography
2. population pyramid
3. political
4. lowest
5. produce; costs
6. one couple, one child
7. zero population growth
8. Urbanization
9. megalopolis
10. human ecology
11. sector
12. peripheral
13. Alienation
14. Cosmopolites
15. less

MATCHING

MATCH THESE THEORISTS/PHILOSOPHERS WITH THEIR CONTRIBUTIONS		MATCH EACH CONCEPT WITH ITS DEFINITION	
1.	a	1.	d
2.	c	2.	e
3.	d	3.	b
4.	e	4.	c
5.	b	5.	a

ESSAYS

1. *State the positions of the New Malthusians and the anti-Malthusians and discuss which view you think is more accurate, based on the information provided about each position.*

The author outlines both positions. Begin this essay by summarizing each side's arguments. For the New Malthusians include the idea of the exponential growth curve, while for the anti-Malthusians, refer to the concepts of the demographic transition and population shrinkage. For both, include some of the facts such as how world population growth does seem to reflect the exponential growth curve (New Malthusians), while the Least Industrialized Nations reflect the second stage of the demographic transition and the population of European countries is shrinking (anti-Malthusians). Finally, draw conclusions about which view you think is more accurate.

2. *Identify and provide explanations for some of the population challenges that affect the Most Industrialized and the Least Industrialized Nations.*

First, for some of the Most Industrialized Nations, populations are shrinking. Of the 42 nations of Europe, 40 are in this situation. As the author notes, they fill more coffins than cradles. The reason for this is a declining birth rate — couples are having fewer children and are not replacing themselves. A second challenge facing the Most Industrialized Nations is the migration of people from the Least Industrialized Nations. As immigrants move into these nations, there is some question about whether they contribute to the economy or are a drain. Regardless, as they immigrate, they create pressures on the receiving society to provide employment and services for them.

For the Least Industrialized Nations, the first challenge is how to feed people. People in many of these nations are starving because the country cannot produce enough food. In some cases, famine is caused by drought, inefficient farming, and wars. In other cases, because of globalization, the major share of agricultural land is committed to producing crops for export rather than for indigenous consumption. A second challenge is to slow population growth. Some nations have successfully reduced the number of children a couple has, but the population continues to grow. The explanation lies in social and cultural factors. In these traditional societies, cultural values encourage couples to have large families, having children confers a status on the parents, and children who will provide for parents in their old age. These factors are strong barriers to effective population control.

3. *Identify the problems associated with forecasting population growth.*

First define the basic demographic equation — that is, the calculation used to project population growth. Then identify problems that make the demographer's job more difficult. These include natural phenomena (famines and plagues), economic factors (short-term booms and busts as well as longer-term industrialization), political factors (wars and government policy), and social factors (educational levels). In your essay identify and discuss the ways in which they make forecasting a challenge.

4. *Discuss whether cities are impersonal Gesellschafts or communal Gemeinshafts.*

For this essay refer to the work of Louis Wirth and Herbert Gans. Wirth talked about the breakup of kinship and neighborhoods with the growth of cities; the result was alienation. On the other hand, Gans found evidence of villages embedded within urban landscapes, which provided people with a sense of community. In particular, he discusses the "ethnic villagers." If you decide to argue for the impersonality of urban life, include some discussion of the norm of noninvolvement and the diffusion of responsibility. If you choose to talk about communities within cities, then refer to how people create intimacy by personalizing their environment, developing attachments to sports teams, objects, and even city locations.

5. *Discuss the factors that fueled suburbanization and consider the impact this population shift had on cities.*

The trend in suburbanization began in the early decades of the twentieth century, but really accelerated after World War II. One of the major factors in this shift of population from cities to surrounding communities was the automobile. As more cars were sold, and more highways built, people had the means to live a distance from where they worked. The rate of suburbanization increased in the

1950s and 1960s, as racial integration of both city schools and neighborhoods increased. Driven by racism, many whites sought to escape these changes by moving to all-white suburbs.

The cities were deeply affected by this shift in population. As more people left, businesses and jobs followed. This contributed to a shrinking tax base, with the result that city governments found it harder to maintain city services. Banks began to redline certain deteriorating, and changing, neighborhoods; people in those neighborhoods found it harder to obtain loans for housing or business purposes. You might also point out how these population changes also contribute to the development of metropolises and megalopolises, which, in turn, leads to increased environmental problems like air pollution.

CHAPTER 15

SOCIAL CHANGE:
TECHNOLOGY, SOCIAL MOVEMENTS, AND THE ENVIRONMENT

ANSWER KEY

MULTIPLE CHOICE

1. d	6. c	11. a	16. b	21. a	26. a
2. a	7. a	12. d	17. b	22. c	27. d
3. c	8. d	13. d	18. d	23. b	28. c
4. c	9. d	14. a	19. d	24. b	29. c
5. a	10. c	15. b	20. b	25. b	30. a

TRUE-FALSE QUESTIONS

1. T	5. F	9. T	13. F	17. F
2. F	6. T	10. T	14. T	18. T
3. F	7. T	11. T	15. T	19. T
4. T	8. F	12. F	16. F	20. T

FILL-IN QUESTIONS

1. modernization
2. steam engine
3. unilinear
4. cultural lag
5. postmodern
6. life
7. social movement
8. reactive social movement
9. redemptive
10. propaganda
11. organization
12. Acid rain
13. green
14. ecosabatoge
15. sustainable environment

MATCHING

MATCH THESE SOCIOLOGICAL CONCEPTS WITH THEIR
DEFINITIONS

1.	d	6.	j
2.	e	7.	a
3.	g	8.	b
4.	h	9.	f
5.	i	10.	c

ESSAYS

1. *According to your text, social change is such a vital part of social life that any significant shift in the characteristics of culture and society warrants notice. Discuss the topic of how social change has affected social life (e.g., regarding social revolutions, capitalism, etc.).*

   Begin by examining the four major social revolutions and the impact they had on society including, for example, a discussion of the plow. Also examine the shift from gemeinschaft to gesellschaft. Finally, include a discussion of the perspectives on capitalism and the impact it had on society; include both Karl Marx and Max Weber in your answer.

2. *Why do societies change? Discuss the attempts to explain the phenomenon of change, and give at least one illustration of each attempt.*

   Discuss the four theories including cultural evolution, natural cycles, conflict, and Ogburn's theory. Be sure to go into detail on each theory and give an example of each.

3. *Choose a particular technology and discuss the impact it has had, and will have, on United States society.*

   Your textbook uses the technology of computers, examining the impacts that it has had on education, medicine, business, and war. Use this discussion to guide your answer.

4. *What is a "social movement?" List the types of social movements and give an example of each type of movement? Discuss and explain the various stages in the development of social movements?*

   Be sure to include in your answer the difference between proactive and reactive social movements. Then discuss the types including alterative, redemptive, reformative, transformative, transnational and metaformative. Finally, conclude with the various stages, including unrest and agitation, resource mobilization, organization, institutionalization, and organizational decline and possible resurgence.

5. *Why is there said to be an "environmental movement" around the worl?. What type of social movement would you call the "environmental movement" and why? What is environmental sociology, and what link(s) do you find between this relatively new field of sociology and the "environmental movement?"*

   Go back and look at your answer to number 4 and use some of the information from it to explain what type of social movement an environmental movement would be. Be sure to explain why. Then explain environmental sociology using Dunlap and Michelson's discussion of the eight assumptions of environmental sociology. Finally, discuss the links that you see between environmental movements and environmental sociology.

NOTES

NOTES

NOTES

NOTES

NOTES

NOTES

NOTES

NOTES

NOTES